Sustainable ceramics

A practical approach

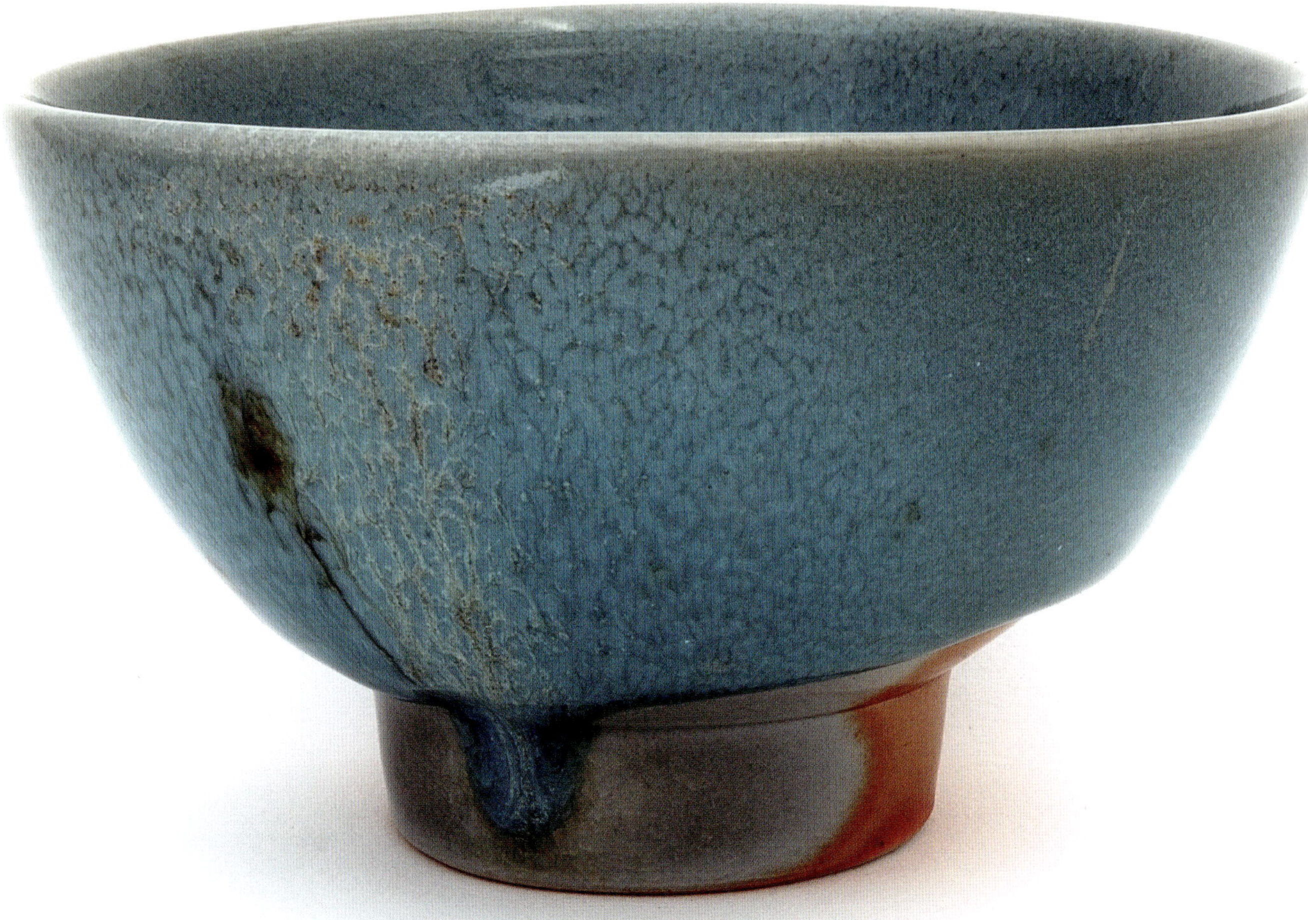

Sustainable ceramics

A practical approach

Robert Harrison

The American Ceramic Society · Ohio

HERBERT PRESS
LONDON · OXFORD · NEW YORK · NEW DELHI · SYDNEY

HERBERT PRESS
Bloomsbury Publishing Plc
50 Bedford Square, London, WC1B 3DP, UK
29 Earlsfort Terrace, Dublin 2, Ireland

BLOOMSBURY, HERBERT PRESS and the Herbert Press logo are trademarks of Bloomsbury publishing Plc

First published in Great Britain in 2013
Published simultaneously in the USA by The American Ceramic Society

A catalogue record for this book is available from the British Library
Library of Congress Cataloguing-in-Publication data has been applied for

Typeset in 10 on 13pt Rotis Semi Sans
Book design by Susan McIntyre
Cover design by Eleanor Rose
Edited by Jim Caunter
Project Managed by Alison Stace
Printed and bound in India by Replika Press Pvt. Ltd.

ISBN: PB: 978-1-78994-030-5; US ed: 978-1-57498-335-7
2 4 6 8 10 9 7 5 3

MIX
Paper from responsible sources
FSC www.fsc.org
FSC® C016779

To find out more about our authors and books visit www.bloomsbury.com and sign up for our newsletters

COVER IMAGES: (Front, top) *The Flight of the Fly*, Jacques Kaufmann, 1994. *Photo: courtesy of the artist.* (Front, bottom) Sanitaryware waste at Armitage Shanks, Staffordshire, UK. *Photo: David Binns.* (Back, top) *Crucible*, Dave Peters, 2011. 24 x 24 cm (9½ x 9½ in), wood-fired local stoneware. *Photo: Vaughn Judge.* (Back, bottom) *Quarry Tile Gateway* (tile detail), Robert Harrison, 2004–06. *Photo: Robert Harrison.*

FRONTISPIECE: Steve Harrison, *Bowl*, 2012. Ht: 10 cm (4 in) x 12.5 cm (5 in), wood-fired bia-tunze porcelain. *Photo: courtesy of the artist.*

RIGHT: Ilana Crispi, *All Sides of a Sphere*, 2006. 46 cm (18 in) x 46 cm (18 in), archival digital print, 1 of 28 different images. *Photo: courtesy of the artist.*

Contents

Foreword by Janet Mansfield 6

Introduction 9

1 Your carbon footprint 15

2 Sustainable ceramic practices for the maker 23

3 Ceramic artists working sustainably 83

4 Working with industry 113

5 Sustainable endeavours: education and networks 123

6 Journal leaders: personal approaches 131

Practical advice – top tips 136

Websites 140

Bibliography 142

Index 144

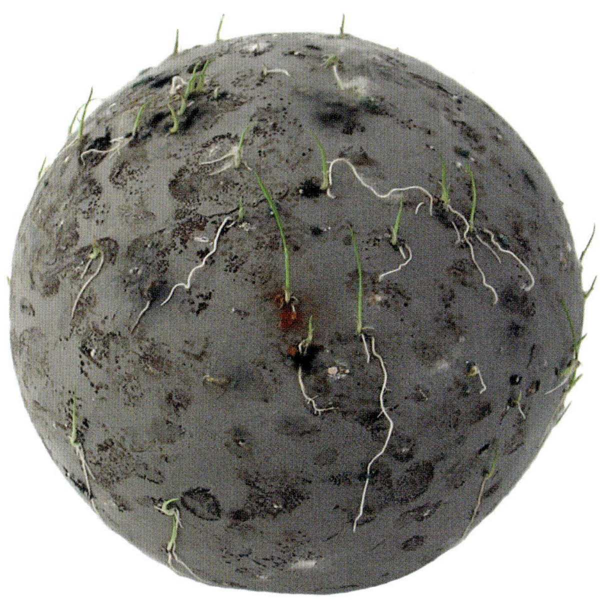

Foreword by Janet Mansfield

Sustainability – a contemporary issue

Sustainability is one of the most talked-about concepts today, one that is being addressed by scientists, mathematicians and ecologists worldwide. Research on this subject takes us to the writings of the UK's Tim Jackson; the US politician Al Gore, who received the Gothenburg prize for sustainable development, as well as a Nobel Prize; Australia's Tim Flannery; and the Israeli Nobel Prize winner, Robert Aumann. We can understand their concerns and read with hope their projections for the way forward, even while recognising that human nature is not as altruistic as they would wish. But what is the stance of the artist, especially the ceramic artist?

Creative ideas are not always technically sound, we need to explore, to experiment, to try out ideas using Earth's materials. We need to progress, reflect contemporary life just as potters have for thousands of years. Most ceramic artists are sensible, aware of Earth's finite resources but we need to be free to follow our individual creative ideas. The issue of sustainability is often used as a political football, and the issue of sustainability in ceramics does not necessairily have the reach to solve the problems of global population growth, hunger and health. The practice of craft, however, is perhaps the most sustainable of all the arts. The work is timeless, made to last, often cherished and passed on through generations in the family. Materials are not wasted but recycled, toxic materials are avoided, disposable products are not favoured, and fashion is not followed thoughtlessly. Clay is a tactile material; there is reality to its mass and weight that reflects the Earth's composition. Its use is not always academic but appeals to the human body and spirit. In that way the work of the artist is logical, individual, sustaining a connection with the planet and our life on it. We need to survive as artists, we need to prosper and advance, and we do not wish to become an endangered species. This publication will offer ways forward in our bid towards sustainable art and life.

When scientists and environmentalists talk about sustainability many are referring back to earlier arguments about ecology. Robert Aumann, one of the authorities on the subject, has a positive approach. In his Nobel Prize biography of 2006 he suggests that we should go forward in a spirit of exploration for its own sake. 'We must go where curiosity takes us, we must go where we want to go. And eventually it is sure to lead us to the beautiful, the important and the useful,' Aumann wrote. I thought such a philosophy might well be a suitable one for a ceramic artist today.

This publication is about sustainable ceramics, and we should look to confirm our stance, what we believe we can change, what good we can do. Or to put it another way, what harm we can avoid. Does sustainability just mean an economically

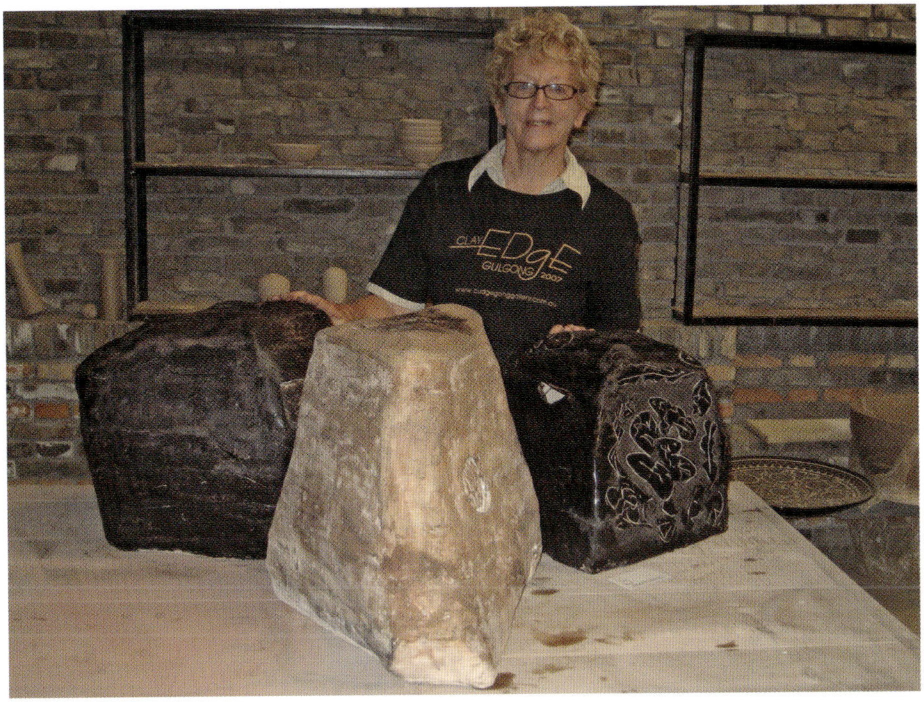

Janet Mansfield in her workshop in Gulgong, Australia, 2012. *Photo: courtesy of the artist.*

sustainable practice? Can I make and sell my work in sufficient quantity to enable me to make more, buy more materials to make it, and fuel to fire it? I need to put food on the table, pay the mortgage, all those mundane and individual survival tactics. Marketing anything has costs, especially in a competitive world, exhibition costs are charged by most galleries, and there are costs in terms of personal energy and travel. These economics only address a local scale, but there are hidden costs that involve the wider community and have to be sustained time after time. Economic sustainability affects us all.

My own work is made from local materials, the area is rich in clays and other minerals and the wood has fallen naturally on the farm and has been collected for firing. Wood left lying on the ground produces methane, which has been proved, and is also a bushfire hazard, encouraging bushfires when left to smoulder in the undergrowth.

I believe that most of us are responsible for what we do, and make objects of worth that will be valued by future generations. Such objects will remind our grandchildren that the ceramicists of the early 21st century were caring, careful and future-thinking artists wishing to sustain the environment and lifestyle in a manner that is answerable and accountable for the future.

The late **Janet Mansfield** was a potter and author who worked and lived in Gulgong, Australia, and sadly passed away in February 2013. She was a past-president of the International Academy of Ceramics and former publisher of the *Ceramics Art and Perception* and *Ceramics Technical* periodicals.

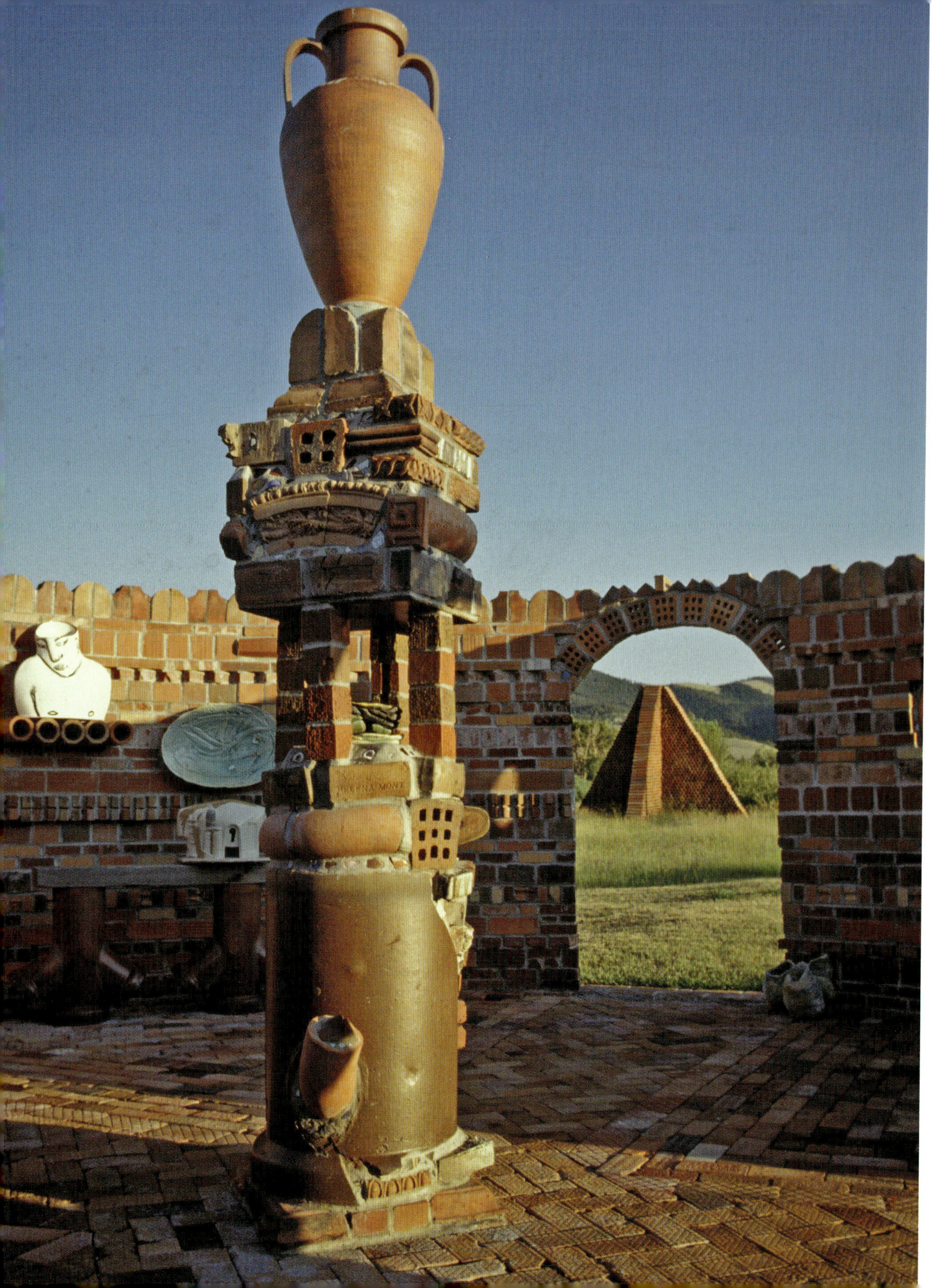

Introduction

Why bother with the subject of sustainable ceramics?

LEFT: *Potters Shrine* interior with *TileX* in background, Archie Bray Foundation for the Ceramic Arts, Helena, Montana, 1987. *Photo: Robert Harrison.*

BELOW: *Green Granitewood,* Author's passive solar home with site-specific sculpture of reclaimed materials, Helena, Montana, 2012. *Photo: Robert Harrison.*

As I approach my sixth decade, the seven billionth human now inhabits the planet. Quality of life is a central issue to most humans. With the revolution in technology of the past two decades, a large percentage of the world's population is now *plugged in* or working to attain *connectivity.* We are in the digital age and as with most aspects of life on this planet, it has both positive and negative aspects.

Most seem to want it all: health, happiness and the ability to enjoy what we work hard for. Some have a desire to contribute, and attempt in their own way to make the world a better place for all, and subsequent generations. Others seem oblivious and free of such responsibilities. I count myself as one of the former individuals. Perhaps it's generational, being a product of the 1960s and 70s when social revolution made anything seem possible. Taking responsibility for one's transactions continues to be inherent to life's daily decisions.

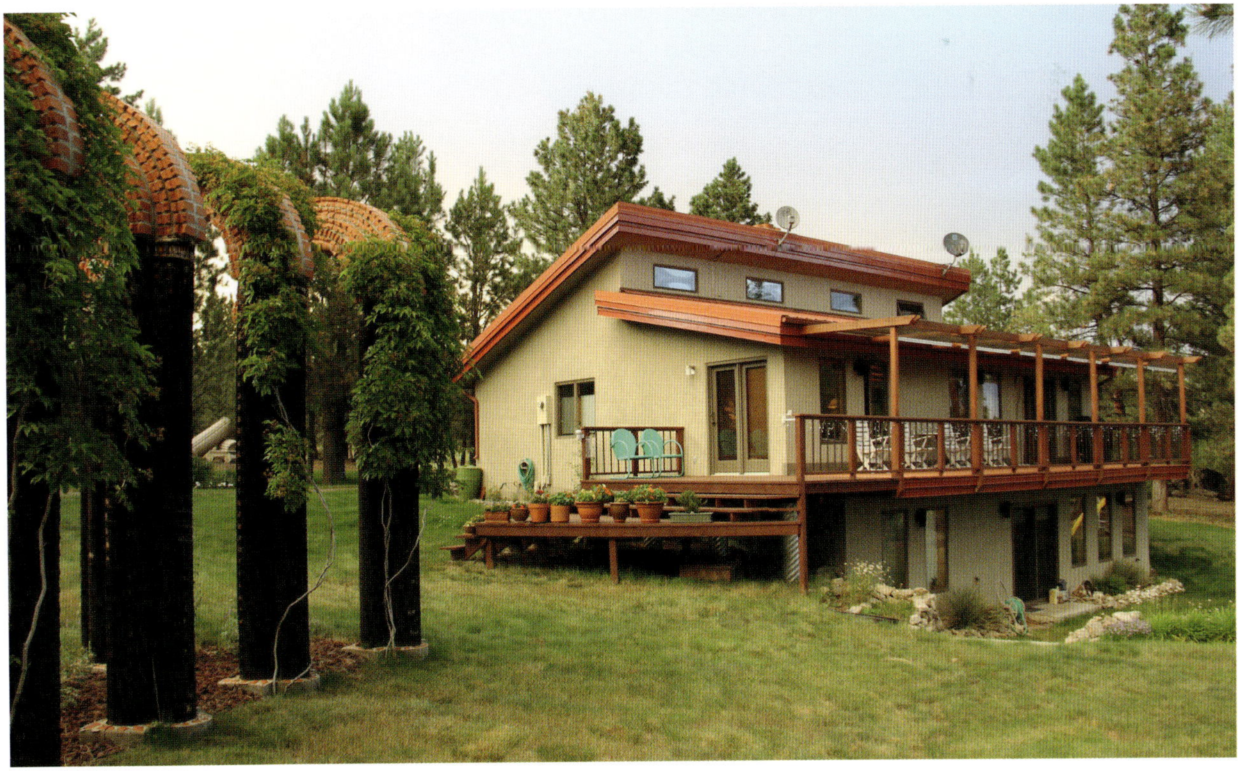

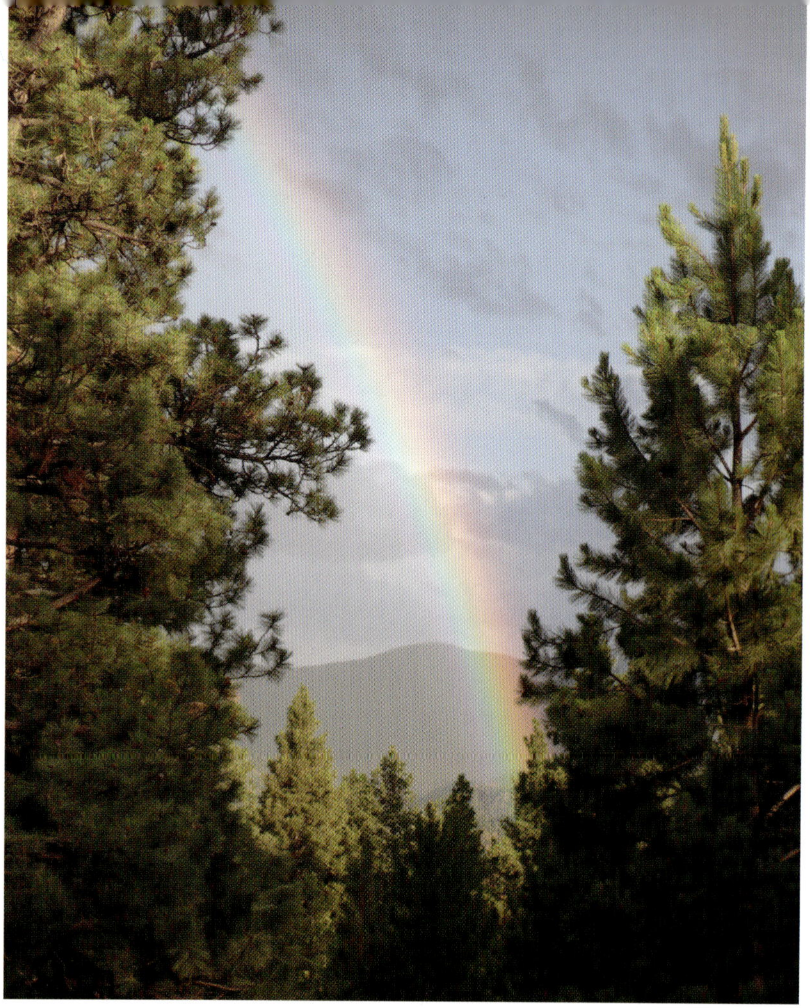

ABOVE: NCECA's Green Task Force logo. *Photo: Robert Harrison.*

LEFT: Rainbow over Granitewood, Helena, Montana, 2012. *Photo: Robert Harrison.*

Individual responsibility

The reality is that everyone is capable of some level of sustainability, whether it comes from necessity or a desire *to help make the world a better place*. It all begins with the individual, and there are a myriad of small everyday efforts that one can do to affect change and maintain a sustainable lifestyle. In fact, if the majority of the western world adopted even a few of these everyday tasks, we would see a dramatic reduction in greenhouse gases and improvement in the eroding ozone layer.

Why go to the efforts now?

Over the last several decades, essentially since the issue of renewable resources became a reality with the mid-20th-century energy crisis, efforts by many individuals have been undertaken to examine aspects of what we do as ceramic makers.

Entering the second decade of the 21st century seems like the ideal time to bring a focus to sustainability issues in the field of ceramics. *Green*, *ecological*, *sustainable*, etc. are descriptive words that have entered our lexicon, and are not only commonplace in western cultures, but have become marketable social identities. Children growing up today are learning from birth that going green is a good thing and they understand the sustainable concept.

Sustainable ethics: social responsibilities

I consider this publication a contribution to the discourse on sustainable practices in ceramics. Over the past decade there have been a number of good articles written on sustainability in ceramics. Research will continue and articles will be written and published to help disseminate evolving ideas and developments in sustainable practices. We can look forward to a brighter future as long as individuals realise they can make an impact and take responsibility for their day-to-day actions.

Every creative field is now involved with sustainable issues. For example, sustainability is driving the world of design, and the 2012 London Olympic Games are a prime example. The world stage for the summer Olympics has staked its reputation on groundbreaking sustainable design as its hallmark. Net-zero building along with carbon neutral footprints is now part of the lexicon for the Olympic Games, perhaps the largest ongoing global event.

Regenerative or restorative design is now part of the field of landscape architecture. These developments have the potential to promote species diversity and slow global warming. Regenerative projects don't just maintain existing ecologies and conserve resources, but can improve air quality, enrich soils and restore biodiversity. Developments in these fields are interwoven into developments in technology and industry.

Ceramic artists are involved in so many aspects of sustainable development from the reclamation of ceramic and glass waste to *growing bricks*, from improvements in design in the ceramic industry to ceramic water filters. We are an extremely bright and conscientious global community, and I predict only more involvement for ceramic practitioners in the sustainability field. The bevy of talented young potters and artists I see locally, nationally and internationally committed to sustainable practices is a testament to the health of the global ceramics field.

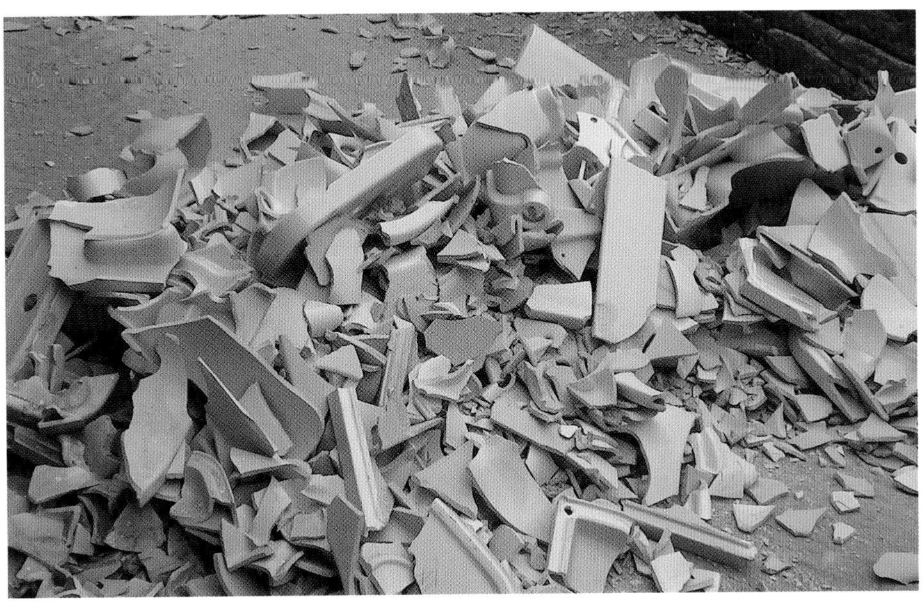

Sanitaryware waste at Armitage Shanks, Staffordshire, UK. *Photo: David Binns.*

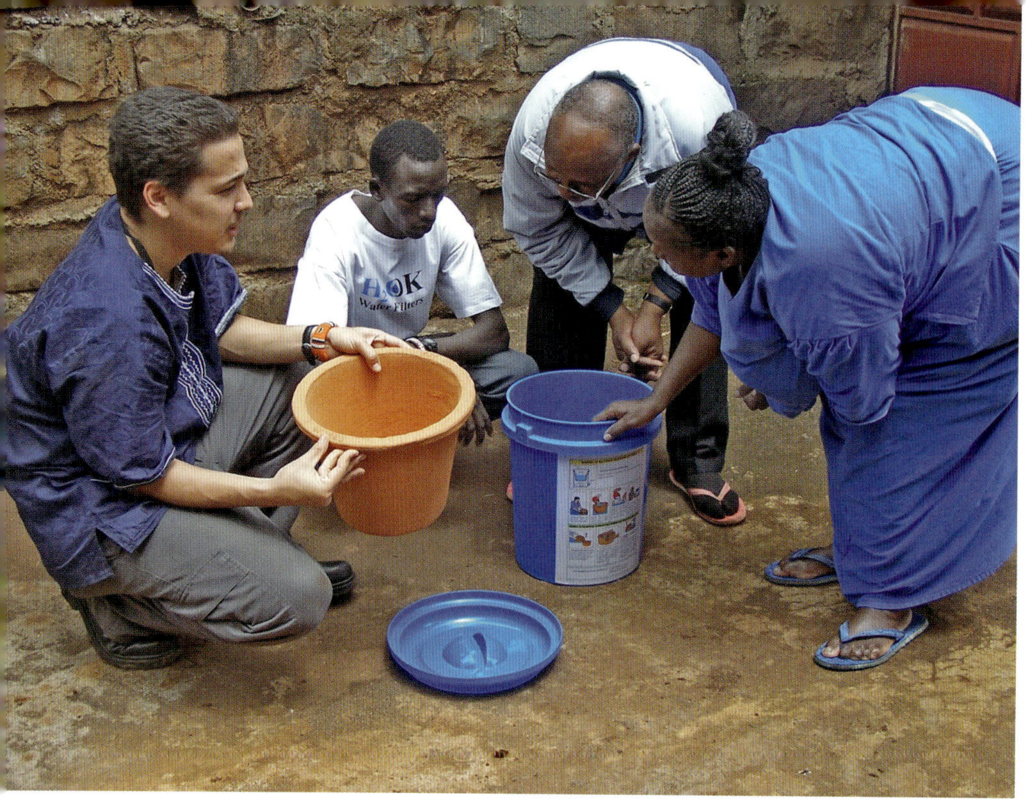

Water Filter developed by Potters for Peace with technician Reynaldo Díaz, Kenya. *Photo: Peter Chartrand.*

This publication is a collaboration between a global group of experts in the field, who have contributed their wisdom on a wide variety of subjects pertinent to ceramic studio practice. I am indebted to their generosity and patience and honoured to consider them my collaborators on this publication.

Environmentally friendly practices in ceramics have been utilised from the very earliest days of ceramic practice. As a human race we have the knowledge and ability to carefully consider the ways we use our resources and make alterations where needed. I have reconfigured my personal approach to eco-consciousness and encourage the readers of this publication to review their own practices and adjust where they can; one small action by many makes a substantial difference for the future of our planet.

A (green) revolution is a process, not an event

My interests in sustainable practices go way back. As a child of the post-Depression generation, I grew up in a working-class family that practised recycling before it was identified as a *green practice*. My family carefully considered their consumption and manufactured goods were repaired when broken and used until they were completely worn out. *Waste not, want not* was a commonly used expression in our family and community. Little did I know at the time that growing up with that understanding had planted the *seeds* of sustainability.

I believe the earth-based nature of the ceramics medium, the malleability and endless possibilities of form and function of the material along with the allure of fire

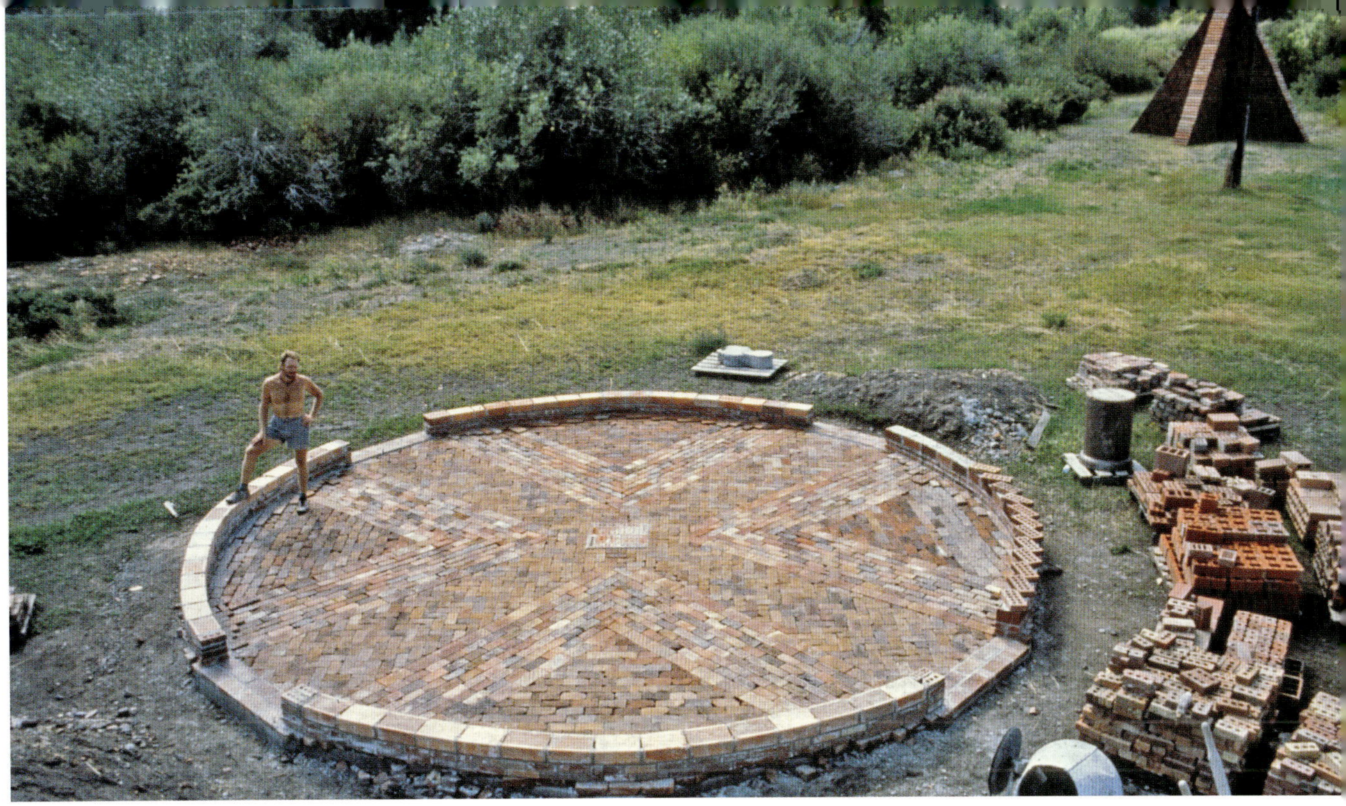

Robert Harrison with *Potters Shrine* under construction (*TileX* in background), Archie Bray Foundation for the Ceramic Arts, Helena, Montana, 1985. *Photo: Robert Harrison.*

drew me to the ceramics studio. Like many, I also found a strong sense of collegiality or *family* present in the studio. In North America, ceramic studios were often relegated to the lower recesses of a facility, both from a practical and perhaps from a philosophical standpoint. Ceramics educators and their students often felt compelled to defend the material and medium through an art school context. Over time, defence of the medium strengthened the bonds of the ceramics communities, locally, regionally, nationally and globally and created a strong, stable, philosophical foundation.

Early in my career financial resources were scarce and I, like many others, took to repurposing materials for my large-scale installations. The repurposed materials I chose to utilise (industrially produced brick and tile) often had acquired a patina, which enhanced the work, but also gave it historic credence. Over the years this aspect of reclaiming, repurposing and recycling has become one of the hallmarks of my work.

I am a professional artist, a maker, not a professional writer. My path to this point was circuitous and fuelled by a passion for the subject. During my presidential tenure with NCECA (the National Council on Education for the Ceramic Arts) the Green Task Force (NCECA GTF) was established and further developed my desire for sustainable practices in ceramics. The publisher of this publication approached me to consider authoring a practical guide on the subject and this is the result.

This publication is an attempt to look at sustainability in the field, and examine aspects that are important to many. It has become apparent to me that even though there have been a number of articles and a few conference journals written on this subject, there is an absence of a more comprehensive publication. This effort is my attempt to gather individual perspectives, a substantial amount of information and present it in an easy to read, understandable format.

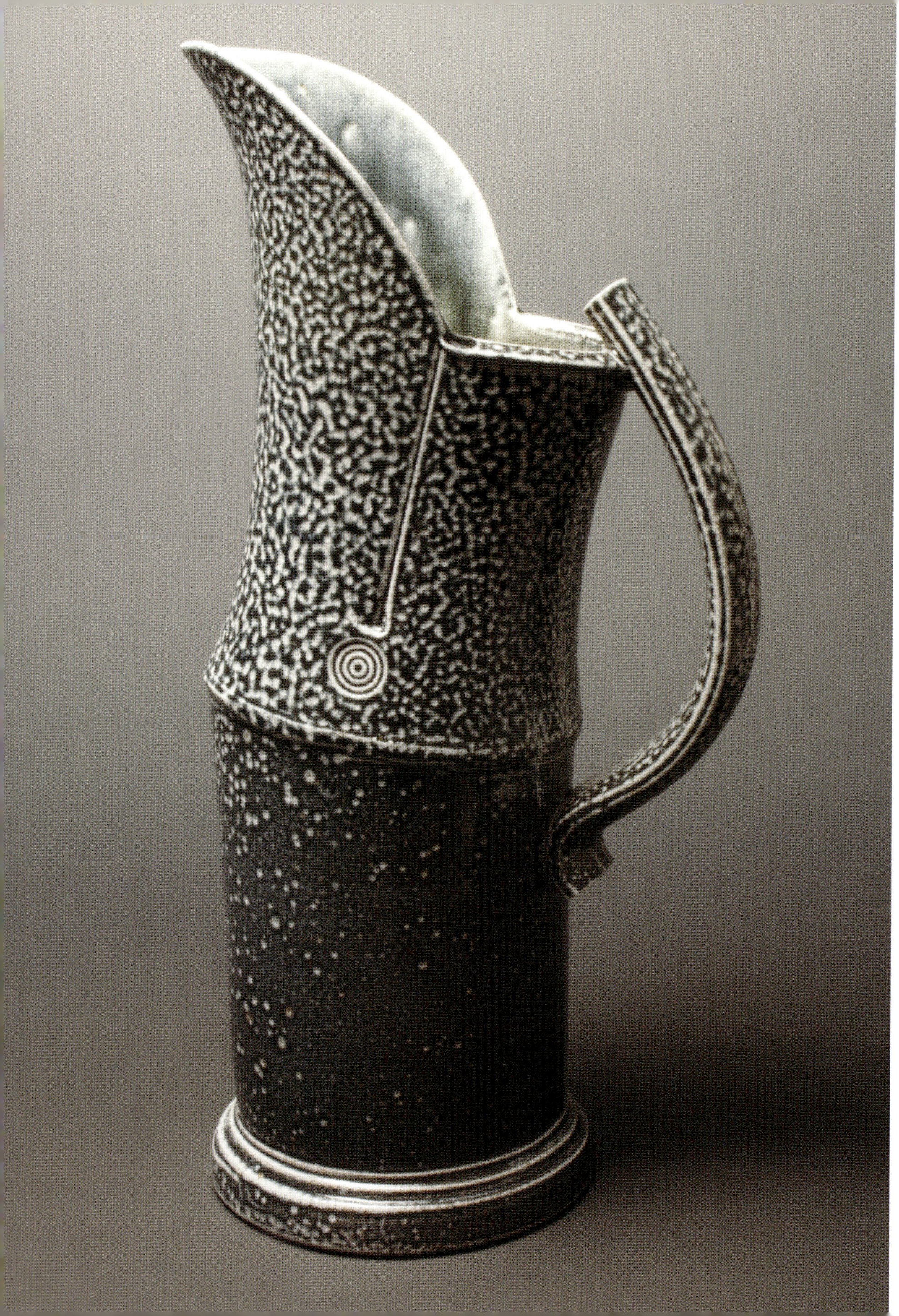

1 Your carbon footprint

Ceramics is dirty: debunking the myth

> *Premise:* Ceramics with all its inherent needs of making, materials, firing fuels and working space is certainly not a *clean/green* medium.
>
> *(Robert Harrison)*

Contrary to this premise, held by numerous members of our community, ceramics can be one of the sustainable and eco-friendly mediums for creativity. It really depends how conscientious you are about your practice. Great advances in research and technology have enabled us to become much more conscious of our carbon footprints as ceramic practitioners.

As we all know the practice of making with clay has been around since the beginnings of modern human existence. Small fertility (Venus) objects are dated to 26,000 years ago, and Japanese Jolmon vessels date to 16,500 years old. The earliest days of modern humans is traced in part to the shards of the earliest cultures that created and fired clay objects and vessels.

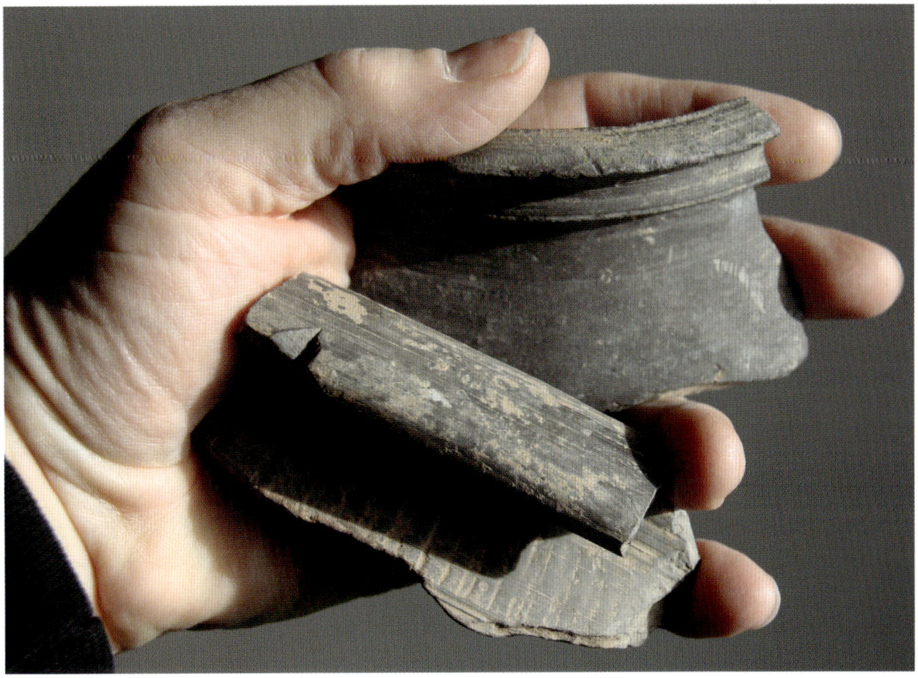

LEFT: *Salt-glazed Articulated Jug*, Walter Keeler, 2012. Ht: 30.5 cm (12 in). *Photo: courtesy of the artist.*

RIGHT: *Ancient Shards*, Robert Harrison. Granitewood Collection, Helena, Montana. *Photo: Robert Harrison.*

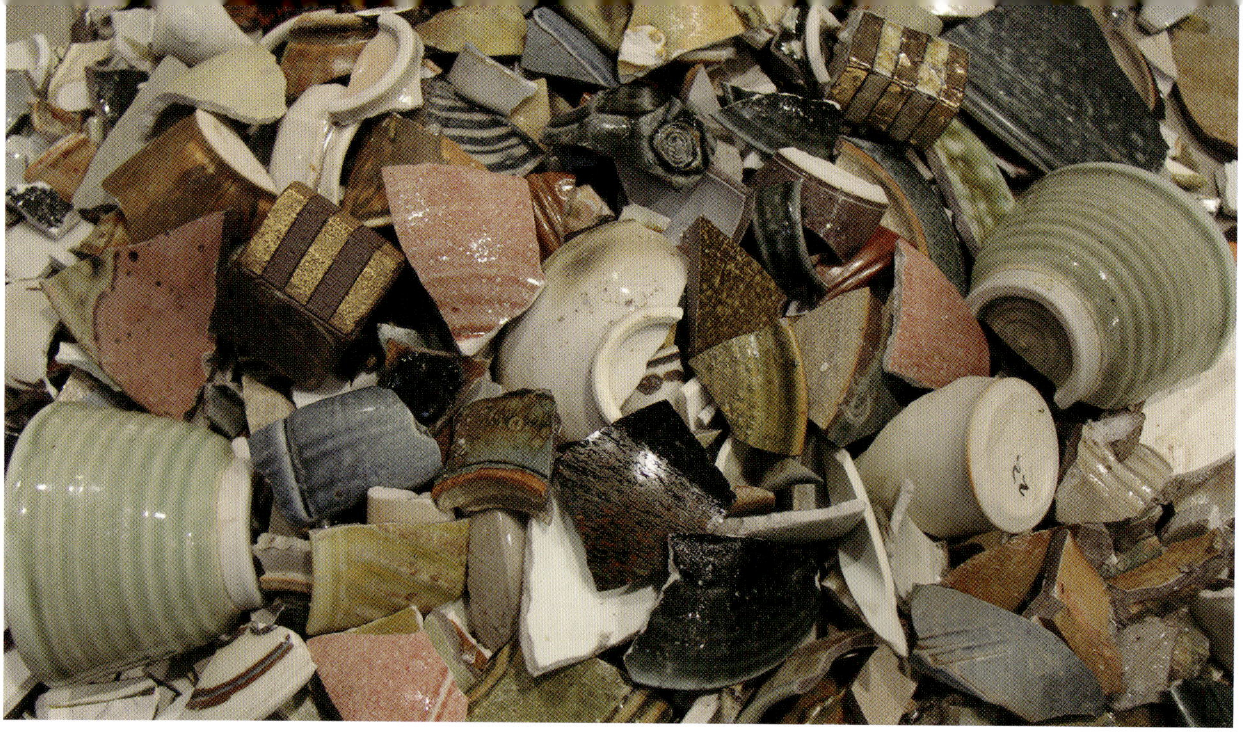

Twenty-first Century Shards, Robert Harrison, 2013. Granitewood Studio, Helena, Montana. *Photo: Robert Harrison.*

Makers today are in fact extending the lineage of ceramic practitioners that dates back through those thousands of years. For the majority of that time, some would argue up until the past few hundred years, ceramic practice was in harmony with the Earth. The Industrial Revolution of the 18th century changed the world. It brought with it great advances and innovation, but also had negative impacts on the environment.

With advances in research, understanding and technologies, we have the ability today to have a zero impact on the environment. One does not have to feel it is a hopeless situation and there is no point in even thinking about it. Ceramic practitioners, like every individual, play a role in this equation.

Any small step is a forward step.

Carbon footprint

What is a *carbon footprint*? The concept originates from the ecological footprint discussion, developed by Rees and Wackernagel in the early 1990s. The carbon footprint is a subset of the ecological footprint and of the more comprehensive Life Cycle Assessment (LCA). The mitigation of carbon footprints through the development of alternative projects, such as solar or wind energy or reforestation, is often known as carbon offsetting.

Inevitably, in going about our daily lives – commuting, sheltering our families, eating – each of us contributes to the greenhouse gas emissions that are causing climate change. Yet, there are many things each of us, as individuals, can do to reduce our carbon emissions. My research has not turned up specific data to the average individual potters/ceramic artists' carbon footprint, perhaps because our individual work is unique and so varied.

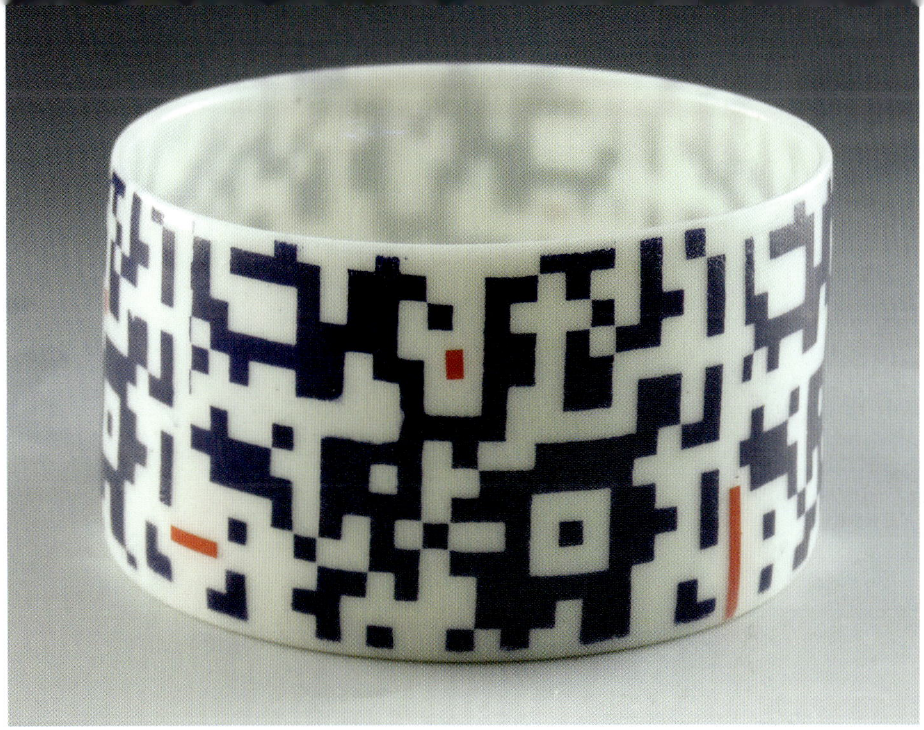

Blue QR Bowl, Aaron Nelson, 2011. Ht: 6.3 cm (2½ in) x 11.4 cm (4½ in), soft paste porcelain. *Photo: courtesy of the artist.*

How much energy does it take to fire a ceramic cup?

Aaron Nelson is the Artistic Director of the Medalta Artist-in-Residence programme in Medicine Hat, Alberta, Canada. Aaron was previously the Clay Business Manager of the Archie Bray Foundation. His extensive knowledge of ceramics materials and his commitment to sustainable issues continue to impress. Aaron writes:

> How much energy does it take to fire one cup? Is the act of turning clay into ceramic a sustainable practice? Are we really using fossil fuels in a responsible way? Where do the raw materials come from? What is the exact relationship between ceramics and glass? These are all questions that I have come to ask myself as my interest in the production of objects (I spent many years as a potter) has expanded to a more conceptual understanding of how these objects are produced and how they fit into contemporary dialogues around consumption. These questions have directed my research towards the formulation of an energy efficient material, which is more glass than clay.
>
> Having worked with porcelain for a number of years I was interested in the aesthetics of translucency. Combined with my interests in energy conservation I have been developing a material loosely based upon the Renaissance prototypical porcelains known as the Medici porcelains. The material that I am currently working with matures at 1045°C [1913°F], is extremely translucent, and has many qualities associated with glass. It fires to temperature in just over three hours. Currently my research has been directed at fluxing the body with over 50% post-consumer material in the form of various types of recycled glass.

Below is a very simple breakdown of the energy required to once fire this small porcelain cup to 1045°C (1913°F).

Energy Audit: 19.98 kWh to fire 30 cups
0.66 kWh to fire one cup = 666 watts

How much energy is 666 watts?

- The energy consumed by an average-size plasma screen television while watching a Super Bowl (North American football) game
- The equivalent to the nutritional energy in three and a half doughnuts, roughly 190.2 calories
- The energy it takes to boil one liter of water.

So if you are watching the big game, drinking a pot of tea and eating doughnuts you are consuming about 2,000 watts of energy, enough to fire three cups!

If you amortise the energy required to fire the cup over the average lifespan of its useful life of an average of 50 years it takes about 13 watts per year, about what a standard compact fluorescent bulb consumes in one hour. Aaron's research has convinced him that the act of turning clay into ceramics can be incredibly efficient and consumes relatively little energy.

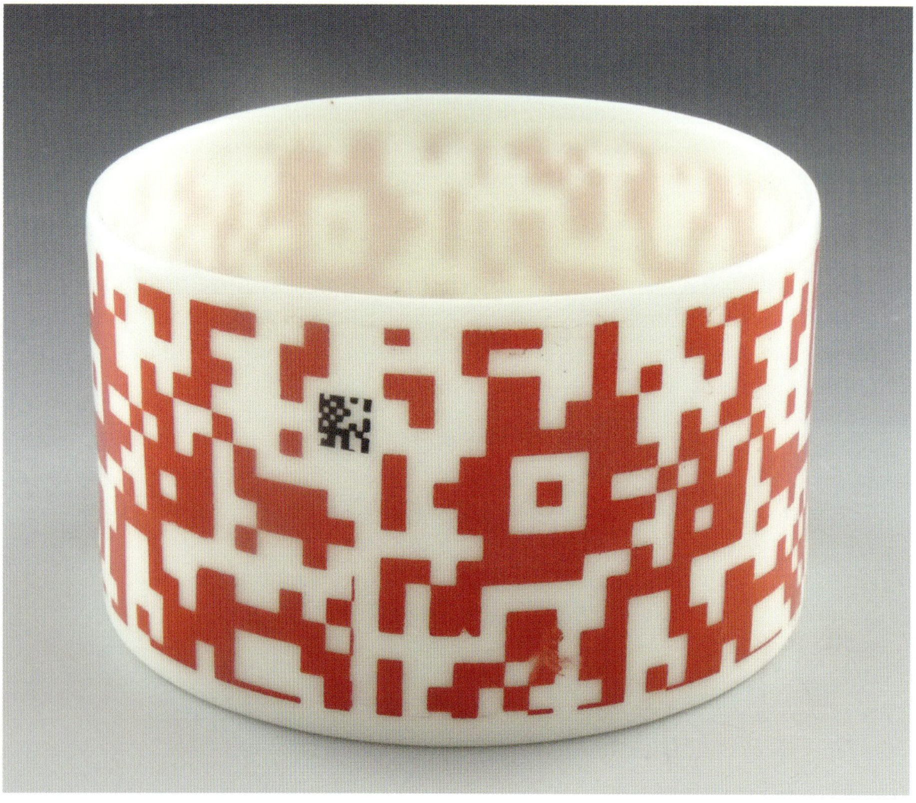

Red QR Bowl, Aaron Nelson, 2011. Ht: 6.3 cm (2½ in) x 11.4 cm (4½ in), soft paste porcelain. *Photo: courtesy of the artist.*

The bicycle kiln

When I heard about Aaron's idea for a human-powered kiln, I needed to learn more! Aaron writes:

> The Idea for a bicycle-powered kiln came out of a trip to the science centre coupled with an energy audit I conducted on my firing cycles. Having determined that I only needed to generate enough electricity to produce about 0.66 kWh, to fire one very small cup I postulated that it would be possible to generate the required electrical energy needed to build a small 27 cubic inch electric kiln with a bicycle-powered generator.
>
> Using a belt-driven permanent magnet motor as a generator the system will be able to produce about 100 watts of energy with one bicycle pedaling at an average speed. This energy then flows into four deep cycle storage batteries and then into an inverter that converts the current to AC to power the kiln. Keeping in mind that while pedalling a bike a human body runs at about 25% efficiency so for every 1 watt produced it takes 4 watts of pedal power. I have determined with the loss of efficiency in various parts of the system I will need to pedal for about 12 hours. If four bicycles were hooked up in series it would only take three hours to generate the required energy.

Obviously a kiln of this sort has little practical applications. The purpose is more conceptual in nature in that it illustrates how little energy it really takes to transform clay into ceramic material.

Leach/Cardew and their sustainable legacy?

Walter Keeler is one of the UK's leading ceramic artists with an international reputation, and some say he is now the pre-eminent British potter. He studied at Harrow School of Art, noted for training production potters, and established his first studio in 1965 where he produced domestic stoneware. In 1976 he and his family moved to Monmouthshire in Wales and created an innovative range of salt-glazed stoneware for which he quickly developed an international reputation.

The following is an interview between the author (RH) and Walter Keeler (WK).

> **WK:** Both Madoline and I came from working-class backgrounds. Madoline's family worked in the coal mines, and struggled; in fact her father left home so there was one less mouth to feed. My father repaired shoes, and my grandfather grew vegetables to feed the family. We repaired, made and mended things to manage economically. Recycling started for practical and economic rather than ecological reasons. I recycled crankcase/engine oil scrounged from local automobile repair shops to fire my kiln instead of allowing them to 'spread the oil on the nettles'. I rationalised that OK, you are burning carbon but preventing other types of pollution; it's a mixed blessing. It was not uncommon to look into

dumpsters or skips for re-useable things; I still have a stool in the workshop I recovered from a skip. It is a post-Depression era thing, like buying second-hand items from junk shops, etc. Most of us go through our day-to-day lives and recycle newspaper, etc. without thinking too much about the ecological aspect. I have never looked at the ecology aspect in my studio practice.

Cardew went to places without a ceramic infrastructure, they had to find and make clay for low fire pots. He prospected, thinking, how can I use the local material? He had some labour, but the prospecting and collecting Cardew did in Africa to find and use local material can be used by anyone, anywhere if you had a mind to. How feasible is that? It depends on your initiative and your locale.

Materials didn't travel a great distance. China clay, feldspar, Cornish Stone were the useful materials in the south-west of England, perhaps that's why there is a concentration of potters there. The reality is that ecology and finance are tied up. If it's cheaper to use, people will use it. On the other hand, there are times you have to invest for the long run, for example low energy bulbs cost more upfront, but in the long run save you money and reduce your carbon footprint.

RH: My research leads me to believe that many processes that were utilised by Leach and then Cardew were early innovations in sustainable practices. Perhaps many of these practices came out of tradition or necessity, but then laid the groundwork for our current efforts to develop healthy sustainable practices for the individual as well as workshops and schools.

WK: Leach had that philosophical attitude that you should use raw materials that you could relate to and that would sustain some sort of integrity in the work. He probably wasn't thinking ecologically at that time but by coincidence it makes sense ecologically. Cardew stressed the idea that you could source materials that are close at hand and process them yourself, which reduces the industrial impact of producing refined materials at a distance and importing them.

I also think of Harry Davis and the Crowan Pottery. He used the old mill as a pottery and generated his own electricity from the water mill. There's a great story about David Leach who was quite thrifty and was visiting. David would go around switching off the lights at night in the mill. Then Harry would get up and storm around putting them back on. The early technologies required using the electricity as it was being produced. The system there was pretty 'Heath Robinson'.

This leads on to the Harrow Studio Pottery course, which was set up by Victor Margrie and Michael Casson in the late 1960s. Students were very good about using materials at hand and would often find the timber for building their own wheels.

There existed a mentality of not buying what you could find, so that recycling was not for ecology reasons but for economic reasons. A lot of potters are infected with that sort of thrifty nature, with most not having a lot of money; you find a way of doing it with materials at hand.

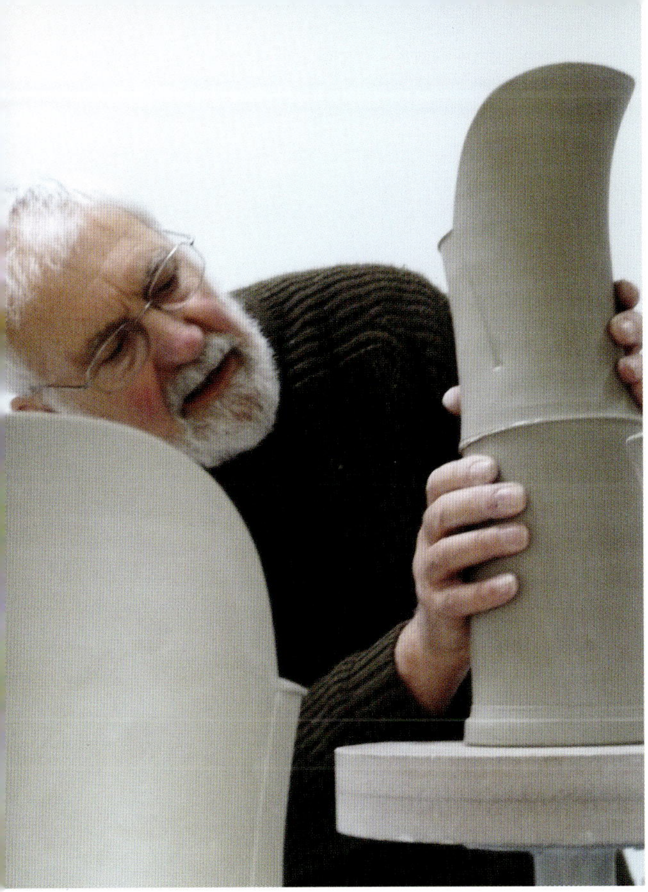

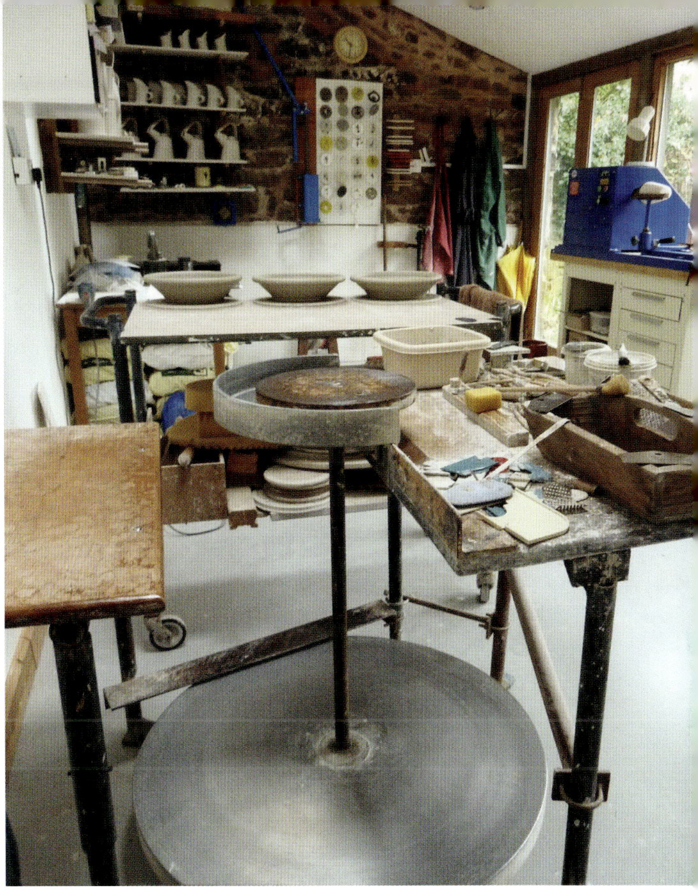

LEFT: Walter Keeler making an *Articulated Jug*, 2012. *Photo: courtesy of the artist.*

RIGHT: Walter Keeler's making shop/studio in Monmouthshire, Wales, 2012. *Photo: courtesy of the artist.*

Pioneer Pottery was a key and a very important publication of the time (60s) and the students were very serious about that. Potters still used materials that were available locally. That cut down on refinement (of the materials) at the time. Some people made that their way of life. We were using fireplace (wood) ash, using clay from underfoot and adding feldspar to make glazes. That practice eliminated buying refined materials. It does mean you have to grind and ball mill your materials and that could be more or less ecological. [Harry Davis wrote *The Potters Alternative*, advancing these types of ecological practices.]

A new generation seems ready to carry on and implement many of the ecological ideas that were discussed years ago but now have the advanced technologies to assist. A lot of people are using ground source heat pumps for their heating, etc. Ground source heat pumps (GHSP) draw heat from the ground or groundwater which is at a relatively constant temperature all year round. The cost of oil is going up all the time. Carbon fuels are expensive and growing more and more expensive. That in itself is enough to look for alternatives. It makes me think back to the days of the Harrow School in the 70s when the students talked about progressive ideas in wind generation and methane use. There was an oil crisis, and people were passionate about it. Ray Finch tore down his oil kiln and went to wood fire. Decisions were primarily made for financial reasons, but now amongst a new generation of young people, these decisions are being made for ecological reasons. The technology has caught up with the dream now.

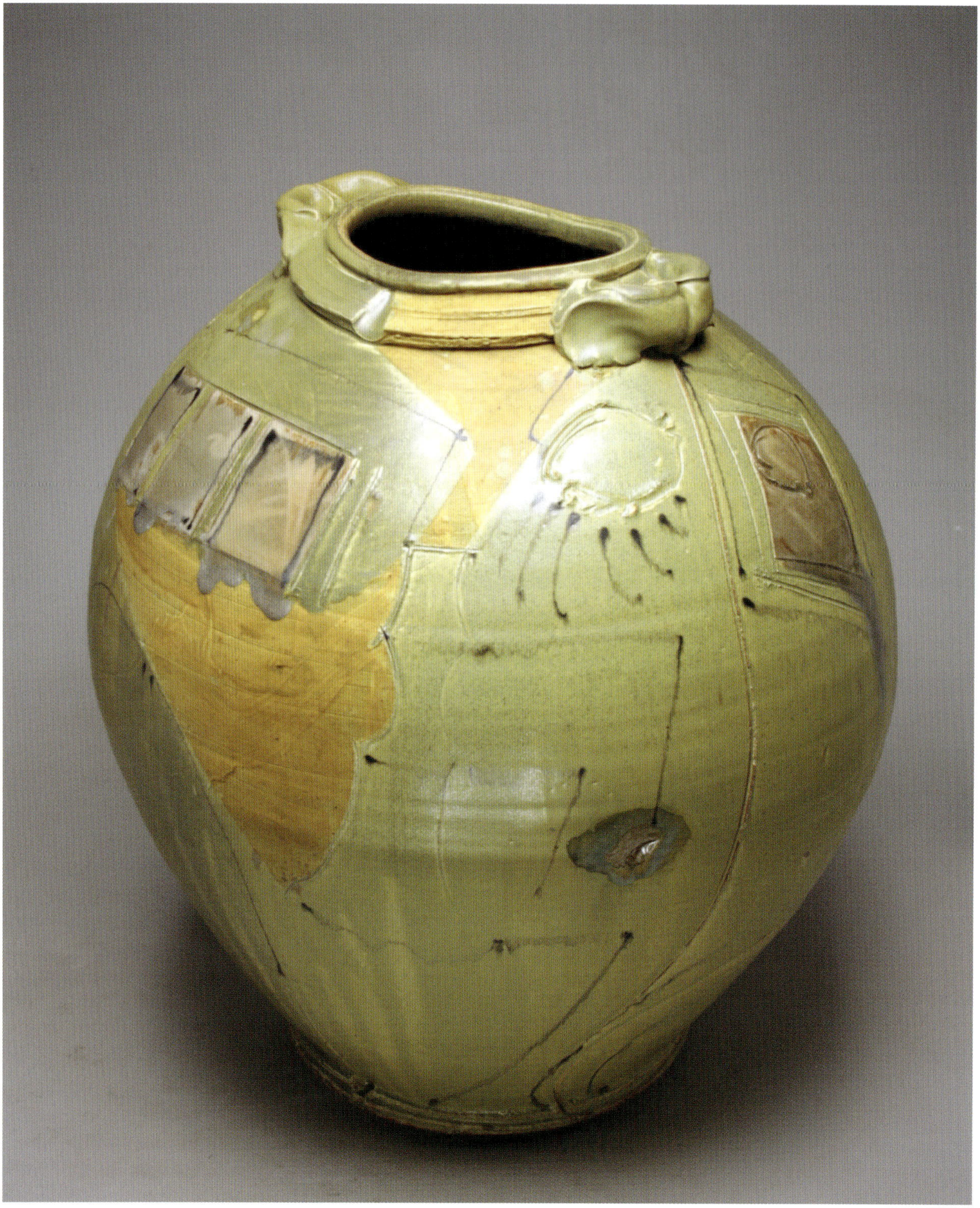

2

Sustainable ceramic practices for the maker

Kilns, fuels and firings

It is understood that the field of ceramics relies heavily on the use of raw materials and natural energy resources. There is no doubt that the impact of the individual maker is minimal compared to that of industry, but I am of the belief that we should take responsibility to evaluate our processes and minimise our impact on the environment. If every maker made one small positive change to his/her practice, the combined result would make a significant difference.

In researching information and contributions for this publication I strove to solicit individuals who had done significant research and made a commitment to sustainable practices. Some are makers, some teach, some administrate, but all are interested in contributing to additional information on sustainable practices in ceramics.

Kilns

The Archie Bray Foundation for the Ceramic Arts: leading by example

The Archie Bray Foundation for the Ceramic Arts in Helena, Montana, has provided studios and facilities to ceramic artists for over 60 years. Artistic Director Steve Lee is convinced that information gathering and analysis is a prerequisite for understanding and implementing sustainable practices. The process for this institution began with a number of energy audits through the local energy provider along with the governmental

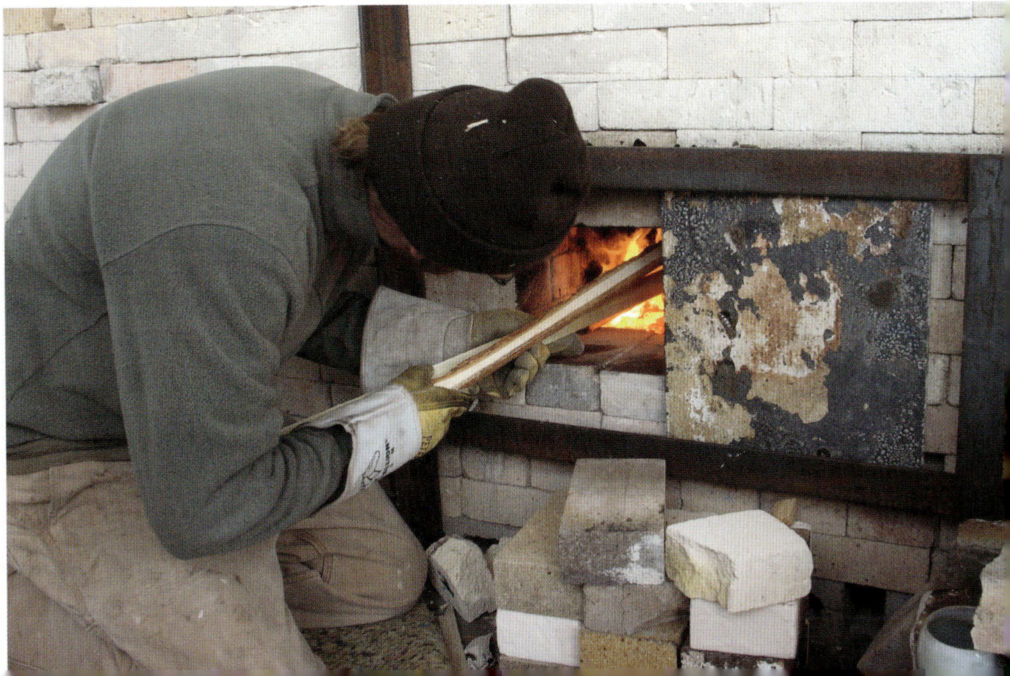

LEFT: *Jar*, Josh DeWeese, 2011. 63.5 cm (25 in) x 58.5 cm (23 in) x 53.5 cm (21 in), wood-fired salt/soda- glazed stoneware using local Trail Creek and Lewiston Pink slip glazes. *Photo: courtesy of the artist.*

RIGHT: Dave Peters wood firing at the Archie Bray Foundation for the Ceramic Arts, Helena, Montana. *Photo: Rachel Hicks.*

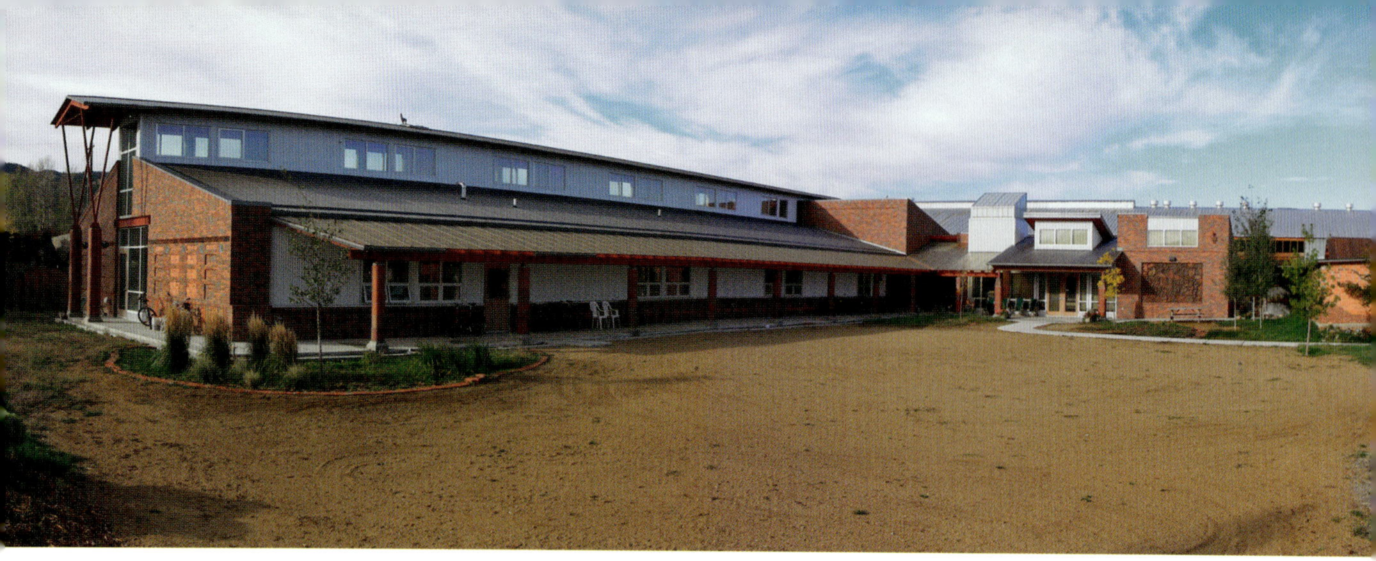

The Shaner Studio at the Archie Bray Foundation for the Ceramic Arts, Helena, Montana, 2008. *Photo: J. David.*

agency on environmental management. Bray maintenance staff used the subsequent recommendations as a guideline to systematically evaluate the facilities and prioritise areas for improvement. Many of the suggestions centred on improving insulation, and increasing the efficiency of communal heating and lighting.

Typically utility or power companies anticipate a certain need for energy to businesses and homes. If additional power is needed they assess an additional demand charge. Because of the increased need for supply, the power company also uses additional energy to generate the amount of electricity needed at one time. A standard electric kiln draws 11.5 kW of energy once it is turned on. Since this increases the need for electricity at one time, the demand charges are approximately £5.20 (US$8.40) per kW. The cost for the power company to provide that volume of electricity is £5.20 (US$8.40) x 11.5 kW or £60.25 (US$96.60) per kiln. If a second kiln is turned on simultaneously, the demand charge will double to accommodate the power needed for the additional kiln. Bray's firing facilities have 12 electric kilns, which led to the conclusion that the most cost-effective way to fire electric kilns would be to create staggered firing schedules. If two kilns are fired in a staggered schedule, the Bray will only incur the single demand charge and still be able to fire the same amount of artwork. This simple adjustment to user behaviour saves financial resources while reducing additional strain on the power company to supply an increased amount of electricity.

Recently, the Bray's community education programme decided to transition from cone 10 to cone 6 firings to reduce fuel costs while maintaining the same quality of clays and glazes in our classes. To track the fuel savings on the kilns, natural gas 'flow meters' were installed to record the amount of cubic feet of gas used per firing. The results were not as expected. In a 12 cubic feet [0.34 cubic metres] gas kiln, five firings were recorded, three to cone 6 reduction (1204°C/2200°F) and two to cone 10 reduction (1288°C/2350°F). The three cone 6 firings were fired by two different artists and used 2,400, 2,200, and 1,700 cubic feet of gas. The cone 10 firings were fired by two different artists and used 2,300 and 2,000 cubic feet of gas. This data in fact shows that the cone 10 firings on average used less gas per firing than the cone 6 firings.

The most important factor in firing efficiency is the operator. Artists often have different methods for firing kilns in an effort to achieve specific results or have been

RIGHT: Steve Lee working in the Shaner Studio at the Archie Bray Foundation for the Ceramic Arts, Helena, Montana, 2012. *Photo: Rachel Hicks.*

BELOW: *Another Time and Place*, Steve Lee, 2012. Ht: 38 cm (15 in) x 33 cm (13 in), porcelain with cobalt inlay. *Photo: Rachel Hicks.*

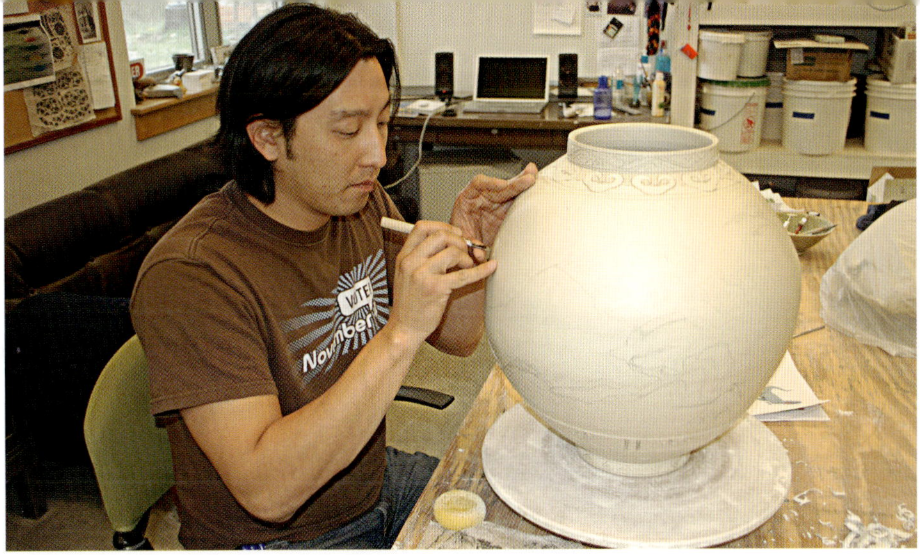

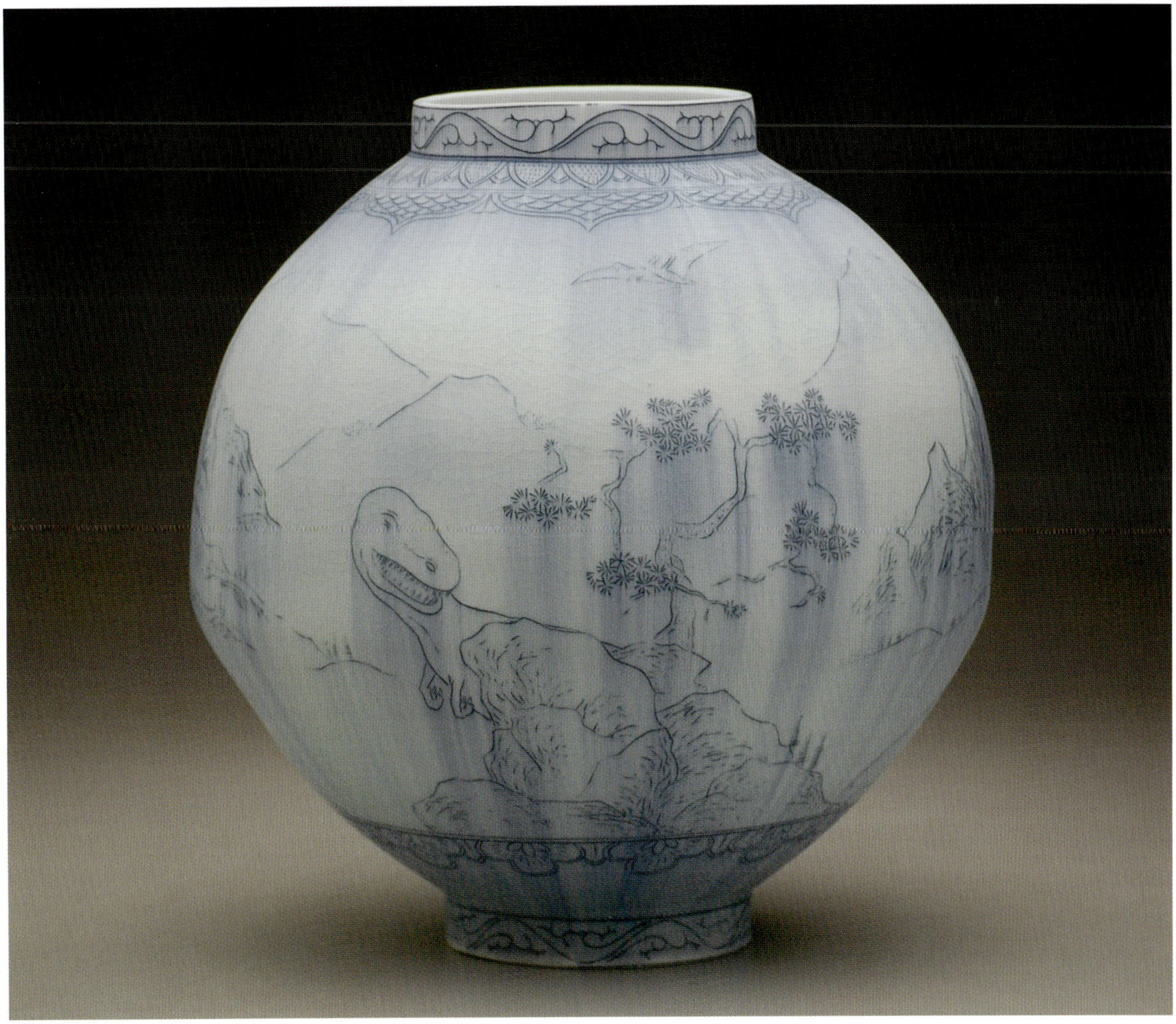

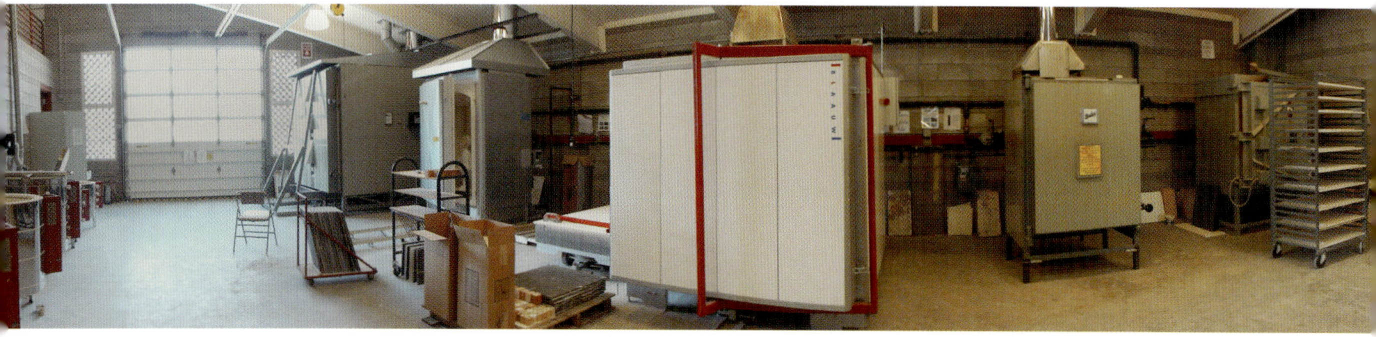

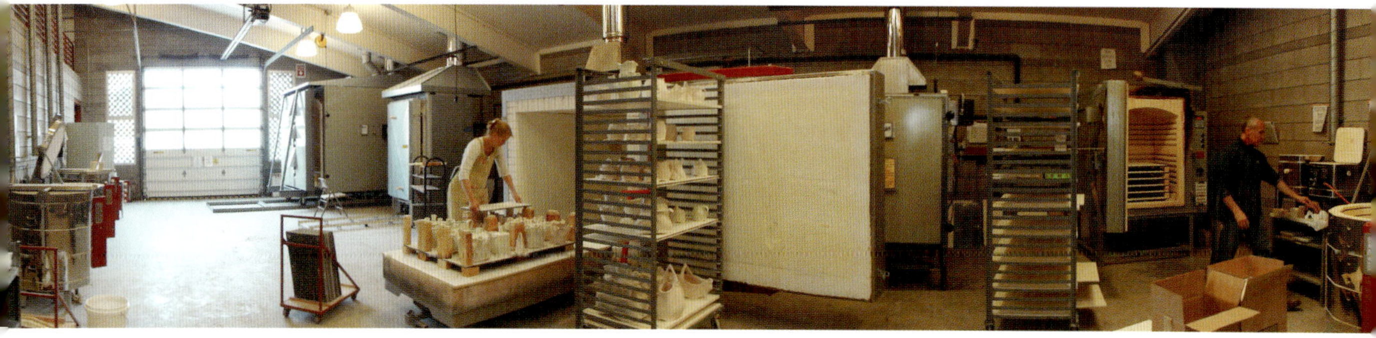

TOP: Archie Bray kiln room in the Shaner Studio, Helena, Montana, 2008. *Photo: Ayumi Horie.*

BOTTOM: Martha Grover and Bobby Silverman in the Archie Bray kiln room in the Shaner Studio, Helena, Montana, 2008. *Photo: Ayumi Horie.*

taught to fire in a certain manner and continue to do so out of habit. At the Bray, artists are encouraged to fire in the manner that will produce the highest quality of work but in some cases similar if not improved results could be achieved in a more efficient way. In Pete Pinnell's article 'Firing Copper Reds', he explains that the amount of gas being used in a reduction firing is often more than is necessary, leading to a waste of fuel. Utilising this information, a standardised firing schedule and kiln settings were created that would produce consistent results and minimise the amount of fuel consumption of each firing. This also reduces the impact of the operator variable to achieve consistent firing results.

The Bray has also initiated a number of energy conservation and waste management practices. The staff looked closely at the recommendations and prioritised them in the context of the budget and available resources. Given the age of the Bray's facilities (60+ years) many of the improvements involved a basic upgrade: such as replacing inefficient heating units; switching incandescent lights with compact florescent light bulbs and LED lighting; sealing air leaks in buildings; replacing and wrapping old water heaters; and creating heightened awareness among staff and resident artists of the efforts to conserve energy. While these seem like small changes, the Bray saw a reduction in its energy costs by 5% for *three consecutive years.*

In 2010 the Bray completed a comprehensive kiln project that focused on upgrading their kiln facilities with efficient, technologically advanced kilns. Many of the kilns previously located on the grounds were home-built and utilised inefficient materials and burner systems and no safety controls. The project added seven new kilns to the Bray studios chosen to make improvements in energy efficiency from the older kilns.

Included in the project are: 3 Bailey kilns (USA), 2 Blaauw kilns (Holland), a Geil car kiln (USA) and an atmospheric kiln built by Master Kiln Builders (USA). Early data has shown a 40 to 60% reduction in natural gas usage between the older and newer kilns of comparable size. The expanded gas kiln facilities also enable the resident artists to use the more cost-effective gas kilns for bisque and glaze firings rather than the electric kilns and subsequent demand charges. It also encourages artists to do group firings which are a much more efficient use of time and energy.

Commercial kilns as energy savers

I was introduced to kiln technology in the 1970s when 'building your own' was standard practice and taught as part of the educational process. Few commercial kilns were available then, and consumption of fossil fuels was just beginning to be understood as an environmental concern. I appreciate my knowledge of kiln construction, and think it is invaluable in understanding kiln operation, but I have come to understand that commercially produced kilns are considerably more energy efficient due to the stringent manufacturing standards that are employed.

Ceramicists today often utilise electric kilns to bisque fire their ware and then employ other kilns (i.e. gas reduction, wood or salt/soda) for their secondary 'atmospheric' firings. A variety of kilns and energy sources for fuel seem the norm, depending on your aesthetics. Installing a 'flow meter' on a gas kiln would give you an accurate measurement of usage and would give you an opportunity to make adjustments for more efficient firing schedules. Electric kiln manufacturers supply spreadsheets that can help you calculate the amount of electricity used in specific firings. You can then use this information to help create more efficient firings.

For decades kiln manufacturers have been striving to improve the energy efficiency of their products. With the invention of refractory ceramic fibres developed for the space industry, insulating refractory blankets have helped to revolutionise ceramic kilns. By wrapping kilns in an envelope of refractory fibre, the heat of the kiln has fewer opportunities to escape. This development has produced a plethora of well-built and energy-efficient kilns. (Initially associated with health risks, the development of ceramic fibre has come on dramatically, and most refractory fibre blankets are applied by the manufacturers and now arrive at schools, art centers and studios completely sealed and with either no or minimal risk for the user.) Consumers have seen great improvements in options for energy-efficient kilns. I hesitate to endorse one manufacturer over another, but many consider Blaauw kilns as the best commercially made ceramics kilns for individuals, schools and art centres today. Those who have made the investment consider the energy efficiency one of the most valuable aspects of the investment.

Blauuw is committed to achieving greater energy efficiency in its kilns, using lightweight insulation materials that make their products 60% more efficient than traditional kilns, as well as committing to kilns with long lives, made from materials that are recyclable. Additionally, they provide *afterburners* that *clean* or *scrub* the carbon hydrogens often produced during firings before they are released into the open air.

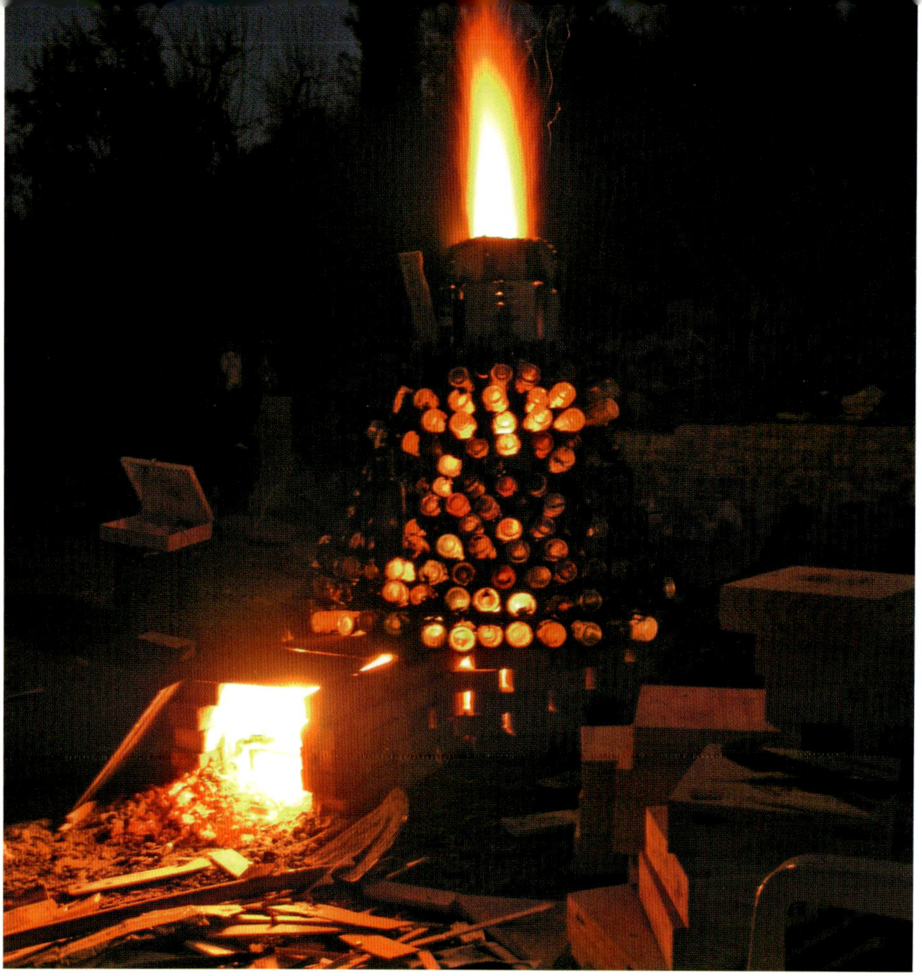

LEFT: Terry Davies and Alberto Cavalini's bottle kiln firing, Italy, 2009. *Photo: Terry Davies/Alberto Cavalini.*

Site-specific recycling: Chianti wine bottle kilns

English potter **Terry Davies** and Italian **Alberto Cavalini** have been lighting up piazzas across Italy with their collaborative kilns built from Chianti wine bottles. This is another great example of an innovative use of local waste material, which in this case also provides a site-specific installation/performance aspect to the kilns.

The principle was simple: glass shares many properties with clay, so just as when clay is heated too fast it will explode, similarly with wine bottles thrown into a bonfire. Their first kiln experiment used about 150 wine bottles. Terry and Alberto explain:

> We marked out on the ground a circle approximately a metre diameter, and lay each bottle side by side, with necks towards the centre. (The thought being, when the necks would become soft from the heat, they would bend down closing the bottle, and creating the closed air space.) In the centre we built a small platform, and placed some raw pots on top. On the side from where we would fire, we built a small simple firebox, using an old kiln shelf as a cover; this is important, as the early flames from the fire must not go into the kiln and touch the glass, until a good temperature is reached, normally around 400°C [752°F]. Next we mixed some field clay with builders sand (the clay mixture is not so important even if it includes vegetation or small stones).

OPPOSITE

TOP LEFT: Bottle kiln construction, Terry Davies and Alberto Cavalini, Italy, 2010.

TOP RIGHT: Fired bottle kiln interior, Italy, 2010.

BOTTOM LEFT: Terry Davies and Alberto Cavalini (centre) with bottle kiln under construction, Italy, 2011.

BOTTOM RIGHT: Terry Davies inside fired and partly dismantled bottle kiln, Italy, 2011.
Photos: Terry Davies/Alberto Cavalini.

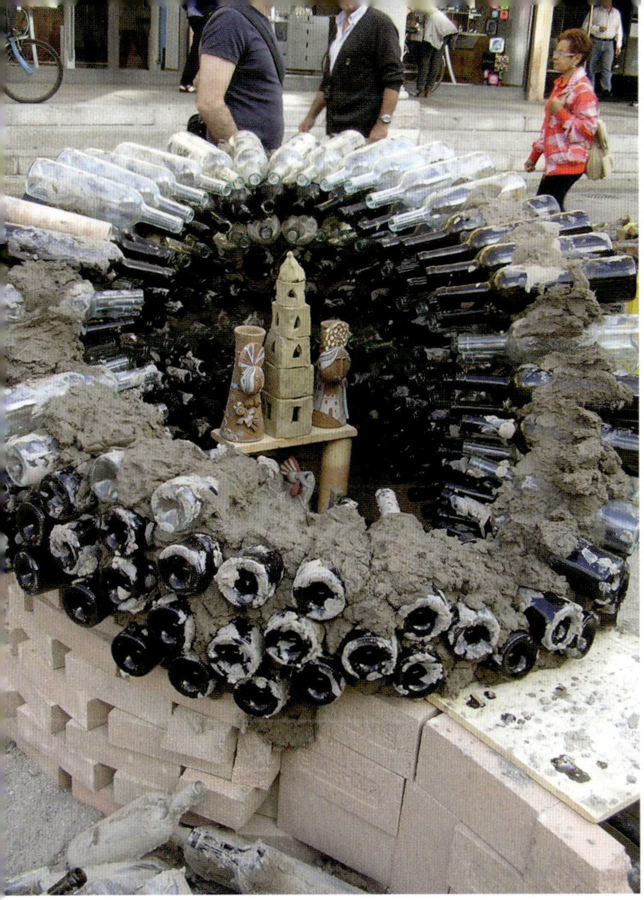

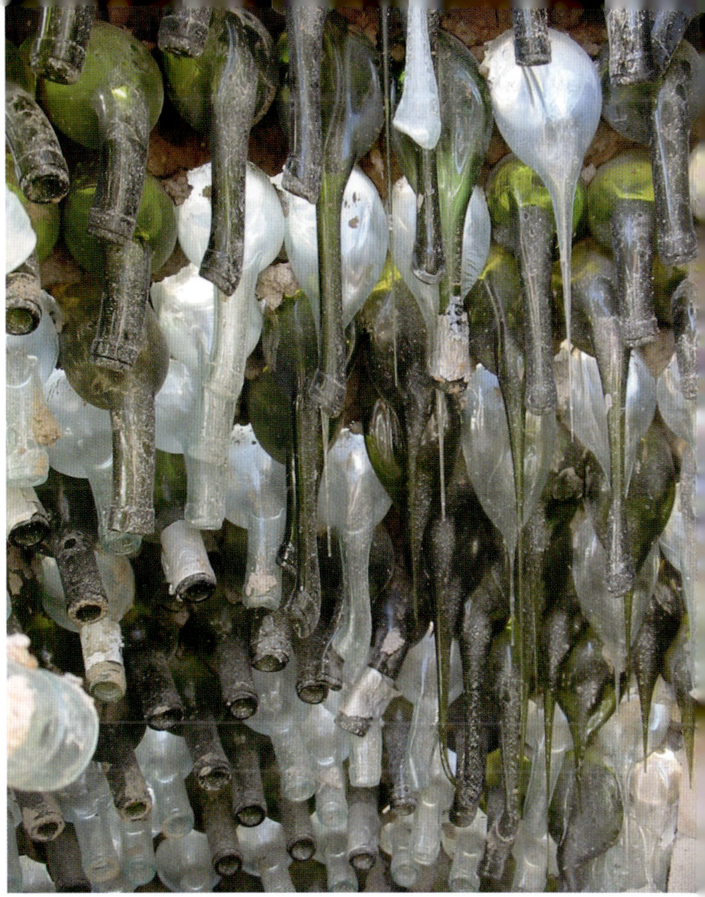

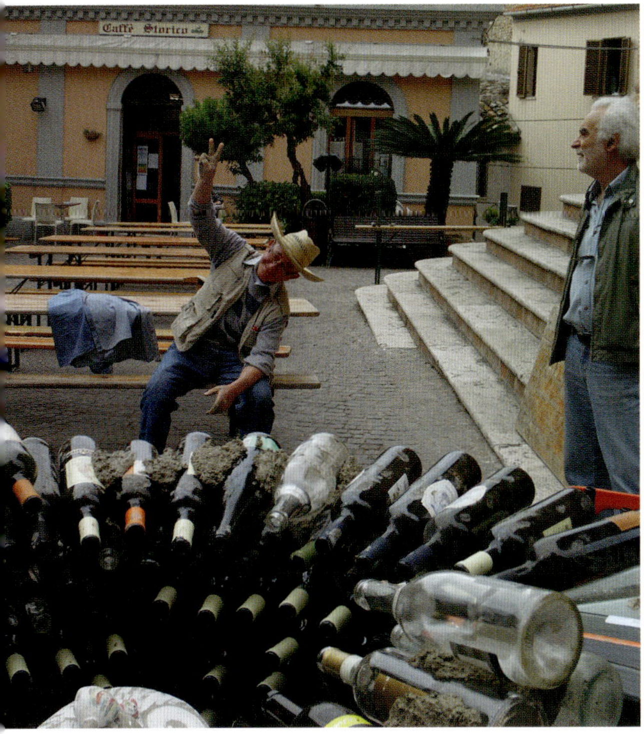
Caffè Storico

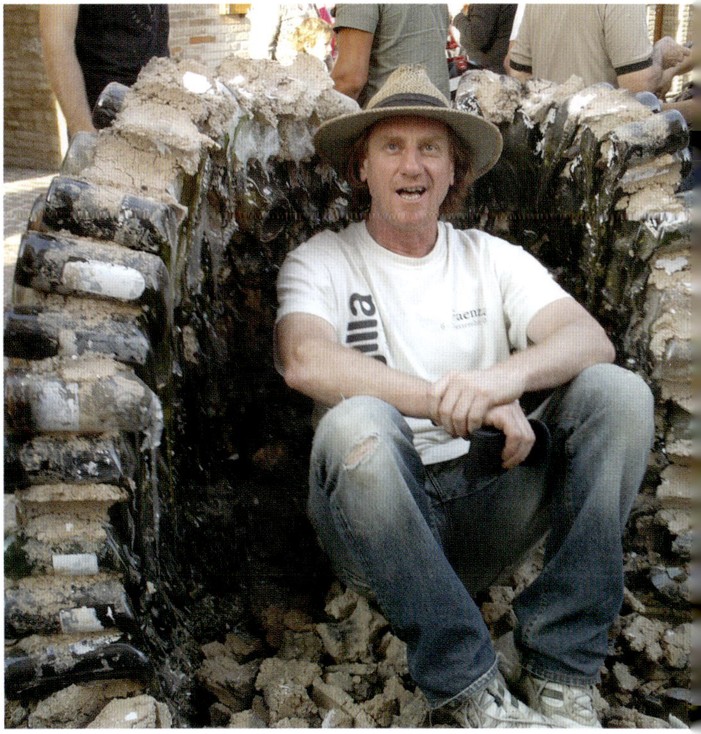
faenza

> A ring of clay was placed around each bottle shoulder, helping to hold each bottle in place, and also closed up the air gap between bottles. With each level the ring becomes narrower, and an igloo shape is formed.

During that first firing, Terry and Alberto took safety precautions and wore eye protection in consideration of a small chance that a glass bottle might explode. They were delighted and surprised to reach 600°C (1112°F) without any explosions. Buoyed by the relative success of the first firing, they built a second kiln with a number of adjustments. They increased the kiln capacity by using 500 wine bottles and enlarged the size of the centre hole for better draw by reversing the bottles (necks point outward) from the 1.5 metre (5 ft) height. They also added a final ring of bottles standing up on their bases to create a chimney and included a firebrick base to help slow the cooling process and provide a firm ground for the glass 'dome'.

As the kiln approached 1000°C (1832°F), they witnessed the glass beginning to melt. The following day, they opened the kiln and found bottles on the outside intact. On one side they had begun to melt, forming a 'cave' of melted bottled necks, and the pots they had fired were decorated with drippings of glass 'icing'.

Terry and Alberto have experimented with the shape of the kilns, some built as large ovals and some as tall bottle shapes. They found it necessary to support the 'waist' of the kilns utilising wooden sticks and wire to prevent the 'belly' from slumping outward (the wooden sticks and wire can be removed prior to the firing once the clay 'mortar' has dried). A small iron grate has also been employed in the firebox to allow improved temperature control. These kilns can be re-fired by simply repairing the small access door created to get the fired work out.

Sadly, Alberto Cavalini passed away during the production of this book.

Firings

Common-sense firing efficiency

John Britt is a potter and educator, conducting workshops regularly and authoring articles on his research into glazes and energy efficiency for the ceramicist. His glaze research for a particular effect can take him from low-fire electric firing to high-temperature gas firing. John states:

> However I work, I try to employ the principles that I teach in glaze chemistry and firing classes to maximise the efficiency of what I am doing.

John's knowledge of the firing cycle allows him to make adjustments for maximum efficiency. Many electric kilns have pre-programmed firing cycles that are easy to use but generalised to work for most potters. For example, a slow bisque cycle may be good for most applications but if you are firing very dry, thin porcelain perhaps a slightly faster cycle would work just as well, while with thicker stoneware you need to make sure to allow more time.

John also eliminated long pre-heats or overnight warm-ups. This is generally done out of tradition or fear but is often a waste of energy. Most kilns, especially

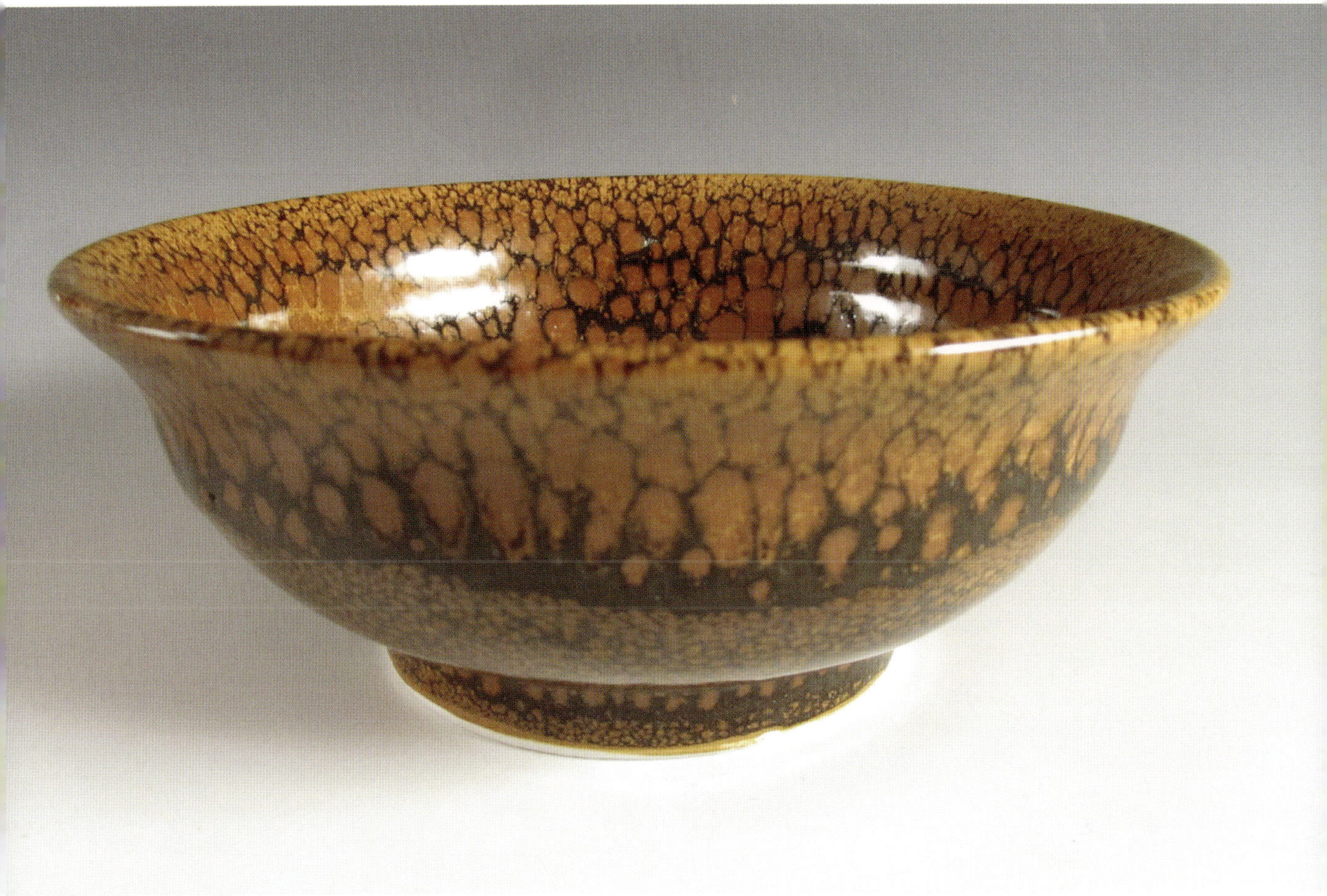

Yellow Oil Spot Bowl, John Britt, 2012. 7.5 cm (3 in) x 15 cm (6 in), thrown. Porcelain, fired at cone 10. *Photo: courtesy of the artist.*

manufactured ones, can be started cold and fired off in 10 to 12 hours. Once the water is out of the glaze coat or bisque, kilns can be fired pretty fast without fear of exploding the pieces. We have a tendency to think of our precious artwork as a baby that must be pampered. But in industry, kilns are routinely fired in less than eight hours. This should give you confidence that you can fire faster without fear.

John offers another specific example of adjusting kiln settings for his own personal needs:

> Another thing I discovered that saved a lot of energy was to pay more attention to my damper settings. In the early stages of firing a gas kiln, I was taught to leave the damper fully open at 23 cm (9 in) to get full oxidation. Later I discovered that the damper at 11.5 cm (4½ in) allowed more of the heat to stay in the kiln and yet was fully oxidising. Then, after many years of firing oxidation in my gas kiln, I realised that at peak temperature, if the damper was at 6.5 cm (2½ in) it was oxidising, so I reasoned that at the lowest gas setting, under 816°C (1500°F), having the damper at 7.5 cm (3 in) would surely oxidise. This change alone knocked about three hours off the firing time.

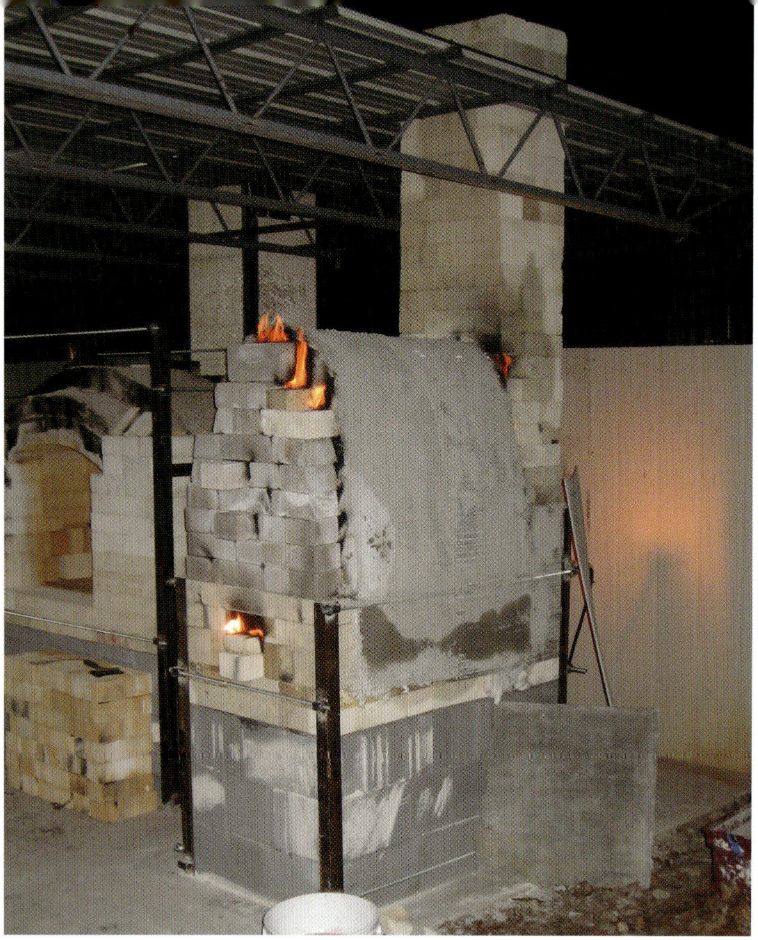

John Britt's experimental soda kiln test firing, kiln walls 29 cm (11½ in), cast refractory shell with stainless steel pins and 12.5 cm (5 in) of refractory fibre with top coat, 2012. *Photo: John Britt.*

Another easy way to save energy and time in bisque firings is to minimise the number of shelves. Shelves contain a lot of mass and take time and energy to heat up. In his bisque firings, John tries to tumble stack (stacking pots on top of one another in a kiln, separated only by wadding) and eliminate the need for shelves. You can take this concept further by using new thinner shelves in gas glaze firings to lower the mass and allow more space for work. The old shelves might be 1 to 1½ inch (2.5–4 cm) thick so with 10 shelves that is 10 to 15 inches (25.5–38 cm), but with the new nitride bonded silicon carbide shelves at ¼ inch (0.6 cm) this would be 2½ inches (6.3 cm) for 10 shelves.

One can also save energy in firings by exchanging the hard brick bag wall in your gas kiln with soft bricks or eliminating the bag walls altogether. Instead of using whole bricks as stilts, try using soaps or extruded stilts. In short anything you can do to reduce the mass but still support the shelves and work.

The best investment you can make is in education. Knowing the firing cycle and the chemical processes that are taking place will allow you to maximise the efficiency of your firings. For example, understanding that carbon monoxide is the cause of reduction effects rather than carbon, will allow you to waste less fuel. Realising that carbon monoxide has to circulate within the kiln will keep you from packing the kiln too tightly. Even though you may think that the tightest pack is the most efficient because you get more work into each firing, you may find that a few less pots in the kiln will allow a more even temperature and reduction, thus a higher percentage of successful pots.

Fact and fiction: environmental impacts of salt/soda firing

Wil Shynkaruk, potter and educator, has been on a quest to explore the safety and environmental implications of salt firing. As western understanding of pollution as health hazard increased, concerns about the health and environmental aspects of salt firings also increased. Wil writes:

> By the nineties, fears of the environmental and health dangers of salt firing had inspired near hysteria in some corners of the ceramic arts community. Many were calling for the complete discontinuation of salt firing. In the face of these calls, Gil Stengil did an extensive search of industrial records to determine what research had been done regarding the impacts of salt glazing. Surprisingly, he found no significant studies. The very few references I have encountered came from Europe and seemed to be inspired more by the visual cloud produced in salt-glazing, rather than by actual health or environmental concerns.

Wil teamed up with a chemist looking for answers. They devised a series of tests that allowed them to calculate the amount of sodium that reacted with the clay surfaces, assuming a 'worst-case' scenario in which all the liberate chloride combined with water vapor to create hydrochloric acid, a brand new kiln is being used, and salting is very generous. The results were that, under these circumstances, only 1.7% of the salt added to the kiln actually reacted with the clay to liberate the chlorides, while the other 98.3% recombined and exited the kiln as salt crystals. In fact, the cloud that emanates from a salt kiln is actually caused by water vapor in the atmosphere condensing around these salt crystals and creating a fog. Wil explains in more detail:

> In our worst-case scenario, firing a salt kiln with 24 cubic feet of stacking space would produce 348 grams of acid. *Put into perspective, a kiln could be salted once a month for an entire year, and introduce only as much acid into*

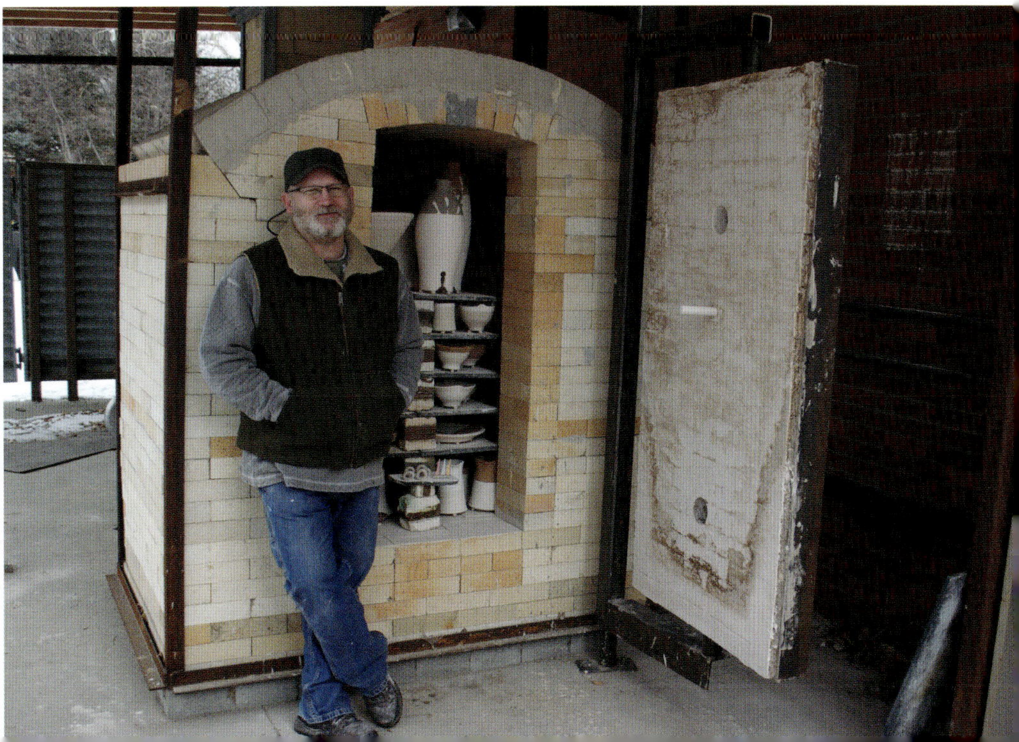

Wil Shyankaruk with his rebuilt salt kiln in Moorhead, Minnesota, 2013. *Photo: courtesy of the artist.*

> *the environment as produced by a single vehicle during two months of typical driving in the United States.* As these calculations were done on a worst-case scenario, we were assuming that the kiln was new and that 45 pounds of salt were added in the salting process. Anyone that salt-glazes regularly knows that this is an excessive amount of salt for a seasoned kiln of this size. In my experience 6 to 10 pounds would be sufficient, so the actual amount of acid produced would be significantly lower. Also, we assumed that all the chloride liberated when the sodium reacts with the clay combines with water vapor to produce acid. It is far more likely that some of the chloride reacts with the metal oxides in the clay and glaze, to form metal chloride compounds like iron chloride (ferric chloride) and cobalt chloride, effectively reducing the amount of acid entering the environment. When one considers that firing a large gas kiln can produce upwards of a ton of carbon dioxide from the combustion process, a few hundred grams of acid diluted in the large volume of air moving through the kiln seems rather inconsequential.
>
> Calculating from our worst-case scenario, we determined that for every 100 grams of salt added to the kiln, only 1.028 grams of acid would be produced. To put this into the practical context of daily work, my most recent salt firing resulted in a release of approximately 20 grams of acid stemming from the addition of 2000 grams of salt into the kiln; this is a fairly trivial quantity of acid.

Interesting parallels and differences exist between soda firing and salt firing. In the early days of soda firing, it was promoted as an environmentally friendly alternative to salt glazing. With evidence of salt glazing's minimal environmental effects however, the motivation for soda firing has shifted away from emulating salt glazing towards the continued development of its own related but distinct aesthetic. There is somewhat more controversy about determining the theoretical chemical reactions that occur in a typical soda kiln. Additional testing of actual emissions of soda kilns is needed.

Wil carried out parallel tests with soda, and results indicated that *'soda firing is similar to, or likely somewhat environmentally worse than salt firing'.*

Over the past number of years there has been a surge in the number of potters seeking to fire at lower temperatures in order to conserve fuel. The number of successful artists firing at cone 6 has proliferated along with several new books on the subject. This strategy has also been successfully applied to salt glazing, with several artists now doing beautiful work in this range.

There are also methods by which salt firing can be made more efficient. Wil explains:

> Salt kilns have traditionally been made of dense firebrick or of a hard-brick lining with an insulating brick exterior. With the use of surface coatings such as Maycoat and Greenpatch 421, it is now feasible to build a salt kiln entirely out of insulating brick or ceramic fiber. With the superior insulating properties of these materials protected by one of the many coatings now available, salt kilns can be built to be far more fuel efficient.

Salt-glazed Jug, Wil Shyankaruk, 2012. 43 cm (17 in) x 16.5 cm (6½ in), stoneware. *Photo: courtesy of the artist.*

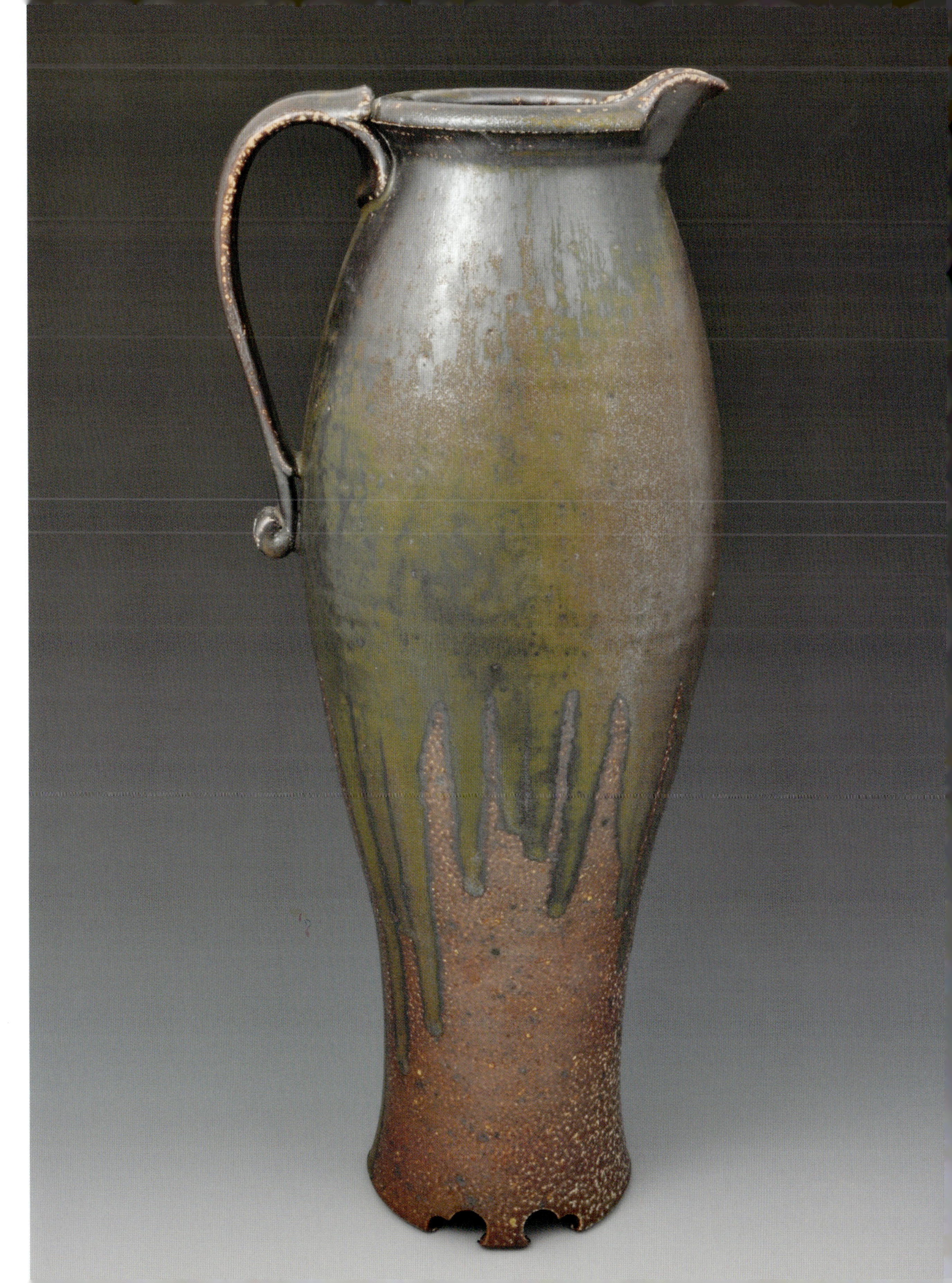

Fuels

Wood firing (as an act of respect)

Steve Harrison is a potter and author, and for over 40 years has been developing techniques using local materials for short, fuel-efficient, clean-burning wood firing. He is the author of several books, most notably *Laid Back Wood Firing*, now in its 5th edition, which has been continuously in print for the past 35 years. Steve epitomises the *holistic potter*, constantly curious and in touch with every aspect of his environment.

Steve utilises the materials he discovers in his local area. He investigates his local geology and has discovered some unusual ceramic bodies, in particular a deposit of white bauxite refractory clay that he used to make his own firebricks for his kiln. After his 42nd test, he came up with a good recipe that included coffee grounds from his local café. The coffee grounds created very small air pockets in the finished firebricks, creating insulated refractory bricks that are therefore more fuel efficient. By utilising local ceramic materials, Steve has developed his own unique wood-fired porcelains, proto-porcelains and blackware.

Steve is well aware of how globalisation has provided us with the best of everything available to us every day of the year. The costs for this complete availability are enormous, not only financially, but also environmentally. Steve writes: 'Nearly everything that I use is obtained locally, by me, by hand or personally operated machine, collected, crushed milled, blunged, flocculated and sun dried, here in this locality, on this spot. I know where my clay and glazes come from; I know where my food comes from.'

Steve fires his wood kiln to stoneware temperatures, to create his native *bai tunze* porcelain. He has spent years developing the concept of the down draft firebox, in an attempt to fire cleanly and minimise his effects on the environment. He also attempts, whenever possible, to recycle firing materials.

LEFT: Steve Harrison, stacked wood for the firing, New South Wales, Australia, 2012.

RIGHT: Steve Harrison's wood kiln firebox during firing, New South Wales, Australia, 2012. *Photos: courtesy of the artist.*

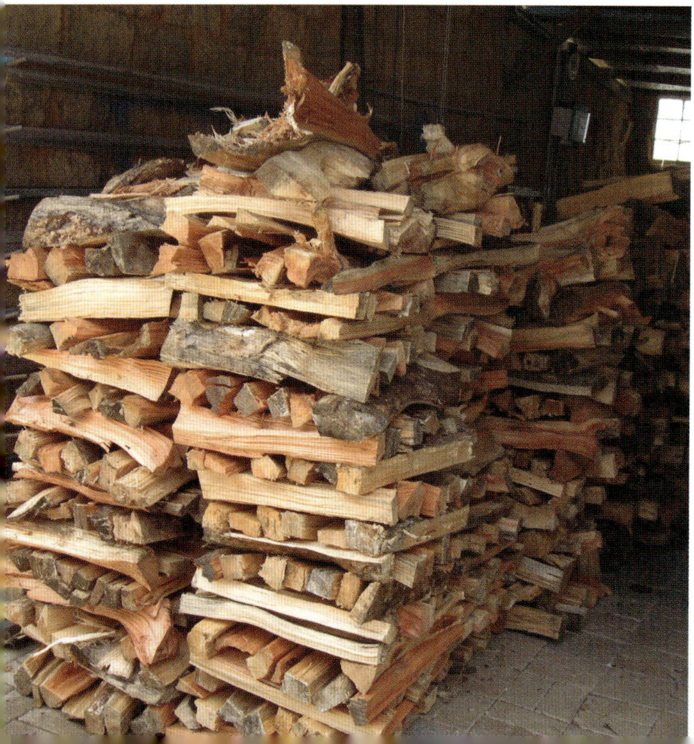

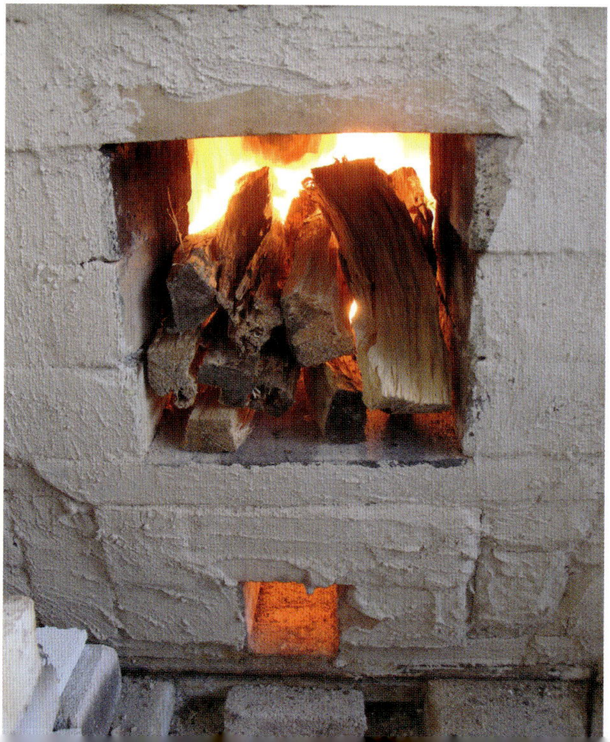

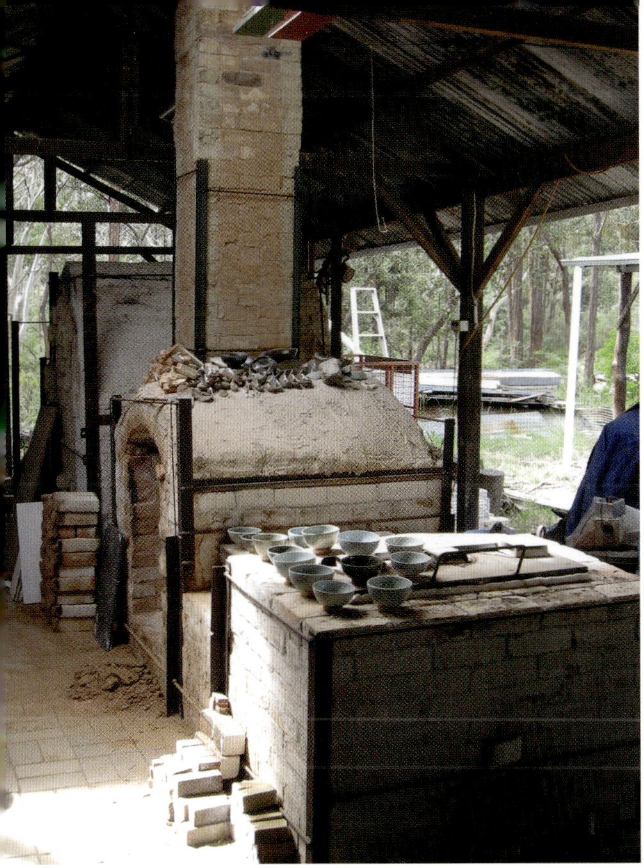

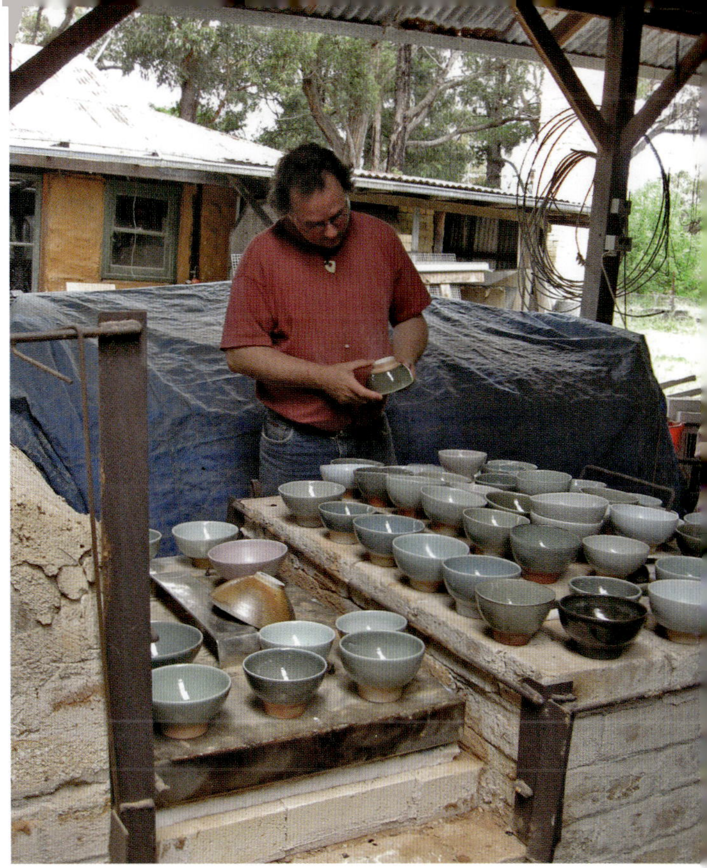

LEFT: Steve Harrison unpacking the wood kiln, New South Wales, Australia, 2012.

RIGHT: Steve Harrison examining pots from the wood firing, New South Wales, Australia, 2012.
Photos: courtesy of the artist.

I'm deeply committed to the integrity of this endeavor, to consume as little as possible, to be as resourceful as possible, to be self-reliant. In building my own kiln from my own firebricks in our own shed, made from local mud, fired with timber that we have grown ourselves on our own land, which has more trees on it now than it had when we first came here 35 years ago. All the waste rock glaze and wood ashes cleaned from the fire, if not used to make new glaze, is respectfully returned to the compost heap, where it is used to fertilise our organic garden.

Veggie oil as an alternative fuel

Ben Culbertson, Ceramics Professor at Shippensburg University in Pennsylvania, has been firing with vegetable oil for a number of years. This renewable fuel source often ends up in landfills and is known as waste vegetable oil (WVO). However, it is possible to convert vegetable oil into a biofuel that is compatible with kiln firing, or to use WVO in a straight, filtered form as a kiln fuel.

WVO on its own, or converted into biofuel, is a recycled waste product that produces fewer harmful emissions than fossil fuels. Both are biodegradable and are usually considered 'carbon neutral' fuels. The plants that produce the oils pull carbon from the atmosphere in the growing process and we simply return that carbon when we burn them. They may also be less expensive than fossil fuels.

Despite the advantages, using WVO or biodiesel comes with a unique set of challenges so they will never match the ease of natural gas and propane as a kiln fuel.

They can, however, offer a more environmentally friendly alternative to those who have access to waste vegetable oil. Many colleges and universities are producing biodiesel from campus WVO as part of their sustainability initiatives. This creates a terrific opportunity for ceramic programmes to become an important part of those initiatives by using some of the WVO and biodiesel produced in instructional programmes. WVO might be accessed locally at restaurants and institutional kitchens.

Numerous 5 gallon (19 litre) lidded buckets to collect the WVO are necessary, along with considerably larger (50+ gallon/190+ litre) storage containers for the firings. Ben explains his use of WVO for biodiesel:

> In 2006 I started making biodiesel. I collected WVO from the dining halls on the campus of Shippensburg University where I teach ceramics. I was concerned that rising fuel prices might eventually force the administration to put restrictions on our ceramics programme. A group of students and I began experimenting with ways to use biofuels for kiln fuel. We started with the biodiesel I was making since it had been working fine in my diesel vehicles. Later we moved to WVO as a fuel. Our goal was to demonstrate that it was possible to fire a stoneware reduction kiln to 2350°F [1288°C] from start to finish with biofuels (which we did!). The WVO was virtually free and the biodiesel I produced was less expensive than heating oil. So, honestly, one of the first motivations to try biofuels for our high temperature ceramic kilns was cost, but we were also motivated to reduce our carbon footprint on campus.

There are several considerations for using vegetable-based fuels that differ from petroleum-based fuels. Firstly, vegetable fuels have a much higher flashpoint than petro-fuels. This is a good quality in relation to flammability. The flashpoint for biodiesel is approximately 300°F (149°C); for vegetable oil, it is higher, approximately 600°F (316°C). The high flashpoint for biodiesel makes it a 'combustible' as opposed to a 'flammable' liquid. This means it is much safer to handle than petro-diesel, which has a flashpoint of 140°F (60°C). Biodiesel is also biodegradable. While the safety benefits are comforting, vegetable fuels do pose challenges for combustion.

The second major difference is that vegetable fuels, unlike petro-fuels, do not contain aromatics or behave the same way petro-fuels do. This is why biodiesel will not work well in traditional kerosene lamps because it doesn't volatilise into a gas at the tip of the wick. Instead it forms a carbonised crust that inhibits capillary action of the wick and the flame eventually dies. Therefore, the most efficient way to burn vegetable fuels is to increase surface area to encourage oxygen mixing so that it behaves more like a gas or to heat the fuel to its flashpoint or auto ignition point to vaporise it. This is achieved in two ways: either by atomisation (pressure nozzle or compressed air nozzle) or by heated surfaces (metal drip-plate burner – acting something like a frying pan fire).

The third major challenge is viscosity. Vegetable fuels tend to be more viscous and thicken or gel more quickly in cold weather. This necessitates preheating the fuel in many circumstances. WVO at 175°F (79°C) has a viscosity comparable to diesel. Cold weather poses a unique challenge because getting the fuel out of the storage container can become impossible without some heat source. Biodiesel can also gel in cold temperatures. This may necessitate placing the fuel tank indoors or providing a heat source (e.g. heating element or solar enclosure) in cold weather.

Ben continues:

> We started with a modified furnace burner using biodiesel as the fuel. Because of the tendency for vegetable fuels to have a longer flame we added an extended blast tube to the furnace burner. Additionally, we inserted a perforated stainless steel pipe at the end of the blast tube. The perforated tube is smaller in diameter and about two-thirds the length of the blast tube extension. It sits at the centre of the blast tube with bolts that act as standouts to hold the tube in place. This perforated tube heats up to red hot within the blast tube and aids combustion of the biodiesel vapour. Using two of these modified furnace burners, we fired our 30 cu. ft [0.85 cu. m] soft brick cross-draft kiln to 2350°F [1288°C] in six to seven hours using approximately 23 gallons [87 litres] of biodiesel. Approximate cost of producing biodiesel was US$1.20/gallon [£0.20/litre].
>
> Using WVO proved more labour intensive and challenging. We fabricated four drip-plate burners with three steps out of one-eighth inch steel plate. Traditionally, drip-plate systems burn smoky in the beginning and then burn cleaner once the kiln is heated up to dull red heat. We have solved that problem by adding a side burner port with a biodiesel burner to preheat the firebox making it fairly simple to start the drip-plate system. The kiln reached red heat in about three hours with one biodiesel furnace burner with a 0.75/gal/hour nozzle. At this point we started the drip-plate burners. A drum filled with WVO that is elevated on a six-foot scaffold fed the drip-plate burners. The drum is equipped with a common water heater element and thermostat that heats the oil. Once the kiln is

LEFT: Ben Culbertson's biodiesel burner using modified burner with perforated tube insert, 2012.

RIGHT: Ben Culbertson's biodiesel burners at peak temperature, 2012. *Photos: Ben Culbertson.*

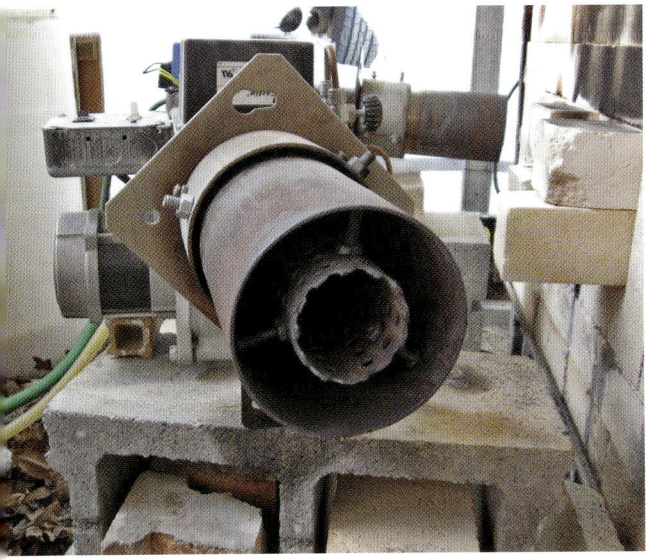

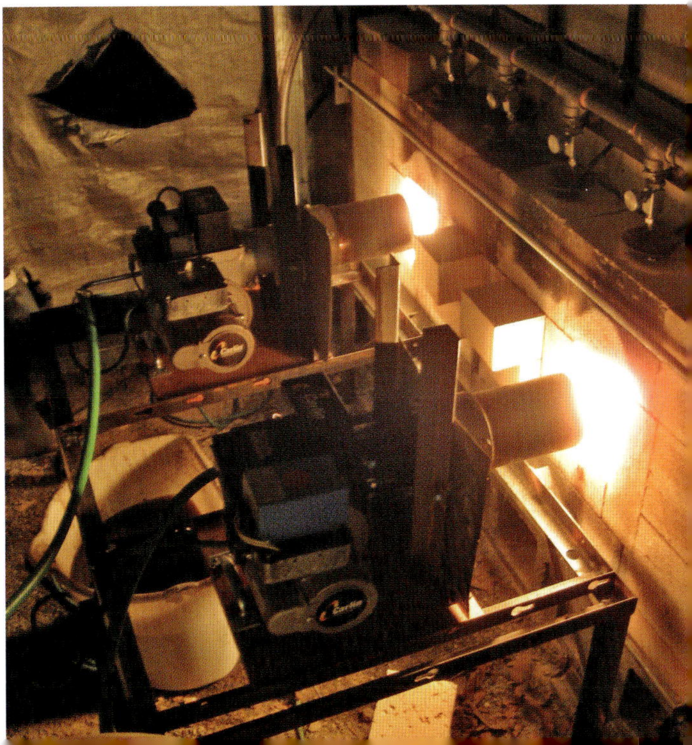

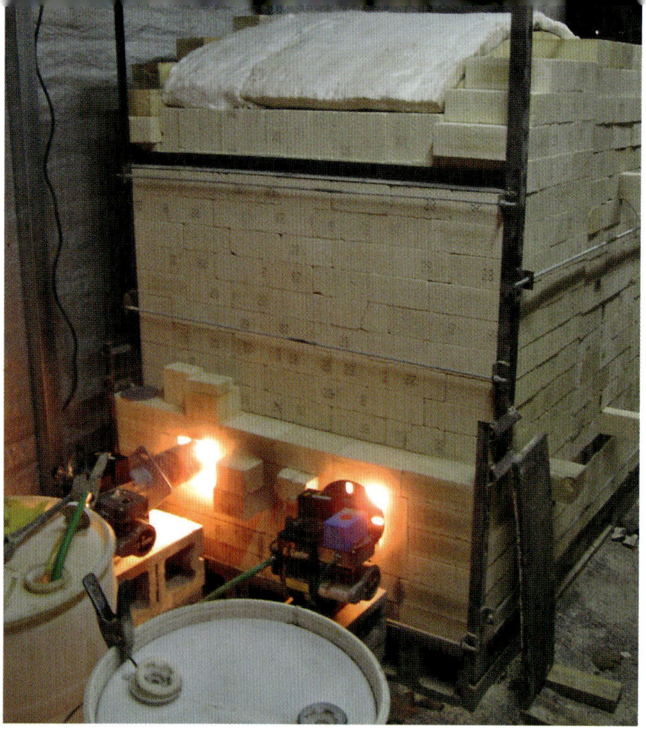

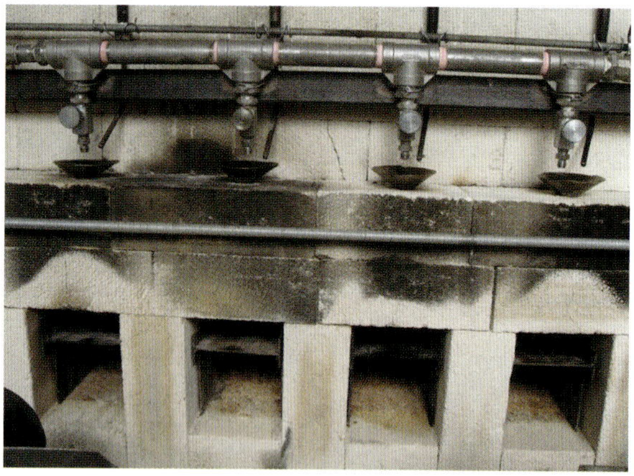

LEFT: Ben Culbertson's veggie kiln with biodiesel burners and fuel drums, 2012.

ABOVE: Drip-plate system for the waste vegetable oil and water drip, 2012. *Photos: Ben Culbertson.*

preheated, one begins 'stoking' the kiln with WVO. The similarity to stoking a wood kiln lies in the fact that fuel and air must be increased gradually as the temperature increases. In addition to the drip valves for oil we added the secret ingredient: water!

With guidance from Sam Clarkson, veggie kiln pioneer, we discovered that water is necessary to get adequate dispersion of the hot oil. We use about 25% water dripped into the funnel with the WVO. The water immediately turns to steam which helps disperse the hot oil into tiny particles to improve combustion. Strange, but true. This was the secret ingredient and we were able to fire up to 2350°F [1288°C] with the drip-plate burners. I mentioned labour intensive because this firing process averaged about 13–15 hours of near-constant monitoring. It surely could be improved. Total WVO consumed was roughly the same as the biodiesel at about 24 gallons [91 litres] in the 30 cu. ft soft brick kiln.

The final system we tried used a special nozzle called a 'siphon-feed nozzle'. It uses compressed air to atomize the WVO into extremely tiny particles. This technology is used on commercial waste oil furnaces that burn used crankcase oil as a fuel. This system is more complex. It requires a 'float tank' which is equipped with a heating element and thermostat. The float tank must heat the oil to approximately 180°F [82°C]. A tube attached to the nozzle pulls the oil into the nozzle through siphon action once the compressed air is turned on. It functions something like a paint sprayer that lifts paint into a spray nozzle with compressed air. We achieved a stable flame with 15psi of air pressure. The advantage of this system is being able to use straight WVO to produce a flame without the pre-heat necessitated by the drip-plate system. While this system will benefit from further improvements, we believe it demonstrates, along with the other systems, the viability of these alternative fuels.

A simple veggie oil kiln

Joe Finch, potter and kiln builder, grew up in a ceramics environment under the tutelage of his father Ray at the Winchcombe Pottery begun by Michael Cardew. He has also been experimenting with waste vegetable oil as a fuel.

Joe previously had used oil in the 1960s, at the beginning of his career when oil prices were low and environmental concerns non-existent. He also turned to oil when establishing the Kolonyama Pottery in Lesotho, as this was the only fuel available in the local area. Once he established his own pottery in 1973, he decided on wood as a fuel, as wood was widely available from a nearby sawmill, and allowed him to achieve exciting results in the kiln. By coincidence, waste wood is also an environmentally friendly source of fuel, but Joe recognised that not everyone has the space for wood firing, or access to a reliable wood source. For this reason, in 2007 he proposed building a kiln that could be fired with waste vegetable oil.

The kiln was a simple down-drought design, very similar to the kiln Joe built for Ruthanne Tudball but without the firebars (plans and photographs are shown in his book *Kiln Construction*), with a firebox on each side and a double internal flue, the one flue being covered apart from a gap at the front (far end from the chimney). Shutting one or the other side of the exit flue to the chimney, with a slide damper, can take the heat to the front or back of the kiln. Two fuel tanks were used, one for the oil and a smaller one for water, pipe work and taps were acquired for the oil and water, and scaffolding used to raise the tanks to allow for gravity feed. Joe explains:

> The principles for oil drip firing are simple. Oil and water are fed by gravity onto the hot drip-plate burner where the water turns to steam atomising the oil, which then vaporises and burns, the air being supplied by the natural draught from the chimney. The water not only improves the combustion of the oil but also reduces

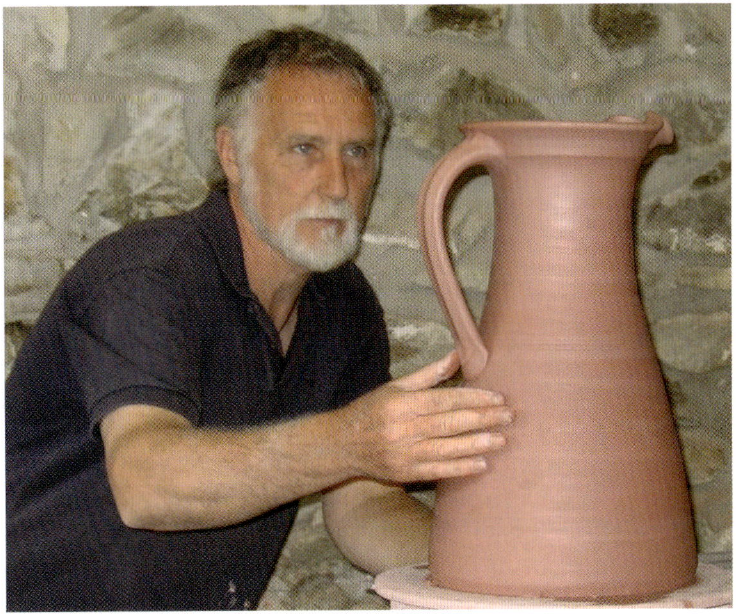

Joe Finch handling a large jug in Wales, UK, 2011. *Photo: courtesy of the artist.*

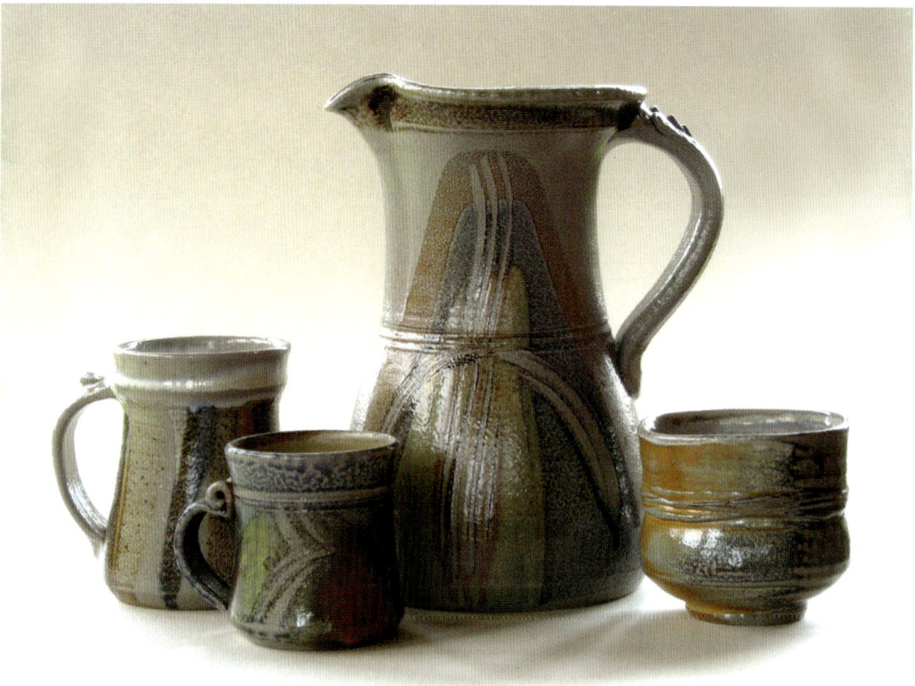

Slip decorated and soda-glazed pots, Joe Finch, 2012. *Photo: courtesy of the artist.*

the amount of carbon clinker that would build up on the plates (the carbon mixing with the steam producing carbon oxide and hydrogen). The cooling of the plates by the water will also prolong their life and the energy lost by the cooling is given back when the carbon oxide and hydrogen burn.

The delivery system for the oil and water needs to be fully adjustable and finely tuned. Simple water taps can be used as long as the flow can be controlled enough to allow very small amounts of water and oil. The amount of water needed is judged by watching the flame but as a guide it is normally about one part water to five parts oil. A fine stream of water from the tap runs down onto a wire, which breaks down the surface tension and produces many small drops, this then mixes with the oil and drips onto the hot burner plates. (In the initial stages of firing the burner plates need to be kept hot by a small wood fire.)

The burner plates should be made from thick iron otherwise they will warp and disintegrate fast. The size and angle of the plates is not crucial and will depend on the viscosity of the oil but as a guide, plates about 10 x 20 cm [4 x 8 in] and a slope of 15 degrees with the second and third plates slightly less should allow burning on all plates. (By raising or lowering the back of the burner frame the angle of the plates can be adjusted.) When firing with wood the pre-heating is important, as the plates and firebox need to be hot before starting the oil or you will produce a lot of black smoke. Also the pre-heat will take you past the early danger parts of the firing, as once the oil fire is started the temperature will rise quickly. When the oil drip is first started, burning will take place on the top plate

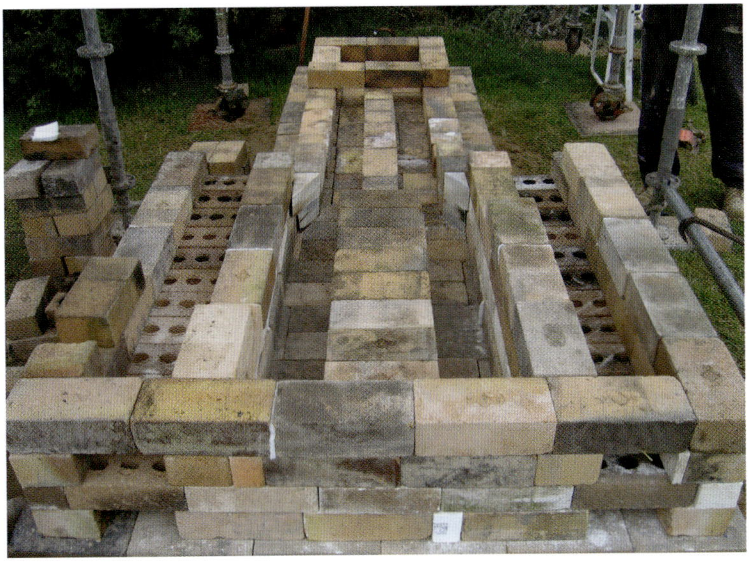

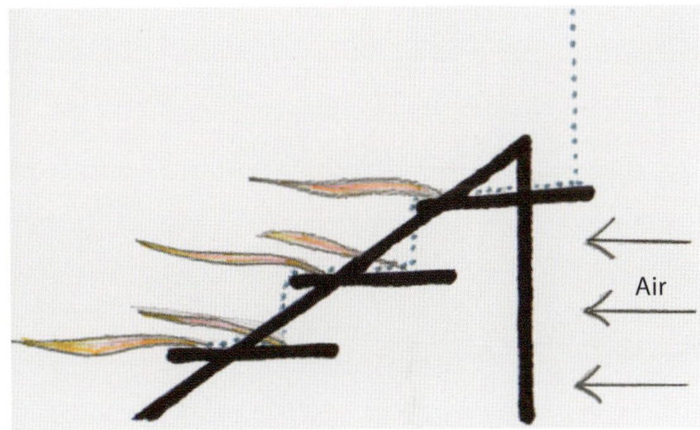

ABOVE: Chip oil kiln under construction in Aberystwyth, Wales, UK, 2007.

TOP RIGHT: Illustration for drip oil and water burner plates, Wales, UK, 2007.

RIGHT: Chip oil kiln in Aberystwyth, Wales, UK, 2007. *Photos: Joe Finch.*

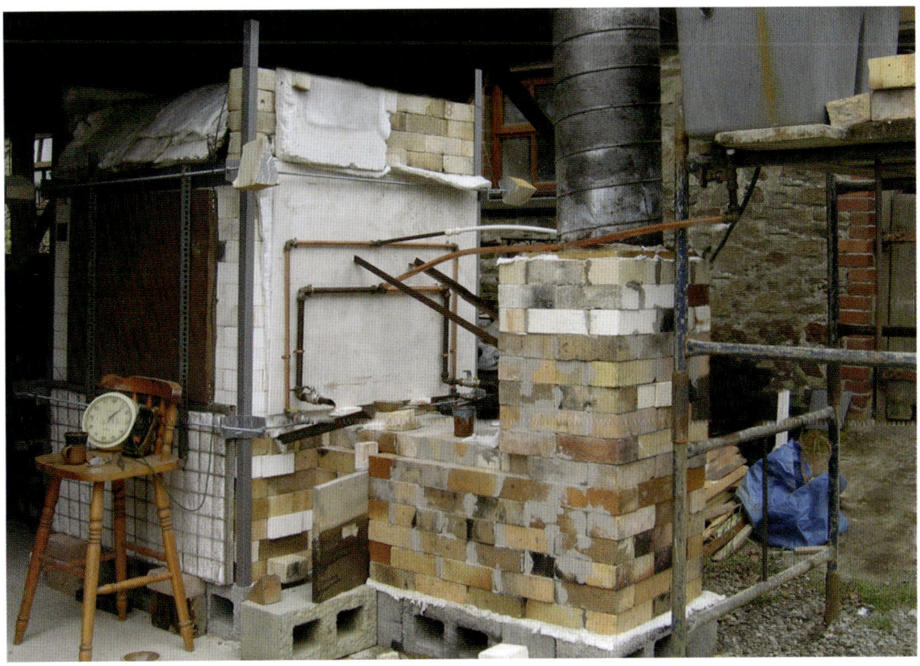

only, but gradually burning will flow to all plates and, as the firebox gets hotter, produce an intense white flame. Care should be taken not to allow oil to drip off the last plate onto the firebox floor as a pool of oil could cause an explosive burn. A mouse-hole, just in front of the burner plates, leading to the outside of the kiln would drain any excess oil or, as shown in the photographs, the layer of bricks with holes at the bottom of the firebox would achieve the same result. Both methods would also allow extra air into the firebox if it is needed.

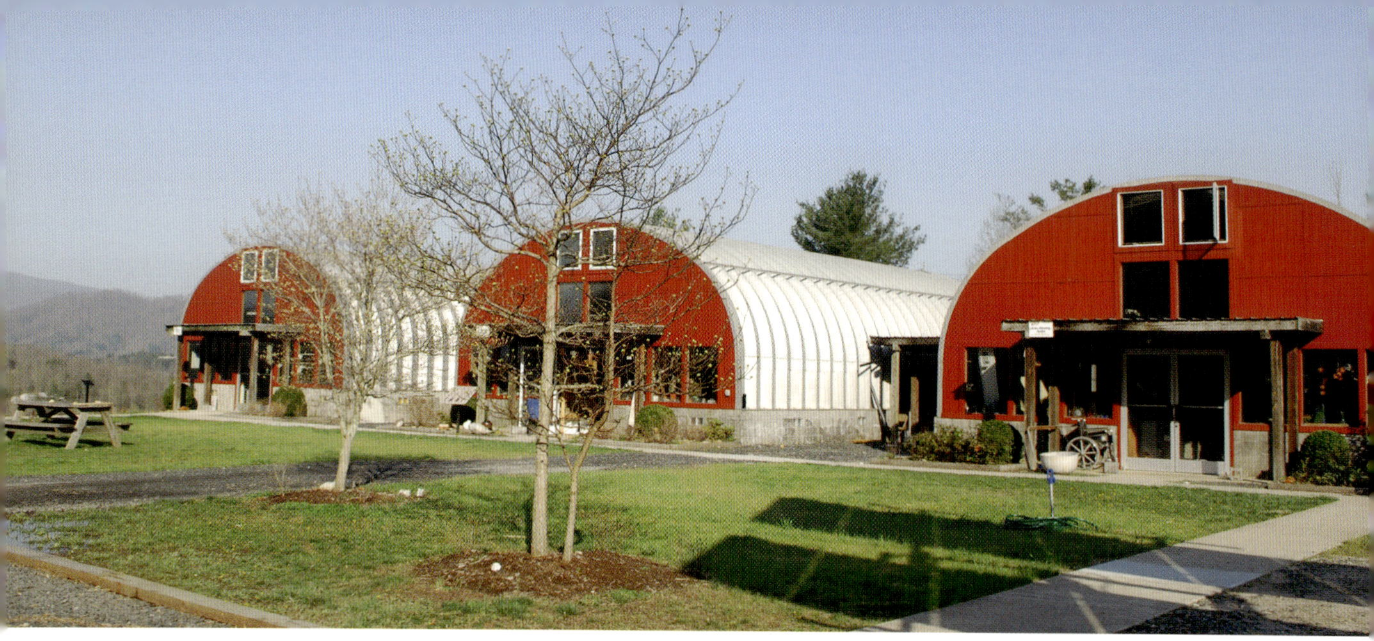

Gallery, clay and glass studios at EnergyXchange, Burnsville, North Carolina, 2011. *Photo: courtesy of the EnergyXchange.*

The EnergyXchange: a model for reclaiming energy

The EnergyXchange is nestled in the Black Mountains of western North Carolina and the area is rich in cultural, natural, and historic assets including the legendary Penland School of Craft. When the landfill that served the residents of the area was closed in 1994, extensive research and discussion took place to find a use for the potential energy. Landfill gas production (approximately 40 to 60% methane) results from chemical reactions and microbes acting upon the waste to break down in the landfill.

EnergyXchange has become one of the US's model energy recovery projects and is used regionally, nationally and internationally as an example of successful small landfill gas projects. Since 2000 the EnergyXchange has provided rental studio space to over 20 resident artists in a Glass studio and a Clay studio, and become known for the goal of turning unused landfill waste into fuel for these craft studios. For the ceramic artists most of the attention has been focused on the gas-fired ceramic kiln, which is fuelled with the methane gas captured from the landfill.

The Methane Kiln

The landfill gas (LFG) used throughout the campus is extracted through several wells drilled into the sealed-over landfill site. The pipelines run from the collection wells to a central manifold and blower station. The blower pulls the gas out of the landfill, and pushes it through the pipeline towards the sites on campus where it is used.

The original ceramic kiln at the site is still in operation over 10 years after it was built. In most aspects it resembles other 'typical' gas-fired reduction kilns in the area. It has 67 cubic feet (1.9 cubic metres) of volume, with around 27 cubic feet (0.76 cubic metres) of stacking space. The working floor of the kiln is built out of hard firebrick, while the rest is composed entirely of insulating firebrick nine inches (23 cm) thick (*firebrick* is commonly used to describe a brick capable of repeated firing to high temperatures and used in kiln construction. Lightweight, insulating brick are typically used for wall and arch construction). After initial firings, a layer of fibre blanket and 'mud' coating was added as extra insulation. The kiln's original chimney was six feet of brick topped off by another eight feet of metal pipe, which was recently replaced with brick entirely. The kiln is powered by forced air burners, purchased from Ward Burners, and designed to operate on the low-pressure and low-heat content gas. This situation required that the orifice commonly used to restrict high-pressure gas be left out of the burners. As a result the burners have no orifice, and instead the half-inch (1.3 cm) pipe is left open to deliver the landfill gas at as high a volume as possible.

Over the years it has been used to fire everything from bisque ware to stoneware, and under current conditions the kiln can be fired to cone 10 in approximately 14–18 hours. As an estimate, a kiln of similar size fired with propane (LPG) might require around 45–50 gallons (170–190 litres) to reach cone 10. This represents not only significant financial savings for a potter, but also a sizeable amount of landfill gas that would otherwise escape into the atmosphere as an unused resource.

The Pallet Kiln

In 2010 a wood-fired soda kiln was added at the EnergyXchange, designed by Mark Peters to take advantage of a supply of discarded wooden pallets. The Pallet Kiln represents not only a second innovative use of local waste material, but also provides a model for others on a scale smaller than that required for landfill methane gas.

The Pallet Kiln is built of a hard brick interior and insulated brick exterior, with a firebox and stokehole large enough to accommodate full pallets. The kiln is 167 cubic feet of total volume (38 cubic feet of stacking space) and consumes approximately 100–120 pallets when fired to cone 10. The kiln's oversized firebox and abundant inlet flues make it possible to stoke the kiln repeatedly with a full pallet (approximately 40 x 40 in (102 x 102 cm)) nails and all. Initial concerns of nails suspended on the sides of pots proved unnecessary, thanks perhaps to the depth and width of the internal firebox.

Over the course of the first year the kiln was fired to cone 10 six times, typically lasting around 18–20 hours and consuming around 120 pallets each time.

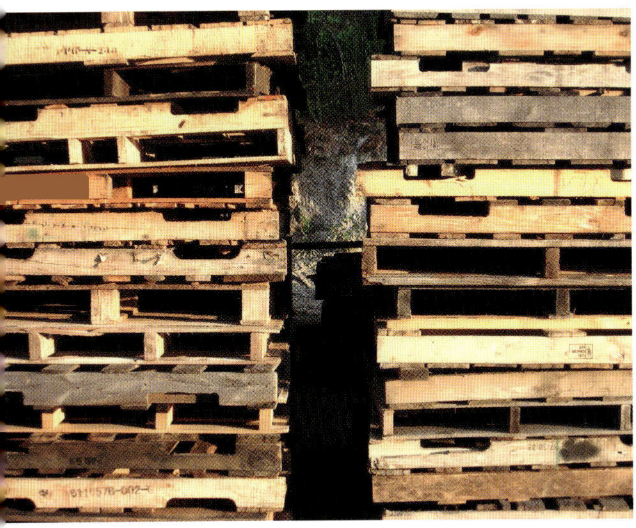

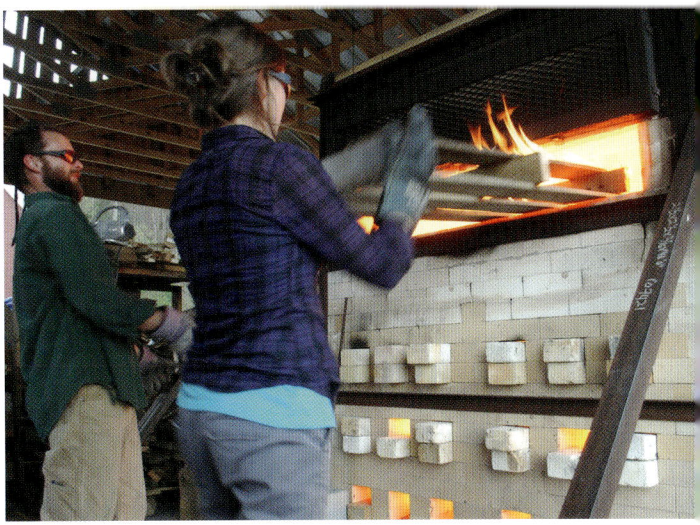

LEFT: Reclaimed wood pallets stacked for firing at EnergyXchange, Burnsville, North Carolina, 2011. *Photo: William Baker*

RIGHT: William Baker and Joy Tanner firing the pallet wood kiln at EnergyXchange, Burnsville, North Carolina, 2011. *Photo: courtesy of the EnergyXchange.*

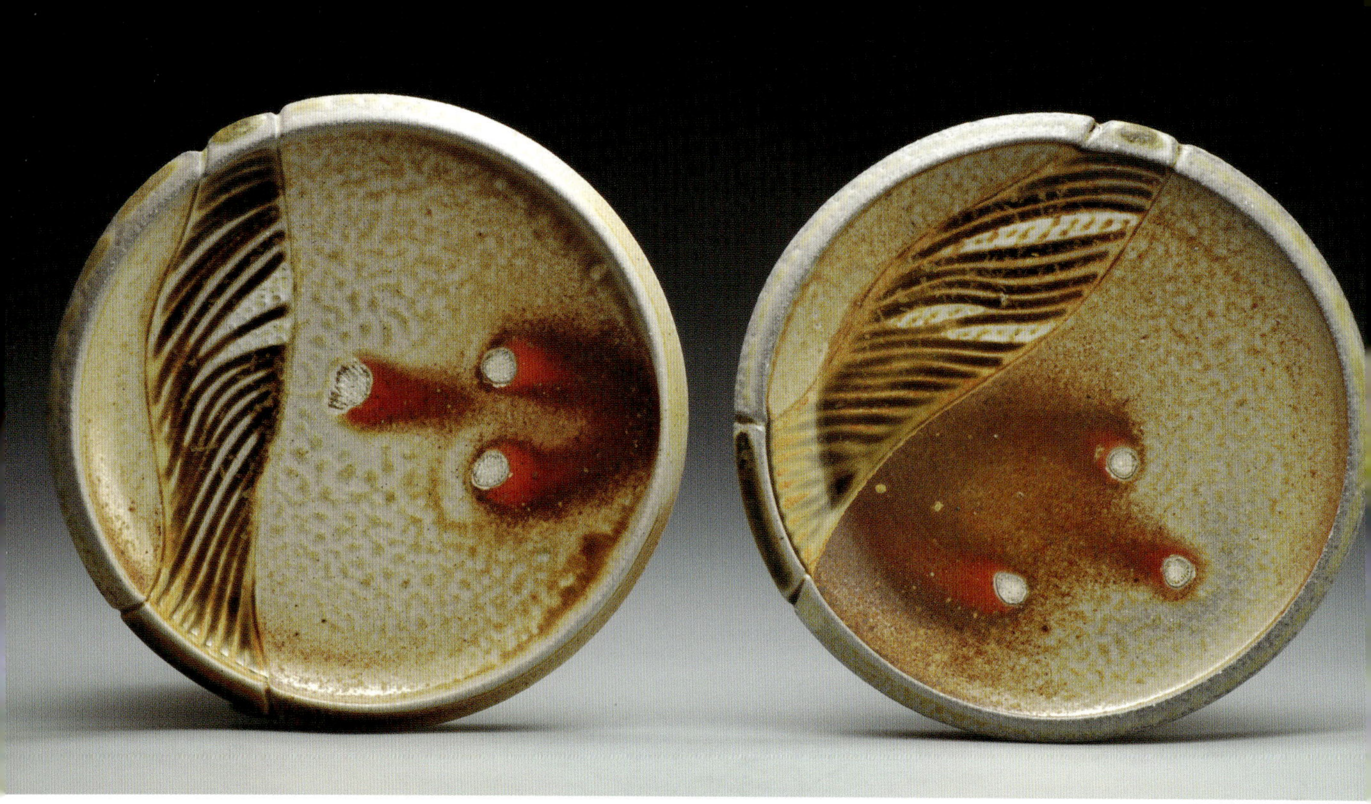

William Baker and **Joy Tanner**, who compiled this information, are resident artists at the EnergyXchange, a rural energy and not-for-profit art residency centre for ceramics and glass.

Carved Plates, Joy Tanner, 2011. Ht: 3.8 cm (1½ in) x 19 cm (7½ in), wheel-thrown and carved stoneware, wood/soda fired to cone 10. *Photo: courtesy of the artist.*

Sustainable materials: backyard resources

Next to fuels and firing, the materials we use as ceramic practitioners have perhaps the greatest impact upon our sustainable practices. Do you know where the clays and glaze materials you are using originated? How far did they have to travel to get to your studio? Are there local/regional materials available that might work just as well as the ones you import from great distances?

These are just a few important questions to be asking yourself regarding your ceramic materials. A good resource to get some of these answers is your local clay supplier. Area geologists are also a resource for those looking for naturally occurring clays typically found around streambeds or where earth strata has been disturbed or exposed. More and more individuals, studios and schools are looking for options to imported materials. By using local materials you help reduce the carbon footprint of your studio.

I am heartened by the fact that younger generations of ceramics practitioners are researching and using materials that might be sourced locally. Accessing these materials can be an effort, which in itself can be rewarding. Bernard Leach and Michael Cardew were advocates of finding and using local materials surmising that the effort puts one in contact with their locale and informs the work on both aesthetic and

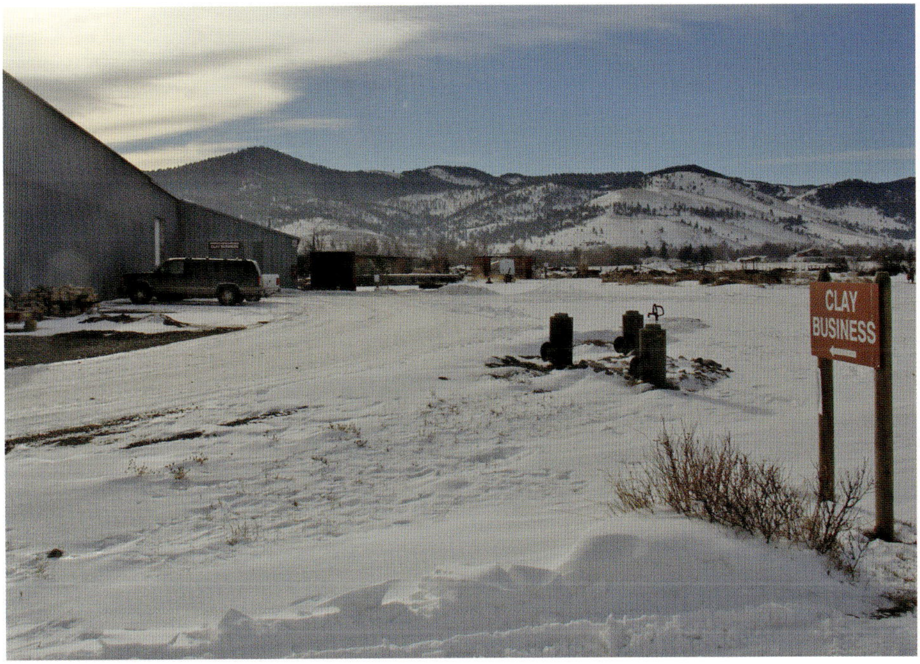

Archie Bray Foundation Clay Business, Helena, Montana, 2013. *Photo: Robert Harrison.*

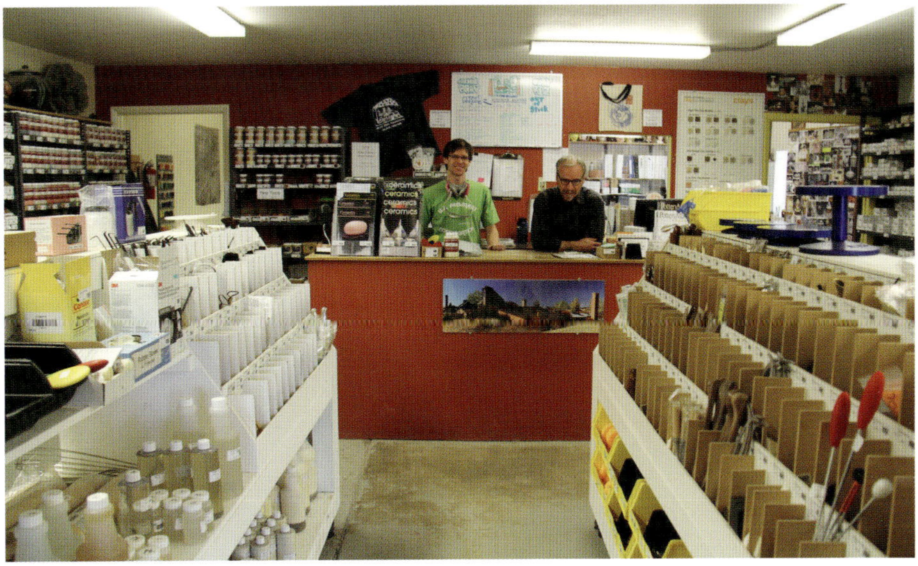

Archie Bray Foundation Clay Business sales room with retail manager Josh Rysted (left) and manager Chuck Aydlett, Helena, Montana, 2012. *Photo: Robert Harrison.*

inherent levels. Going out and gathering local materials is not for everyone; carefully consider the benefits to you and your work in advance.

The materials we use as potters and sculptors bind us together in the expansive field of contemporary ceramics. Clay bodies are typically comprised of dry processed clay with the addition of feldspar and flint, depending on maturing temperature and can often be found close to home. Glazes however, are combinations of numerous dry materials, carefully measured, combined and applied to form a secondary surface

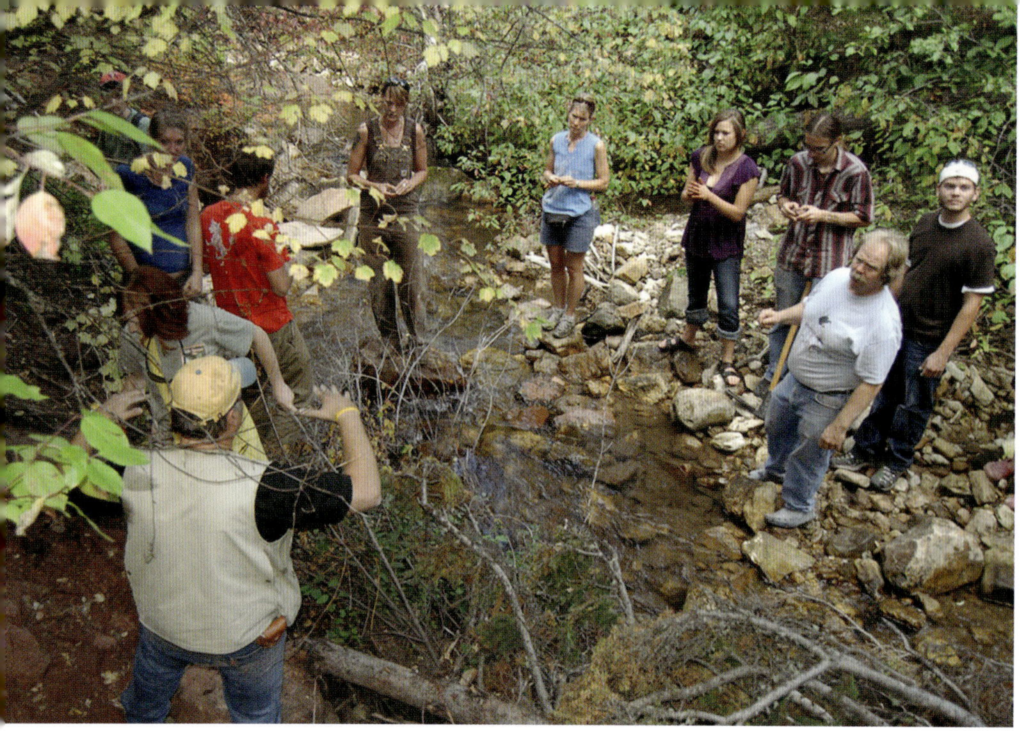

LEFT: Geologist Tim Stepp lecturing Montana State University students on wild clay at a local clay deposit near Bozeman, Montana, 2011. *Photo: Josh DeWeese.*

on the clay. The majority of these glaze materials might originate farther afield and require transportation to the potter/ceramic artist.

From clay and glaze materials to plaster and materials for fuels, along with numerous other materials we utilise in our creative pursuits, I believe it is essential to examine our *material resources*.

Adobe: ancient and totally underutilised sculptural material

Clay is one of the oldest building materials on Earth, among other ancient, naturally occurring geologic materials such as stone and organic materials like wood. Between one-half and two-thirds of the world's population, in traditional societies as well as developed countries, still live or work in a building made with clay as an essential part of its load-bearing structure. Also a primary ingredient in natural building techniques, clay is used to create *adobe* bricks and rammed-earth structures as well as building elements such as plaster, clay floors and clay paints.

Adobe is an organic, sustainable building material traditionally made from sand, clay, water and some type of additional fibrous material like straw or sawdust for binding and strength. It is air dried and sun baked. Adobe can be made into bricks in simple wooden molds, ram-pressed into larger wooden forms or used as a freeform hand-building material. It can be mixed as a mortar or trowelled, brushed or spread by hand to enhance a surface; the possibilities are literally endless.

Adobe structures are extremely durable, and account for some of the oldest existing buildings in the world. In hot climates adobe structures with their significant thermal mass offer considerable advantages although without some form of reinforcing are susceptible to damage in areas prone to earthquakes. Adobe brick making was employed in southern Europe in the Late Bronze Age and Iron Age, and from the 8th century BC on.

OPPOSITE

TOP LEFT: Old adobe church exterior in Taos, New Mexico, 2012. *Photo: Robert Harrison.*

TOP RIGHT: Old Adobe Church exterior detail, Taos, New Mexico, 2012. *Photo: Robert Harrison.*

BOTTOM: Robert Harrison with *Tex-As-X*, 1986. 1.2 m (4 ft) x 6.1 m (20 ft), rampressed stabilised adobe, indigenous limestone, University of Texas, San Antonio. *Photo: Robert Harrison.*

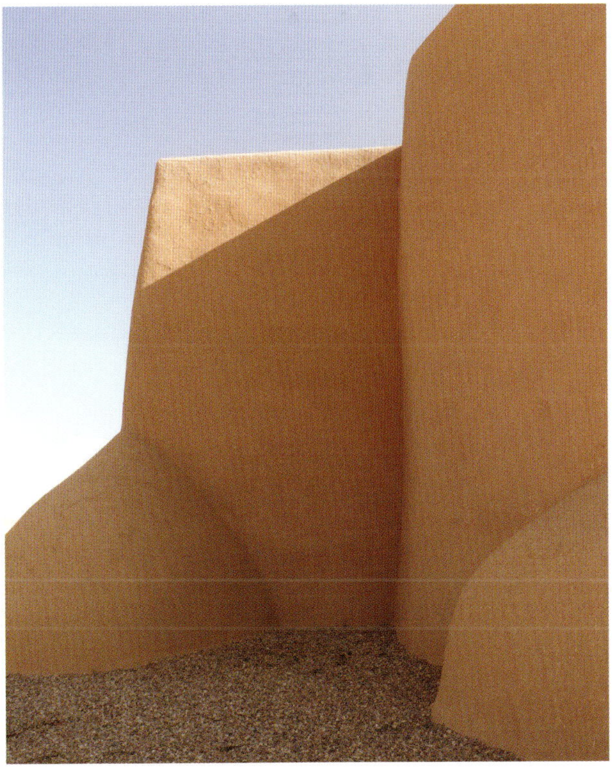

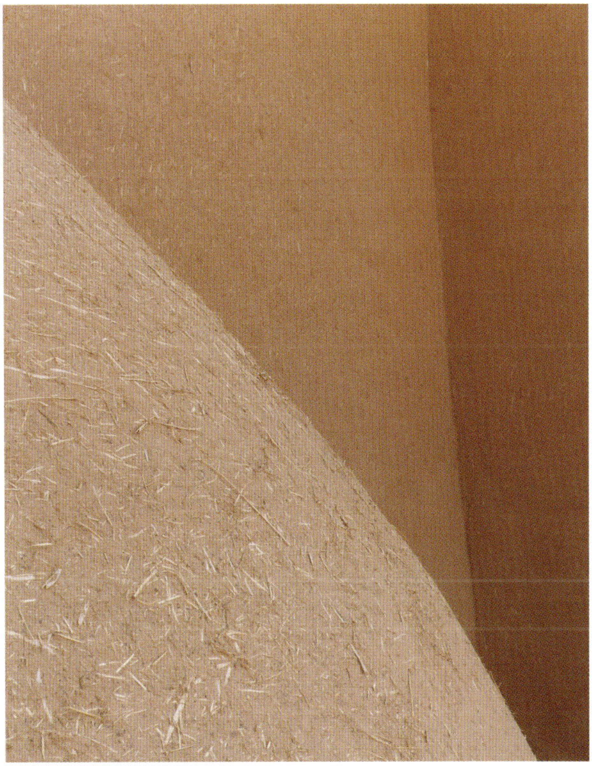

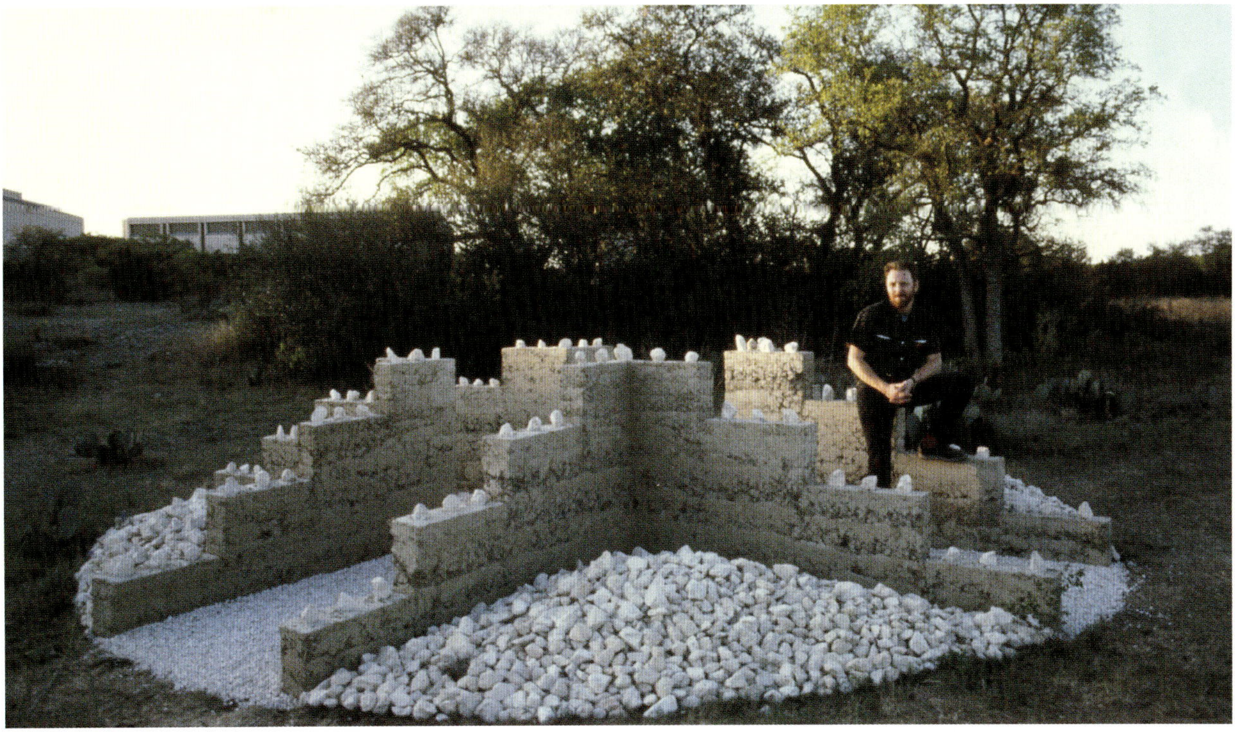

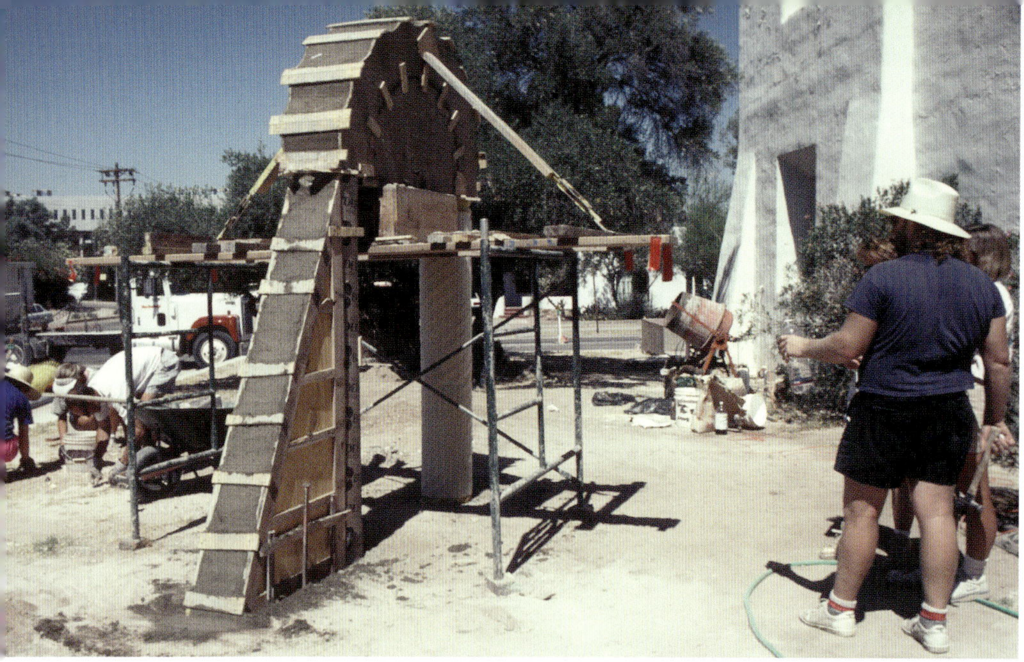

Tucsonarch under construction with the author and ceramics students, University of Arizona, Tucson, 1991. *Photo: Robert Harrison.*

Since I began working with this elemental building material over 25 years ago, I have used it in a wide variety of my large-scale outdoor and indoor installations. I have used it in temporal installations where the sculpture deteriorates naturally with wind/sun/rain eroding the surface over a period of time depending on environmental activity. I have also added a stabiliser like Portland cement to the mix to harden and toughen the material, which extends the life of the structure considerably. The more stabiliser you add the tougher the material is. I have also used a lime/cement/sand stucco to coat the adobe surface and add texture and colour.

BELOW: *Australian Gateway*, Robert Harrison, 1992. 30.5 x 30.5 m (100 x 100 ft), recycled corrugated iron, recycled timber, indigenous lava rock, cast stabilised adobe, concrete, University of South Australia, Adelaide, Australia. *Photo: Robert Harrison.*

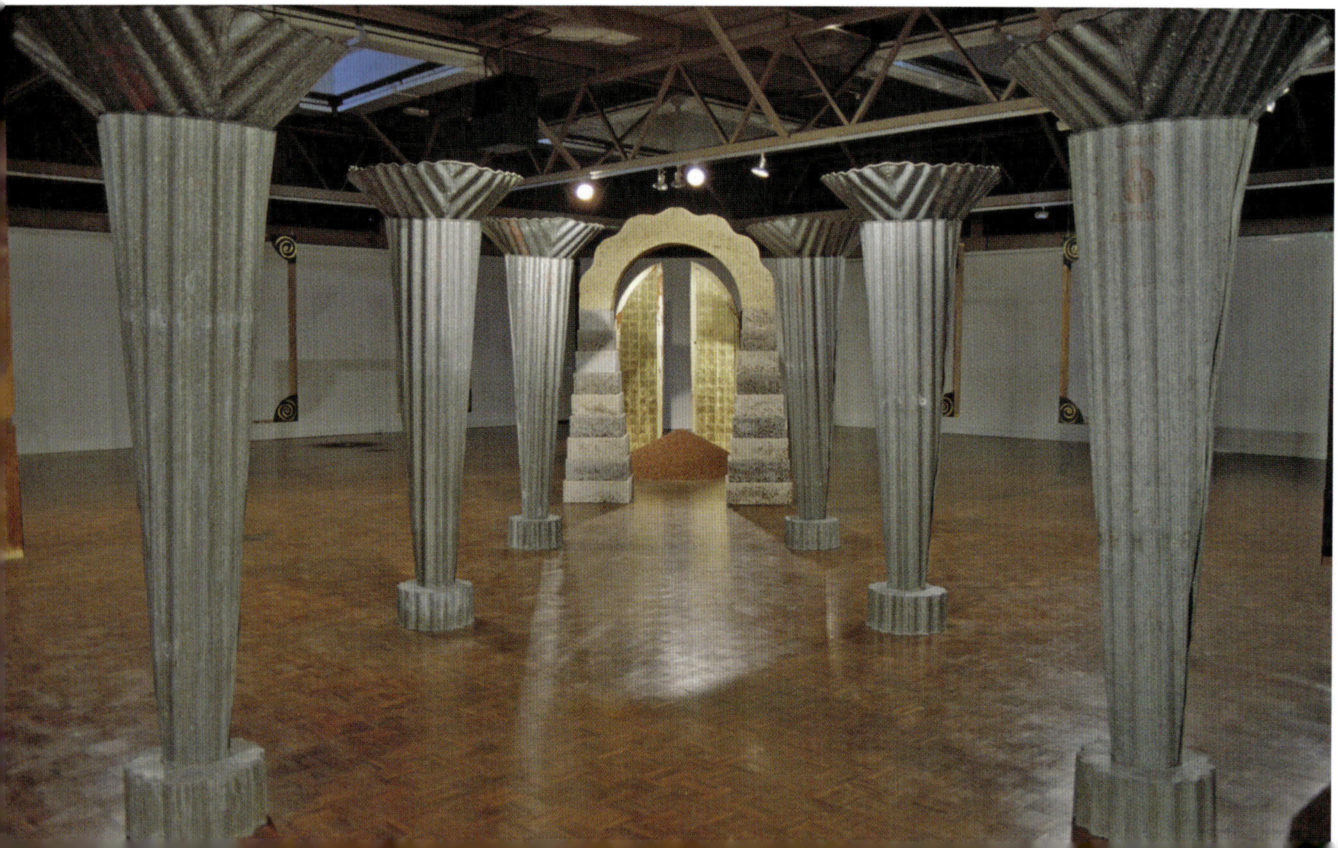

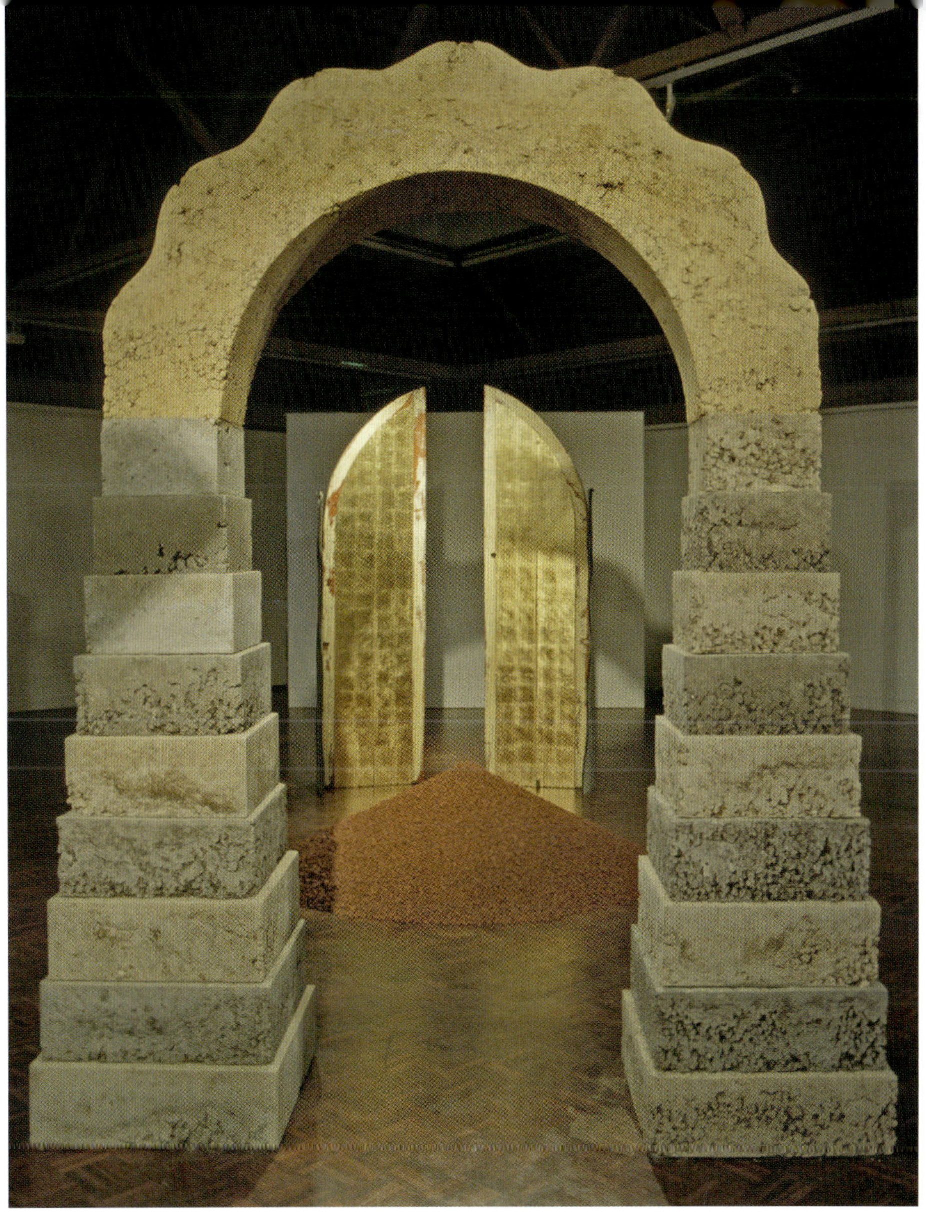

Australian Gateway Arch, Robert Harrison, 1992. 2.7 x 1.8 x 0.6 m (9 x 6 x 2 ft), cast stabilised adobe, concrete. *Photo: Robert Harrison.*

Sourcing local ceramic materials

Modern convenience certainly has its benefits, giving us more freedom to explore new ideas and direct our energy in different ways. As ceramic artists we are now able to use materials from around the globe, custom-blending clay bodies to meet specific needs using clays from the other side of the world. The endless possibilities are phenomenal, and in many ways the accessibility has nurtured an explosion of creativity.

Historically, the great works in ceramics came from a specific location and were tied to the discovery of geologic phenomena unique to that place. Now the look of chunky feldspathic clay of Shigaraki can be recreated anywhere. In our post-modern age anything seems possible as we blur cultural boundaries in search of aesthetic solutions, but perhaps we are losing our understanding of the potential of our own native materials to influence our creativity.

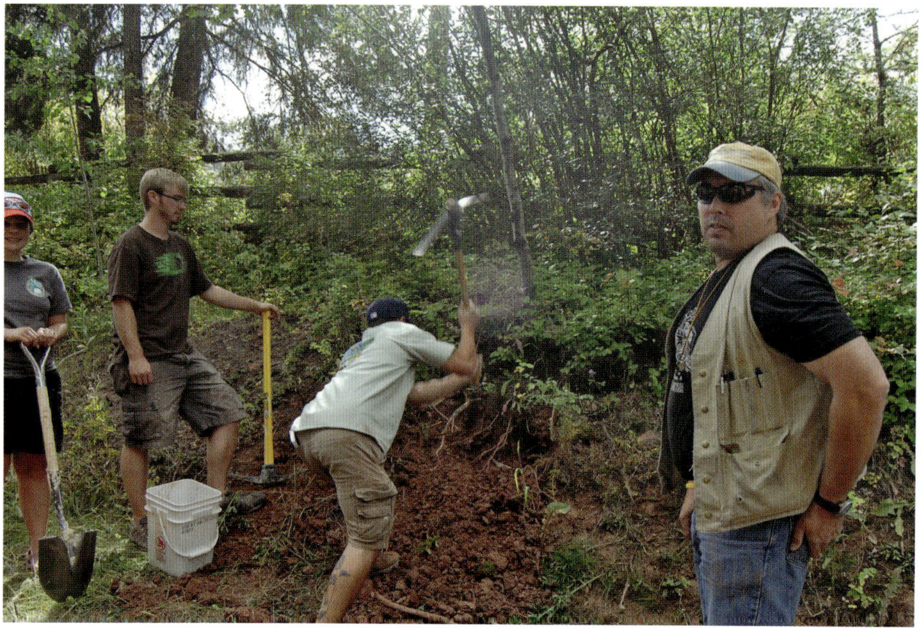

Geologist Tim Stepp and Montana State University digging local wild clay near Bozeman, Montana, 2011. *Photo: Josh DeWeese / Dean Adams.*

Wild clay in Montana

At Montana State University (MSU), **Josh DeWeese** (former Artistic Director of the Archie Bray Foundation for the Ceramic Arts) and his colleague **Dean Adams** have created the International Wild Clay Research Project (IWCRP) to study the use of local, indigenous ceramic materials, and to advance sustainable, efficient practices in the ceramic arts. They are primarily interested in ways that indigenous unique materials contribute to the identity of artwork produced in a specific locality. In Montana there are many unique deposits of clay minerals suitable for the ceramic process, and through the IWCRP they plan to develop ideas and sustainable processes for harvesting indigenous materials unique to the area.

Student research projects at MSU involve collecting local ceramic materials and developing different processing systems using a hammer mill and ball mill. Students are also involved in developing kiln technology and design using recycled vegetable oil, and developing the potential of using camelina straw waste as a fuel source.

The use of indigenous materials is common around the world and Josh and Dean's research has taken them to both Europe and Asia, as well as throughout their region. Their goal is to establish a dialogue with contemporary artists who are interested in the concept of using indigenous materials and processes, and to develop opportunities for student and faculty exchange between the Montana State University and schools and art centres around the world.

In contemporary western society motivation is partially fuelled by an emerging broad interest in using *local* products and materials in many different areas of life, for example groceries. This movement grows out of a concern for the environment and is a reaction to the mass consumption of a contemporary corporate world. There is a

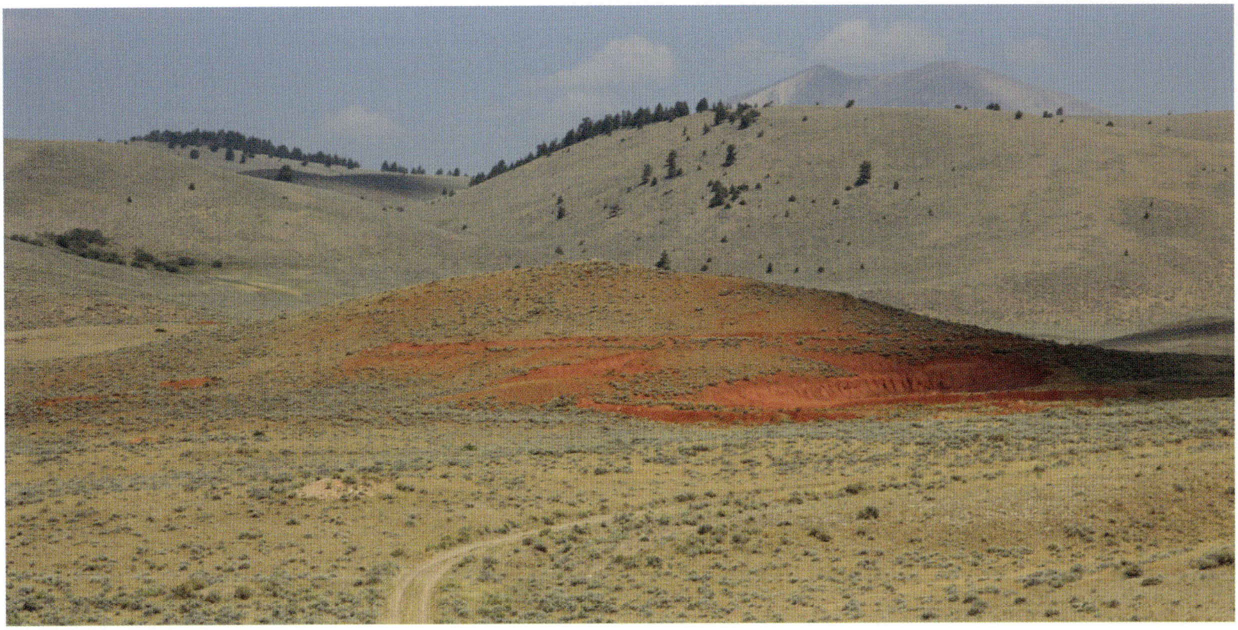

ABOVE: Montana wild clay: Dyce Creek clay deposit in south-west Montana, 2011. *Photo: Josh DeWeese / Dean Adams.*

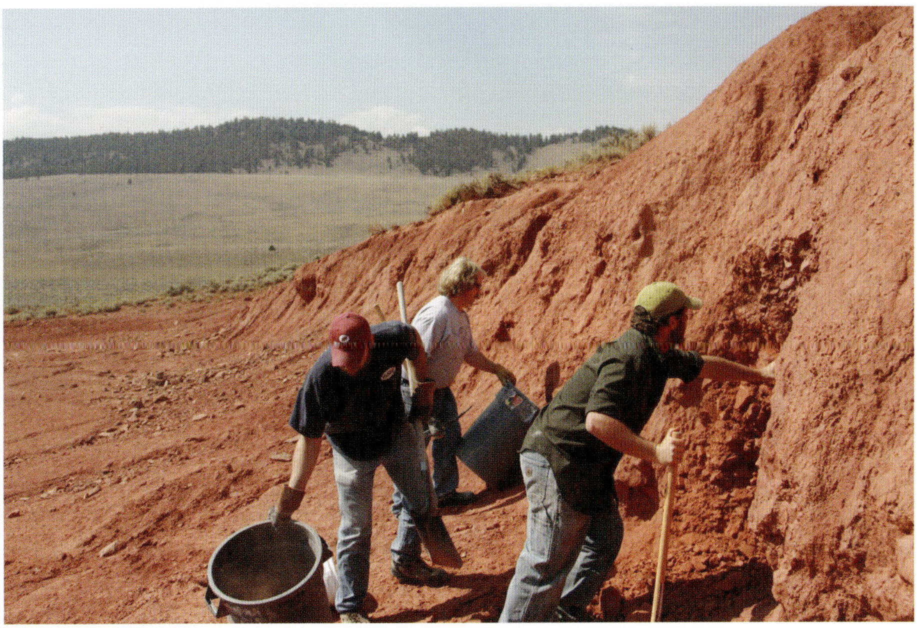

Montana State University's International Wild Clay Research Project members digging in Dyce Creek clay deposit in south-west Montana, 2011. Left to right: Brad Bickell, Josh DeWeese, Joseph Geil. *Photo: Dean Adams.*

willingness to sacrifice the convenience of commercial products for the honesty and integrity of creating beauty with what is available in our backyard. For ceramic artists, we are also attracted to the *idea* of those beautiful clays and glazes that we see in historical wares from a time when the materials were less processed and homogenised, and we are inspired to expend the energy necessary to gather and process materials to attain those qualities.

A potter's 'Clay Threads'

Elizabeth Sparks is a potter and educator working sustainably. She writes:

> I strive to find new solutions in a fast-paced, waste-producing culture while I define myself as a designer and maker. Seeing that simple domestic tasks create the foundation for a lifestyle, I work to create choices to illuminate a new way of life. Because clay has an ancient relationship with food and water in cultures all over the world, it is a sustainable, beautiful material for containment that is rooted in the earth.

Liz finds inspiration in the pre-industrial inventions of early American redware and cultures from around the world that design pottery connected to agriculture. While she repurposes these ideas, she envisions an environment that awakens the senses, identifying the contemporary need to connect with local foods and water supplies. She believes clay to be a beneficial material for domestic uses, transportable containers, interior design, and architecture. She continues:

> Clay is also a common-sense material for storage of our sustenance. Clay Thread Technology (patent pending) is a technique I use to make jugs, bottles, jars and other domestic pots for healthy containment of food and water. My hope is to bring pottery into larger society as a creator of material culture, and to reconsider the territory of where and how pots live in the world. I am currently making water bottles, growlers, milk bottles and small jars.

Spice Jars, Elizabeth Sparks, 2010. 15 x 30.5 cm (6 x 12 in), local Montana clay with terra sigilatta and glazes. *Photo: courtesy of the artist.*

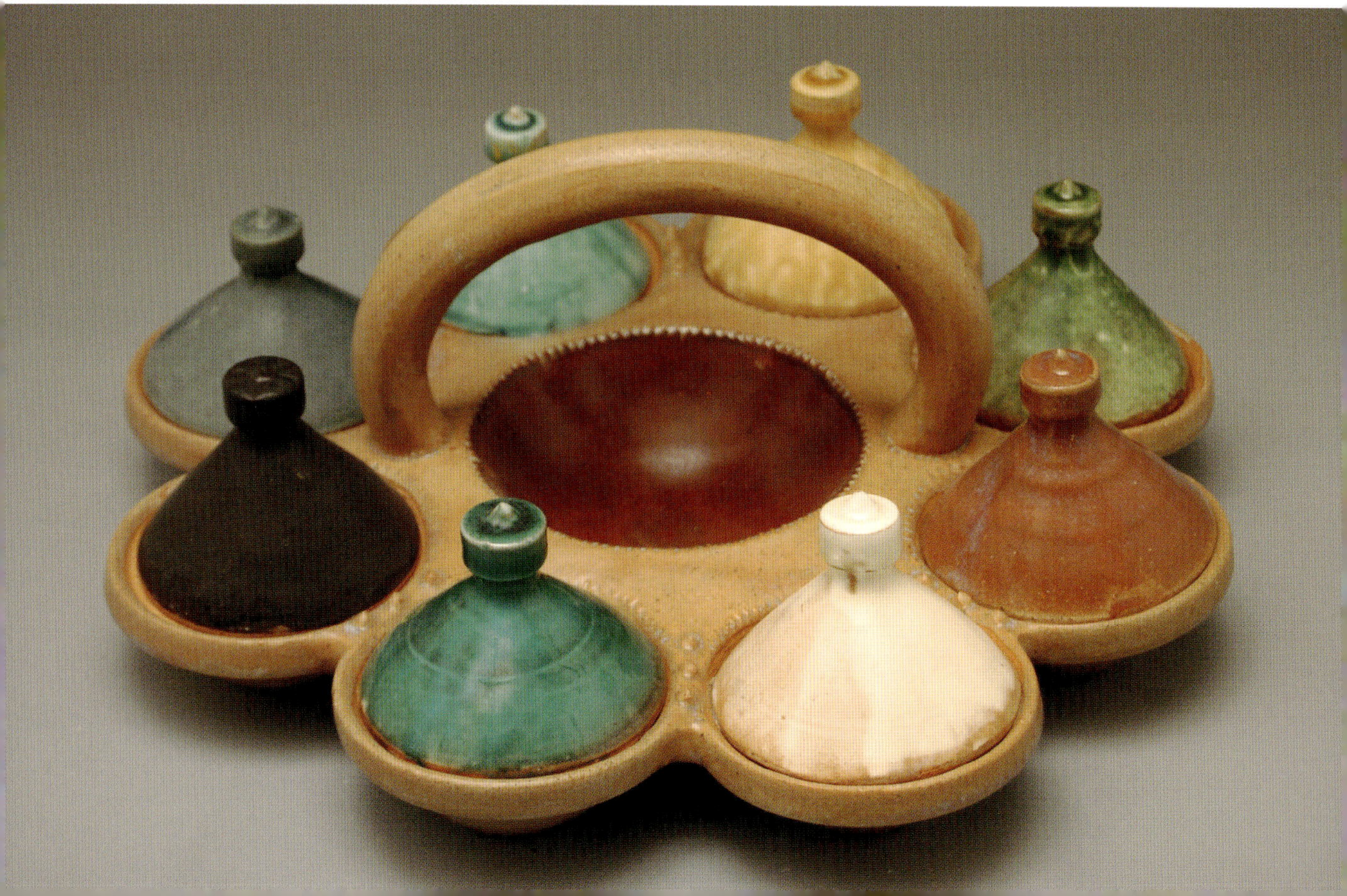

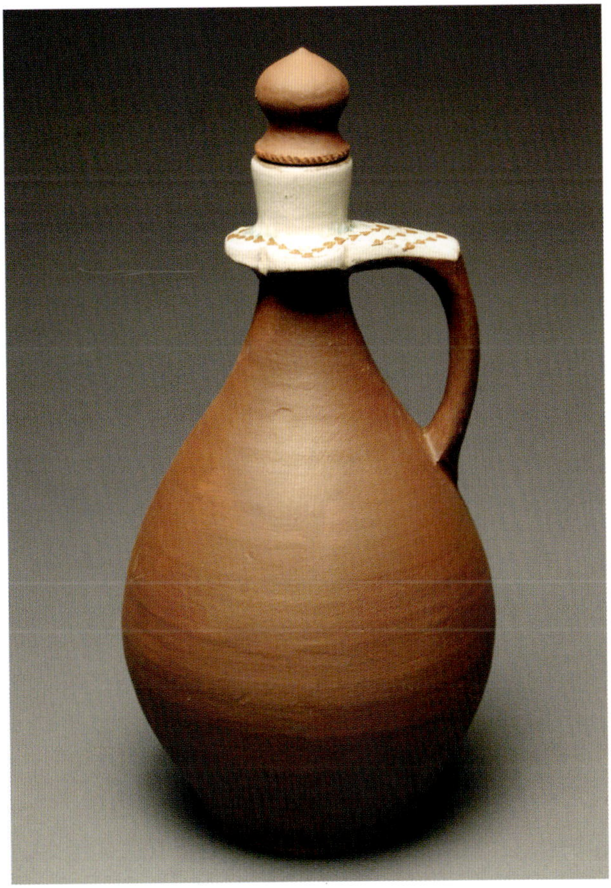

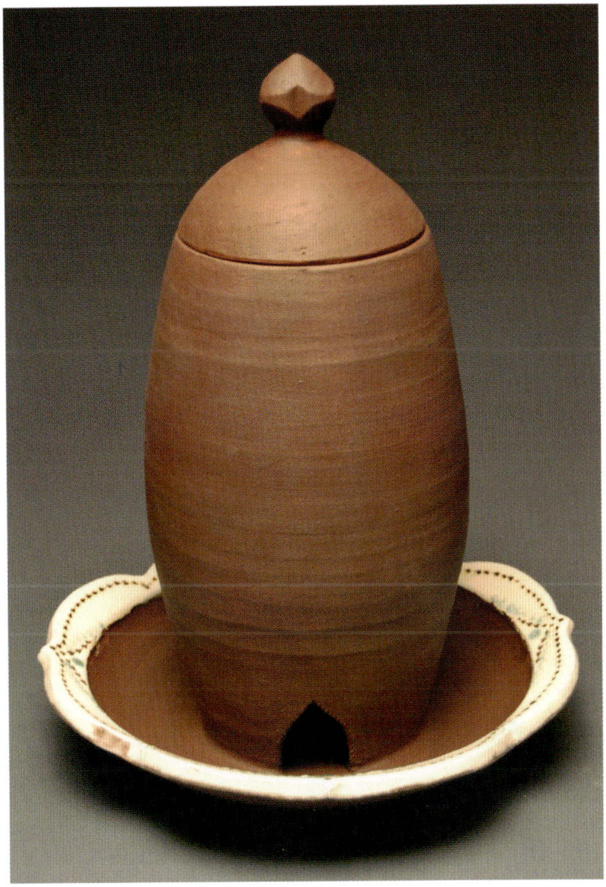

LEFT: *Water Jug*, Elizabeth Sparks, 2011. 30.5 x 12.7 cm (12 x 5 in), local Montana clay with terra sigilatta and glazes. *Photo: courtesy of the artist.*

RIGHT: *Chicken Feeder*, Elizabeth Sparks, 2010. 45.7 x 22.8 cm (18 x 9 in), local Montana clay with terra sigilatta and glazes. *Photo: courtesy of the artist.*

For Liz, sustainability means recognising that some processes which are now becoming the new sustainable techniques in the USA are practices that have stood the test of time in poor countries where pottery is a low-income, working-class job. People use local clay because that is all they have, and the particular traits or aesthetics of the work has evolved from the nature of the materials that are available. True sustainability means taking a global perspective of inclusivity and interdependence.

> I primarily use clay that I find and dig from where I am working at the time. I enjoy the process of discovery and engagement with the outdoor environment that finding clay offers me. I especially enjoy using clays with a specific history tied to a place, such as the roof tiles in Alfred, New York, or the old brick clay at the Archie Bray Foundation. I love being a potter who comes around years later to repurpose the same material for a contemporary need. Since most clay I have found tends to be red or dark in colour, I also use domestic kaolin from Georgia as both a white slip and a clay body. This gives a light surface over the dark clays, allowing the glazes to be brighter. *For me, the practice of using local clays is larger than simply my own preferences; it is a way of being rooted in the earth, with larger potential for groups or communities.*

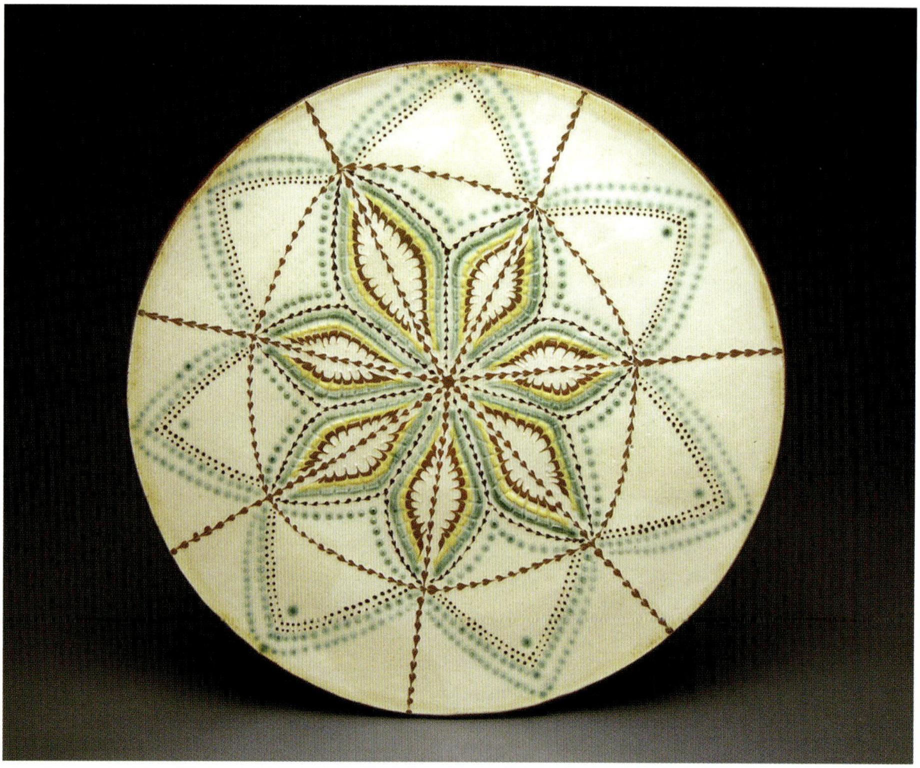

Starflower Platter, Elizabeth Sparks, 2011. 3.8 x 30.5 cm (1½ x 12 in), local clay with terra sigilatta and glazes. *Photo: courtesy of the artist.*

> I keep my glaze recipes as simple as possible, using as many local or free materials as I can find. In North Carolina I used the fines from a gravel-making plant for a beautiful black Temmoku glaze. I gathered limestone directly from a mine in Tennessee, which I used in celadon glazes during that time and created a beautiful satin surface that, was different from commercial whiting. Wood ash is a material that can be found anywhere that there is a wood kiln or wood-stove and I use it in most of my glazes. It acts as both the silica and flux parts of a glaze. Most recently I have begun to use ground recycled glass as a component in glazes, because it is much cheaper than frit and there are places in Montana where glass is no longer recycled. It works well at the mid-range temperature to which I am firing. Old Egyptian Faience glazes and the Alkaline glazes of the American south, both of which used ground glass as an ingredient, also inspire me. I am concerned about the availability of commercial materials in the future, so I am constantly testing and looking for resources.

Liz fires to cone 3, which ranges between 2121 and 2134°F (1160 and 1168°C). She began using this temperature because she wanted the durability of stoneware combined with a shorter firing time and consequently less fuel. At this temperature *mullite* begins to form a crystalline structure within the clay body. This is important to her because it means that the body has an internal strength and structure that low-fired earthenware does not have simply from using talc as a flux.

Heavy clay: working the hard way

David Peters is a potter and educator who has found his path through sustainable ceramics *the hard way*. Dave writes:

> Wet or dry, clay is heavy. It is why historically ceramic styles and technology were tied to specific regions. Moving clay long distances just wasn't worth the cost or the effort, and consequently production centres grew around clay deposits. With the onset of cheaper transportation costs the distribution of materials became much more viable. Technical information and recipes were freely shared amongst artists so the use of a few specific materials became widespread, leading to further global distribution of just a handful of industrial ceramic materials.

Clay is an abundant mineral that can be found almost everywhere. There are a few exceptions of course, but Dave surmises that most people on the planet live within about 200 miles of some variety of clay. However, the clay you find near your home is not likely to be exactly like the bagged clay you're used to using from a ceramics supply business. Each and every clay deposit is unique; its characteristics shaped by the combination of variables of its parent rock, the means by which it was altered, and how it was deposited. On the one hand these traits are a challenge because each material will require some refining or testing to get to know it and learn how to use it. On the other hand, those peculiar characteristics can offer up new possibilities. With a little curiosity and patience new discoveries are made that can feed one's work in fresh ways.

> The first clay I found was a nice size lens of yellow and white clay that seemed to pour out of a road cut of black rock. It reeked of sulphur like a hot spring and it faced a spectacular highland valley. One of my best friends, who happens to be a crackpot geologist, deduced that it was a 2.6 billion-year-old mudstone altered a second time in place by sulphuric acid introduced by a volcanic intrusion. Running that clay through my fingers as I looked out over a sprawling valley of Ponderosa pines, I had a powerful thought; the clay I was using to make my pots acts like it does because of mysterious circumstances and variables combined over a length of time that was as long as the age of life itself. It was as profoundly unique as the fingerprints that were pinching it.

LEFT: Dave Peters digging a mud-stone clay near Armington Junction, Montana, 2011. *Photo: Tim Stepp.*

RIGHT: Dave Peters with a freshly dug piece of volcanic primary clay from Basin, Montana, 2011. *Photo: Mel Griffin.*

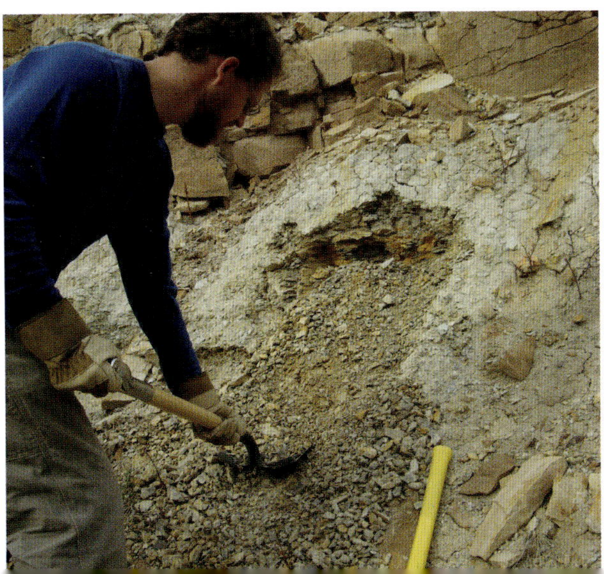

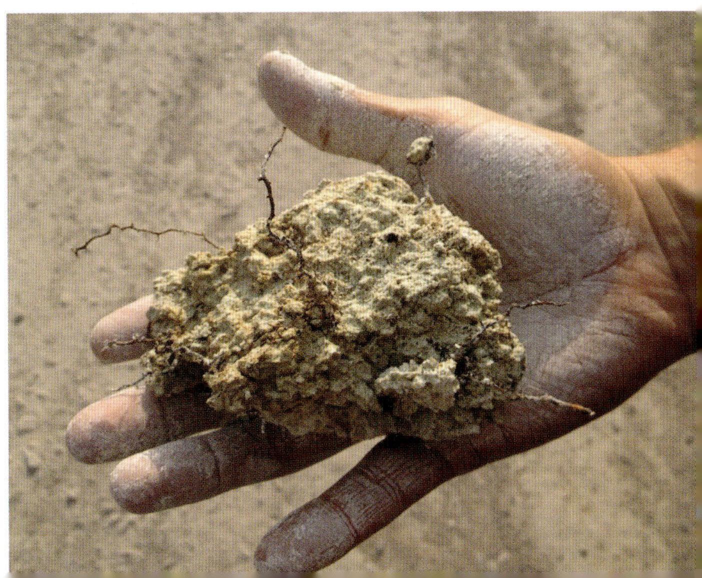

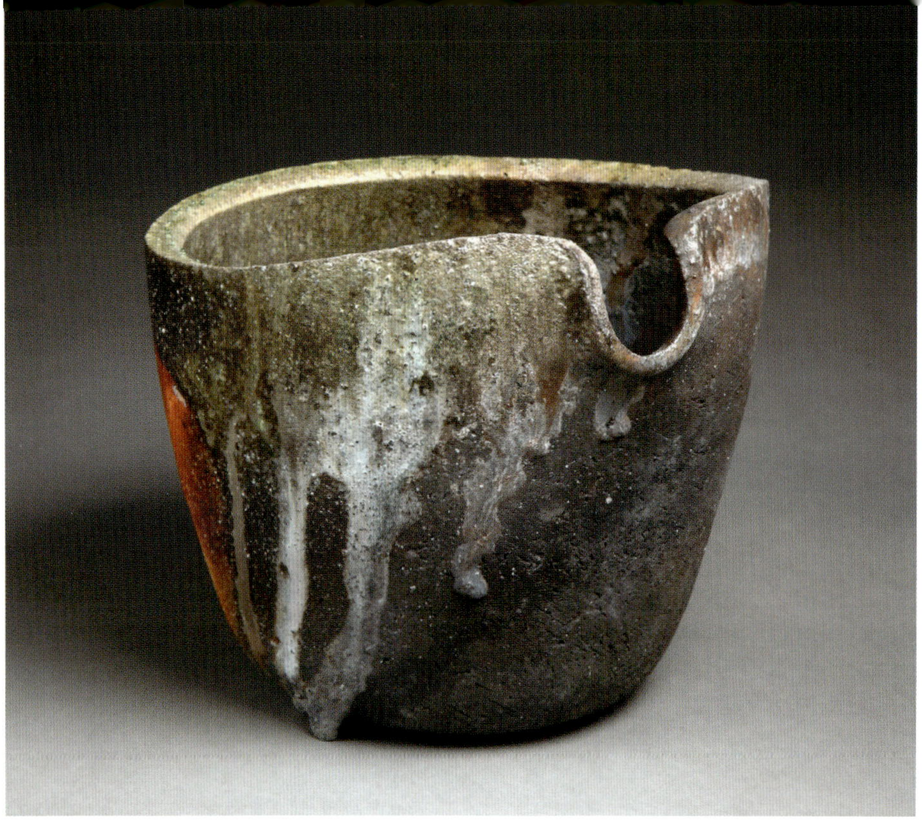

Crucible, Dave Peters, 2011. 24 x 24 cm (9½ x 9½ in), wood-fired local stoneware. *Photo: Vaughn Judge.*

> This clay had taken billions of years to form, and I had used it all in one summer. That experience changed the way I treat clay. I now use all clays with extra care and respect, running numerous tests to make sure I am on the right track, and I never fire a pot if I know for sure that I'm not happy with it. I am scrupulous with trimmings and reclaim, and test fire unmarked bags of materials to figure out what they are instead of just throwing them out. *Although clay in general is abundant, each particular clay is a finite resource and when you use it all, it is gone forever.*

Dave is philosophical when it comes to the efforts required in finding, processing, making and then firing his pots. Each clay is processed in its own prescribed way, some require crushing and milling, but all require slaking, blundging, settling, drying, and wedging. After each year's digs, Dave makes hundreds of tests to find formulas of clay bodies that are agreeable enough to work with and can withstand the test of firing without losing their unique characteristics. By the time he sits down to make a pot, he has already invested a huge amount of time and effort in the process.

His process has also inspired a healthy curiosity towardss what can be done with a variety of other materials and by-products from the process. The sawdust from chain saws and other power tools is mixed into his wadding. He collects the used wads from his firings and grinds them into grog. The wood ash from each firing is saved and is used to seal cracks in the kiln, or is washed, sieved, and added as a flux in glazes. Dave has even swept up rusted dust from ground steel to use as colourant, and collected beer bottles from the studio to pulverise and use as frit. Just about everything can be of some use if you are able to see potential and are willing to try it.

Look who's (literally) throwing stones...

Steve Harrison has devoted his career as a potter, author and environmentalist to sustainable living in his native Australia. His work with materials (and firings) is the result of many years of research in his local area. He writes:

> Some years ago I stumbled across a very small, dense, and extremely hard deposit of rock which could have been a white feldspathic igneous stone – but that only happens in the movies, so I didn't believe what my eyes were telling me. I was told when I arrived here in this district over 30 years ago that there were no white igneous feldspathic rocks in this area. It was potters knowledge, a known fact! Consequently I didn't bother to test this sample straight away, because I knew intellectually that it couldn't be feldspathic stone. Only when I had tested every other sample did I get around to this amazing rock. Of course I only tested it as a glaze material, it was just so hard and dense, it needed to be broken down in a jaw crusher, then reduced further in a disk mill and finally ball milled for 16 hours for it to be reduced to a fine powder. It turned out to produce the loveliest Guan/pale blue celadon although very matt and viscous and quite crawled.

The crawling intrigued him, because crawling is often associated with plastic materials, so perhaps the apparent hard, non-plastic rock could have some plasticity. Steve mixed up a small batch of the ball-milled powder with water and wedged it up. Steve continues:

> Miraculously it was almost throwable into a very thick walled, small, uneven bowl form. I glazed it with the pale blue celadon glaze made from itself and to my total amazement it transformed itself into a translucent porcelain, even though it was 8 mm (⅓in) thick. This porcelain isn't the whitest, or the most translucent, but it

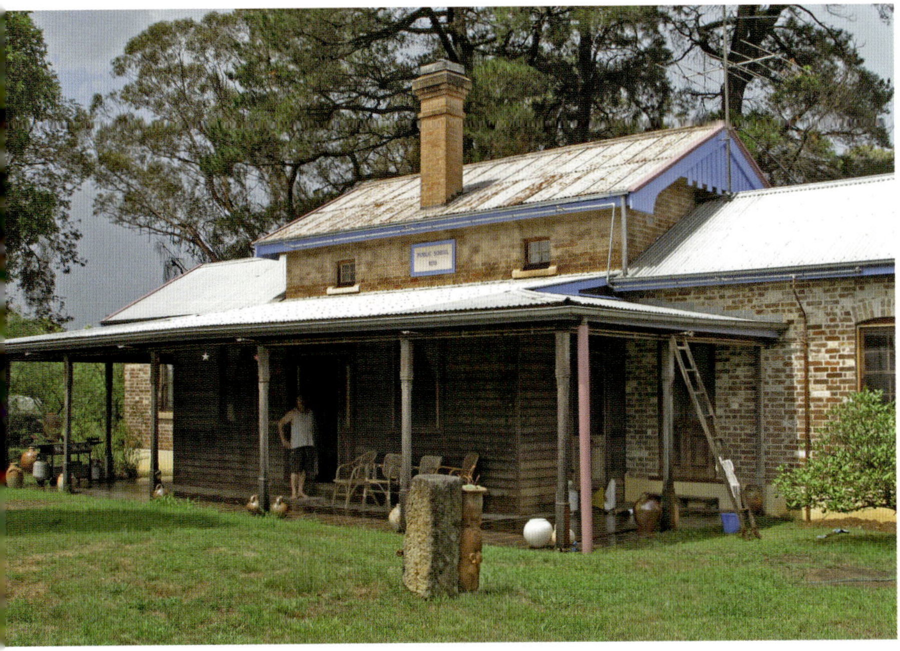

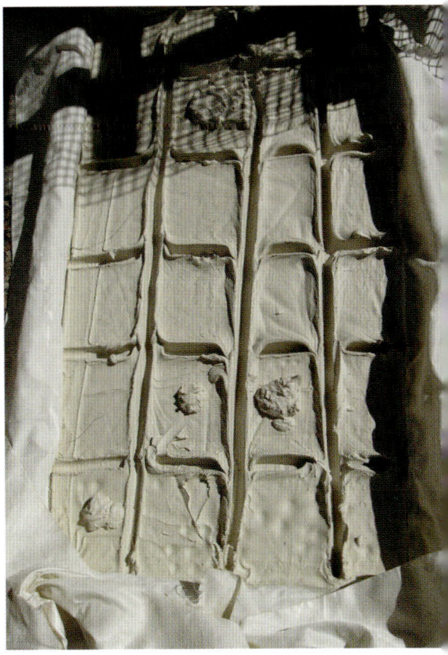

LEFT: Steve Harrison in School House residence, New South Wales, Australia, 2010.

RIGHT: Steve Harrison's ball milled bai-tunze porcelain slip in the drying bed, New South Wales, Australia, 2012. *Photos: Steve Harrison.*

is my porcelain and it is completely local. I could not have imagined that I could discover a white feldspathic porcelain stone or 'bai tunze', as the Song Chinese called it, but I did and it only goes to prove the old adage that 'the harder you work, the luckier you get'.

I now add some bentonite to the mix, which is not local, but it is Australian, and this helps the plasticity along somewhat, but careful ageing for a few years does the same job. I can only make very small items with this material and they need a lot of turning to thin out the base, which needs to be left thick on the wheel to help support the wall, due to the almost total lack of plasticity, but these are minor limitations. I have been able to make what I think are some very lovely bowls by this method, by only using what I find around me, seeing what it can do and then using it in its own way to express something that is unique to this locality. These things can only happen here. They are not great things. In fact they are not even noticed or valued by almost anybody but me. But they are important to me because they can only be done here. If I lived somewhere else, I'd be making different pots.

I have since discovered a very beautiful matt black clay body that is just as unlikely and impossible. I didn't know that a clay body like this existed until I stumbled across it. I wasn't looking for anything in particular, just doing research for the sake of it. I always travel with a few plastic bags and a garden trowel in my car – just in case. On this occasion I happened to come across some rotten

Wheel and porcelain bowls, Steve Harrison, New South Wales, Australia, 2012. *Photo: Steve Harrison.*

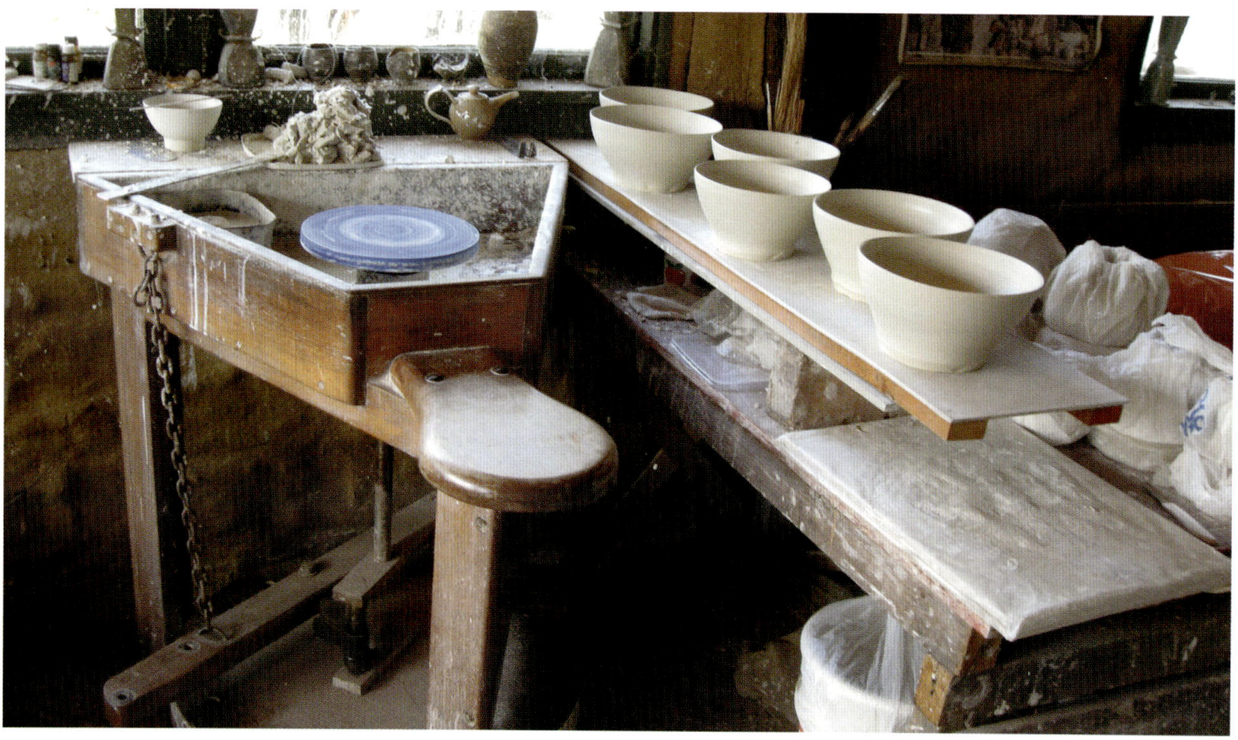

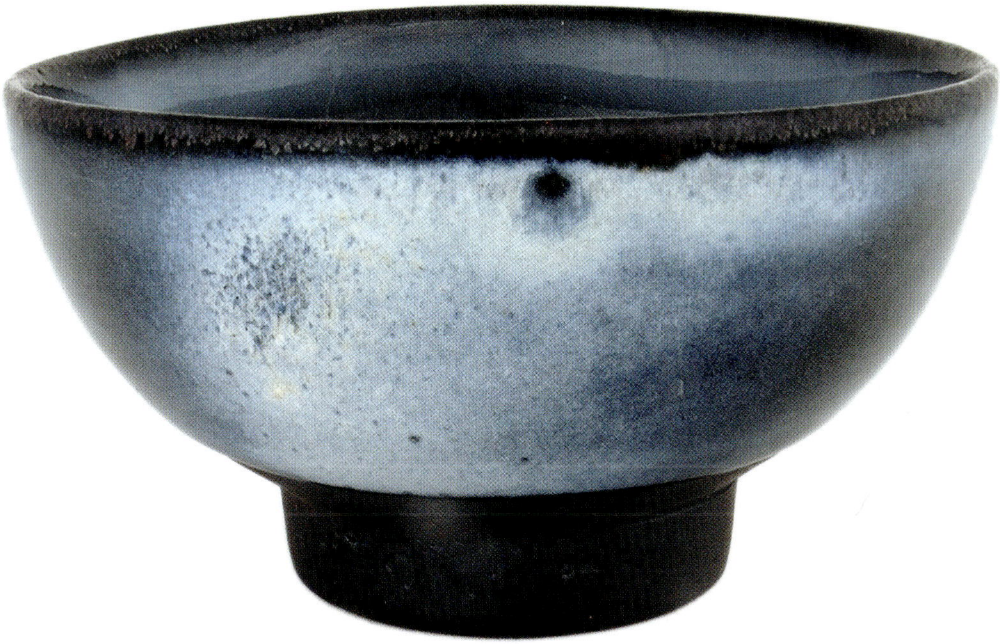

Bowl, Steve Harrison, 2012. 10 x 12.5 cm (4 x 5 in), wood-fired blackware. *Photo: courtesy of the artist.*

basaltic gravel on the side of the road, where it had washed down from the road cutting. It was completely non-plastic, so I tested it as a glaze material – because that's what I always do as a starting point; but because I'm the person that I am, I also tested it as a potential clay body.

The result after stoneware firing this washed gravel body was a stunning dense, matt, black surface that brings out some very rich and beautiful effects from my local stone glazes. Ground rock dust or washed gravel silt aren't the most promising materials to work with, but apart from the limited plasticity, which restricts the scale and form of the pieces, there are many fine qualities that these materials exhibit when wood fired. I am particularly fond of the intense red and orange flashed porcelain body colour.

I have been working with these materials that no one knew existed (including me) until I stumbled upon them by sheer persistence and some luck. My work involves the hand selection of the stones, their crushing, grinding and eventual reforming to produce these unique pieces. Likewise the glazes are all created and fired using the same creative research and attention to detail. Simple stones, ashes, clay and lime can be transmuted to soft pastel translucent colour with the hardness and durability of porcelain.

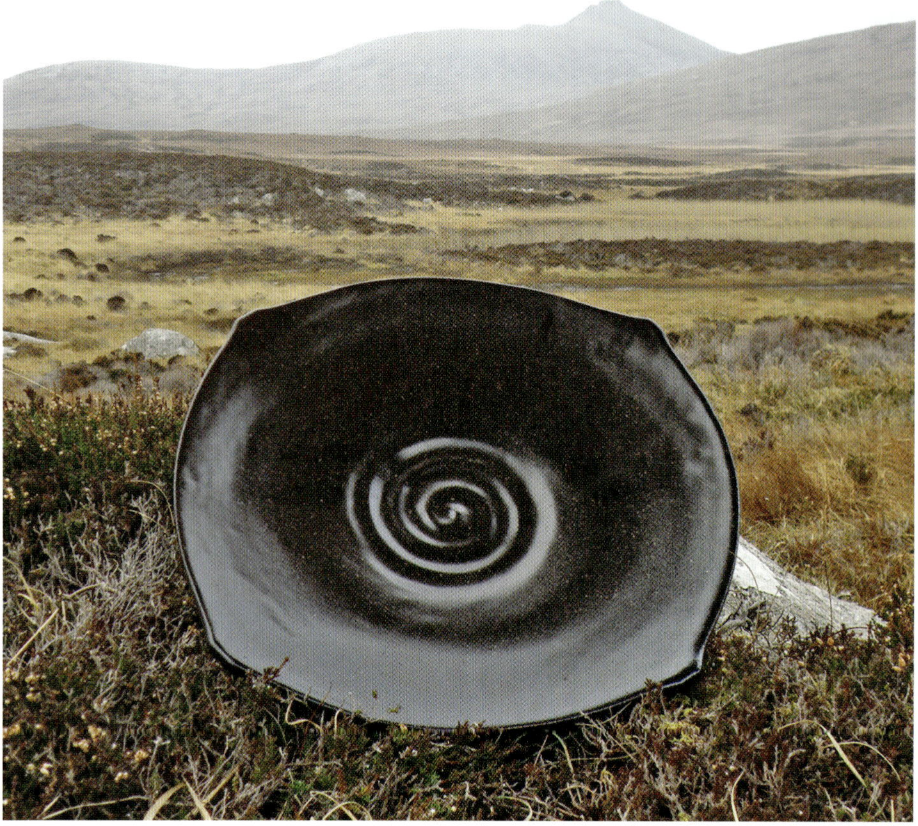

Landscape with Hornblende Platter, Miranda Forrest, 2008. 38 cm (15 in), indigenous degraded hornblende (subsoil) glaze fired to cone 8 oxidation. *Photo: courtesy of the artist.*

Using indigenous materials (Inspired by a remote natural landscape)

In 1999, after years of making ceramics with conventional, purchased materials, **Miranda Forrest** moved to South Uist, one of the Western Isles in Scotland also known as the Outer Hebrides. Interestingly the Outer Hebrides is composed of Lewisian Gneiss, an ancient rock type 'torn off' the tectonic plate that is now Canada, and left behind on the fringe of Europe![1] On South Uist, she felt inspired to experiment with native materials; an unfulfilled intention she had had for some time. Initial successes with Tenmoku type glazes lead to incorporating a wide range of local materials into her work. Although she has found no island clay that she can use as a clay body, her environment yields a surprising amount of material for glazes. Miranda writes:

> Reasons why I use local materials include: my landscape inspires me, and I love linking it directly to my ceramics; my personal unalloyed fascination and satisfaction in using materials I have collected; sustainable and non-polluting aspects of using local materials; my ceramics are site-specific and carry a 'sense of place'.
>
> The Earth is a ceramic body so ceramic materials are natural and abundant in the landscape. However, the particular geological formation of an area will determine in what form the materials are present. How to assess them is not always easy or obvious, but rocks weather naturally into fine deposits, and plants can be used to produce ashes.

[1] Angus, Stewart, *The Outer Hebrides*, White Horse Press, Cambridge UK. 1997. P 13.

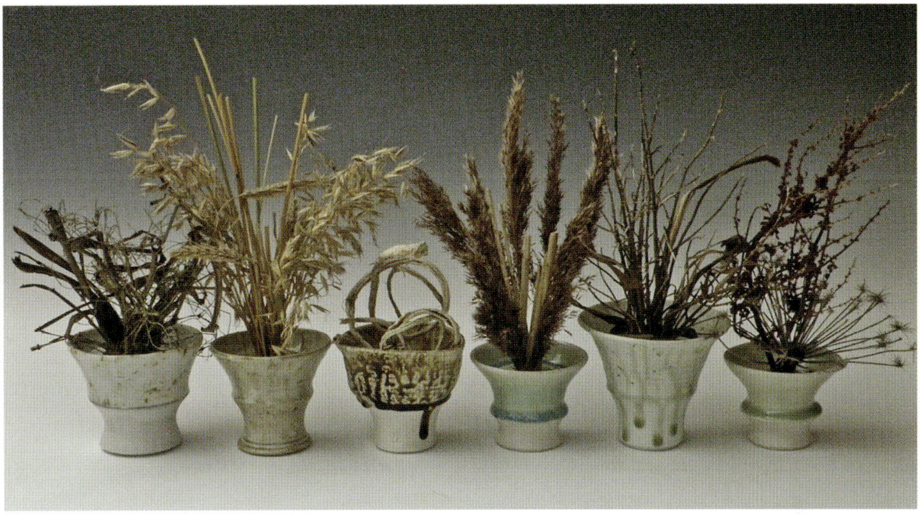

Vases with raw materials, Miranda Forrest, 2008–2012. 7–10 cm (2¾–4 in), indigenous plant materials shown provided the ashes for the specific glazes over porcelain and porcelaineous stoneware clays, glazes brushed or poured on, fired to cone 8/9 reduction. *Photo: courtesy of the artist.*

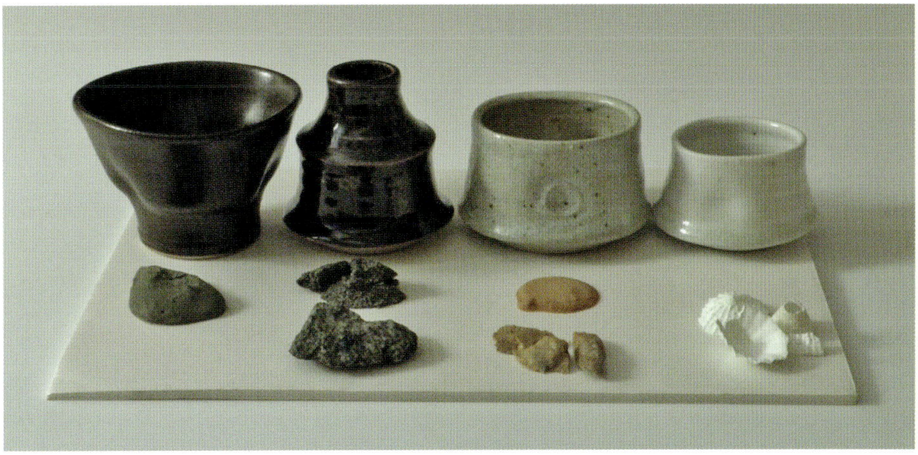

Rock samples and their glaze from Miranda Forrest. Indigenous rocks/shells, left to right: hornblende deposit, gneiss rock (glaze with horsetail ash), impure feldspar rock fragments (glaze with nettle ash) stoneware and right-hand piece porcelain, fired to cone 8/9 oxidation/reduction. *Photo: courtesy of the artist.*

> As a generalisation, for my glazes, rock derivatives provide silica, alumina, flux, iron and possibly titanium; plant ashes provide silica, flux, iron and I suspect phosphorus; seashells provide the flux calcium. I fire to stoneware temperatures (Orton cone 8 to 10).
>
> In my location iron-rich rocks have weathered more freely than the granites and feldspars. Access to fine particle iron-rich naturally degraded rock deposits and quarry dust means that I have no problem producing Tenmoku glazes entirely from local materials that only need a minimal amount of grinding and processing. I regard these glazes as 'balanced' because they have melted but not run, and produce an uncrazed surface.

Miranda only finds feldspars and granites as hard rocks. She looks for them anywhere that rock is exposed, including quarries. If she wants a source of alumina without iron she either uses a purchased (imported) feldspar or puts local fragmented feldspar rocks

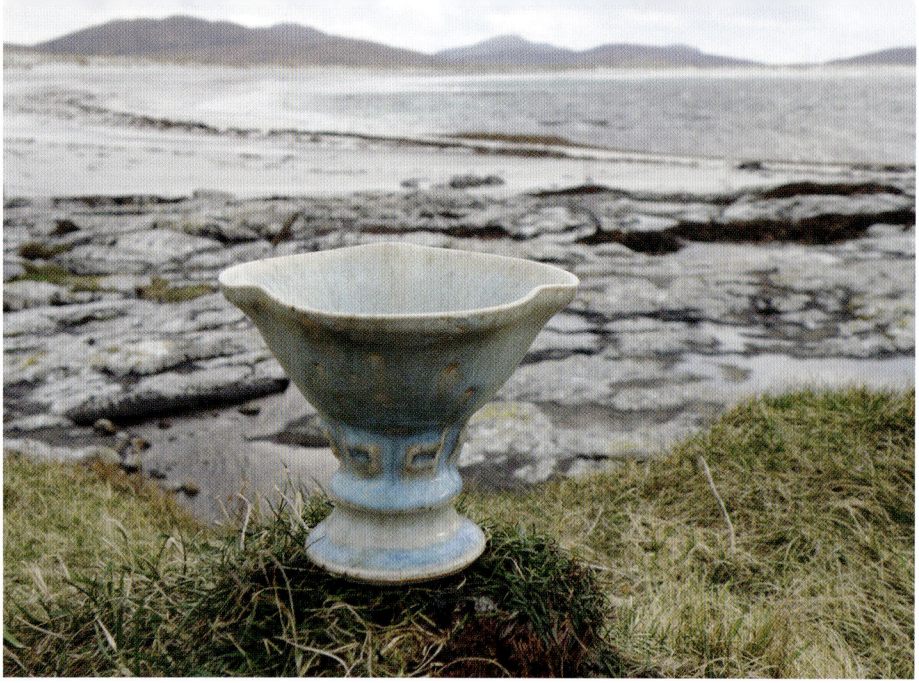

Optical Blue Pedestal Bowl, Miranda Forrest, 2012. Ht: 10 cm (4 in), indigenous reed and driftwood ash with purchased feldspar glaze, fired to cone 9 reduction. *Photo: courtesy of the artist.*

at the bottom of the kiln when biscuit firing (approximately 950°C or 1740°F) which usually enables her to grind them. She process seashells in a similar manner.

> I use several herbaceous terrestrial plants for ashes. As well as their fluxing properties they produce blues and greens that range from subtle to quite intense. For the 'runny' or 'stringy' effect typical of high flux ash glazes I often use only plant ashes, either singly or in combinations. I use ashes to flux iron-rich rock derivatives for dark glazes and add them to feldspar or granite for lighter ones. I find ashes from seaweeds contain very potent fluxes and so use them judiciously.

Other materials she collects are driftwood for wood ash; ash from peat she hand-cuts for winter fuel; and ochre found oozing out of cracks in rocks. All the local materials are ones that she uses regularly. However, when she is on the mainland she often gathers native clay just for the satisfaction of making a piece that is made and glazed entirely from materials she has collected.

The sustainable studio

Building an energy-efficient ceramics studio

For the first 30 years of his career, potter **Lee Akins** produced his clay work in shared studios and a converted garage. When Lee and his wife decided to make a big change and move to New Mexico in 2007,he had a great new opportunity. Over the years, he had become increasingly concerned about the impact we all have on the environment; the move was his chance to build a 'green', energy-efficient, comfortable and healthy studio and home.

Researching materials and approaches to building was an exciting time as Lee discovered so many possibilities. The first and single most important thing he found to being 'green' was to *build it small.* There are many reasons to do this: a small studio uses less land and building materials, takes less energy to heat and cool and, of course, requires less investment cost. *Building small* means carefully calculating exactly what your needs are. Lee researched building plans and measured existing spaces to get a sense of what he required. A great resource was Virginia Scotchie's book *Setting Up Your Ceramic Studio.* Gradually, with research into cost and building efficiency, their plan evolved into a single L-shaped building. The final studio ended up 17 x 20 ft (5 x 6 m).

The next major decision was which material to use for the exterior walls. There are numerous choices available. Countless houses in New Mexico are the standard 'stick' frame construction used throughout North America although often upgraded from 2 x 4 in to 2 x 6 in (5 x 10 to 5 x 15 cm). Even when the framed walls are well insulated each part of the wooden frame becomes a 'thermal bridge' for cold and heat. Lee was interested in a more energy-efficient choice.

The traditional material in their area of the south-western United States is adobe. Adobe is a completely sustainable and recyclable combination of clay, sand and an organic material like straw, which acts as a binder. Adobe appealed to him as a ceramic artist, but had a number of drawbacks. Adobe is labour intensive to lay and plaster, consequently the contractor cost was high. Adobe provides a good thermal mass but is not a good insulator. New local building codes require an exterior foam layer to improve insulation, which detracted from its advantage of being a totally natural material.

Lee was very interested in straw bale construction and attended several workshops on *building your own.* Straw bale is also very sustainable and owner/builder friendly. It has one of the highest insulation R-values for wall materials. He had two reservations; the first problem was that their property is located a few hundred yards from the Rio Grande River. A well-designed straw bale will resist moisture from rain and snow but a 100-year flood could be catastrophic. The second problem became apparent as they interviewed potential contractors. Lee wanted to do as much of the building work as

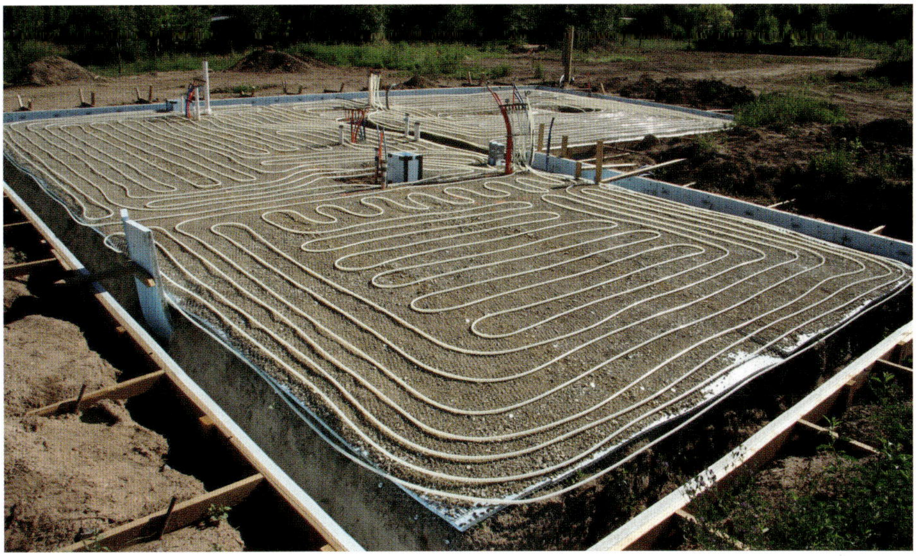

Lee Akins, tubes for radiant heat floors prior to concrete foundation slab, Ranchos de Taos, New Mexico, 2008. *Photo: Lee Akins.*

Material	Time	Cost	R-value	Thermal mass	Sustainable	Pros	Cons
Adobe	Slow finishing	Low material	R-15-22	High	High, Renewable	Locally available; low noise; fire & bug resistant, DIY	Moisture sensitive, thick walls, poor insulation, seismic
Rammed earth	Slow	Low material	R-19	High	High, Renewable	Locally available; low noise; fire & bug resistant	Moisture sensitive, thick walls, seismic
Straw bale	Fast building, Slow finishing	Low material, High finishing	R-28-50	Low	High, Renewable	Locally available; low noise; somewhat fire & bug resistant; DIY	Moisture sensitive, thick walls, not to code everywhere
Cob	Slow	Low material		High	High, Renewable	Locally available; low noise; fire & bug seismic resistant; DIY	Moisture sensitive, thick walls, not to code, poor insulation, seismic
Pumice-crete	Fast	Slightly higher	R-21-28	Medium	Medium	Some local availability; low noise; fire, mould & bug resistant	Limited availability, thick walls
SIP	Fast	Slightly higher	R-15-45	Low	Low	Wind & seismic resistant	Uneven quality, low fire resistance
ICF	Fast	Slightly higher	R-17-40	Medium	Low	Low noise; fire, mould, & earthquake resistant	Low bug resistance
AAC	Fast	Higher	R-12-30	High	Low	Low noise; fire, mould, & bug resistant, easily cut	Limited availability
Standard Frame	Standard	Standard	R-8-13	Low	Medium	Readily available materials and expertise, DIY	Poor insulation

Lee Akins, *Materials comparison chart*, 2007-08.

possible in order to be a part of the entire process as well as saving capital, but felt too inexperienced to be in charge. The two straw bale contractors in their area did beautiful work but neither was interested in working with an owner/builder. Lee still feels straw bale would make an excellent studio material in the right setting: a dry climate with a wide temperature range.

Three other new materials, SIP (Structural Integrated Panel), AAC (Autoclaved Aerated Concrete), and ICF (Insulated Concrete Forms), are all quick to build with and very energy efficient. However, as the manufacture of all three relies on concrete and foam as materials they were not as appealing to him.

The best combination for their situation turned out to be pumice-crete. Pumice is a volcanic rock found in many parts of North America including New Mexico. Pumice is mixed with a small amount of cement to bond it together and poured into plywood forms. The 14-inch (35.5 cm) thick walls serve as both insulation and structure, greatly reducing the amount of wood needed for framing. Lee was able to find a highly recommended local contractor who preferred to build just the shell of the structure. He was able to provide expertise and good local subcontractors that made for a smooth building experience. Lee and his son did the finishing on the house and studio once the main structure was done. This proved to be a good way to reduce their building costs by providing 'sweat equity'.

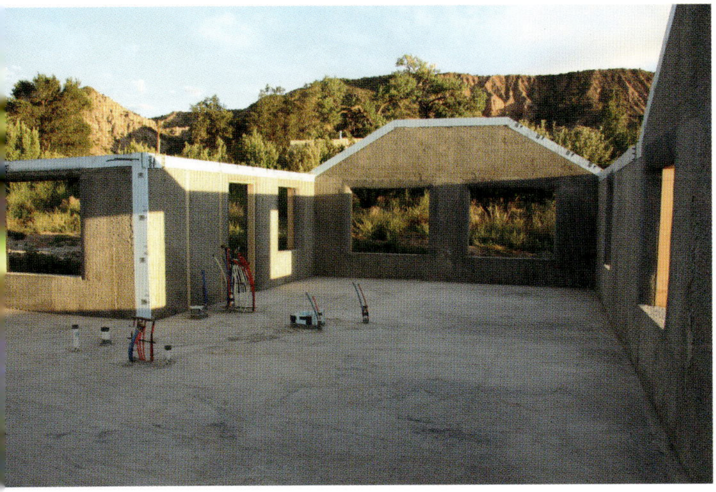

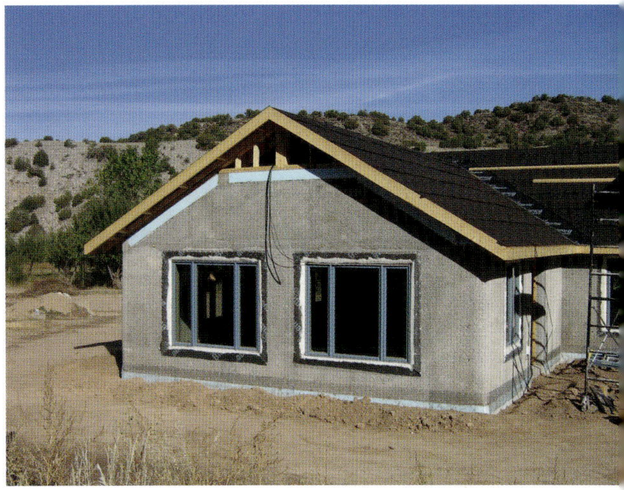

LEFT: Pumice-crete walls and cast concrete foundation slab, Ranchos de Taos, New Mexico, 2008. *Photo: Lee Akins.*

RIGHT: Roof construction, Ranchos de Taos, New Mexico, 2008. *Photo: Lee Akins.*

Heat rises, so the most critical insulation is actually in the ceiling. They used a combination of blown-in cellulose (recycled newspaper) and formaldehyde-free fibreglass bats to achieve the recommended R-38 insulation. Recycled cotton bats are also available now.

Using passive solar principles can save up to 50% on heating and cooling.

Implementing these principles usually adds little additional cost during construction but does require prior planning. Orienting the building on an east/west axis allows placement of windows to take advantage of solar gain. Lee put the majority of the windows, double pane low E, on the long south-facing wall. The sun pours in during the winter, heating the thermal mass of the concrete floor. Deep overhangs over the windows block the sun in the summer and keep the interior cool. The morning and afternoon heat in the summer is avoided by having few windows on the east and west walls. The studio does not have any windows on the north side, reducing heat loss in the winter. A great article on using these principles for a south facing garage studio can be found at: http://builditsolar.com/Projects/SpaceHeating/SolarGarageCollector/garcol.htm.

Radiant heat (hot water pumped through the floor) is ideal for clay studios. It is quiet and does not stir up dust particles or create drafts like a forced-air system. This decrease in air movement is especially suited for drying ceramics evenly. A high-efficiency boiler heats the water for the floor and backs up Lee's solar hot water system on the rare cloudy day. They considered installing solar panels (photo voltaic) to provide their electrical power as well, but were deterred by the high initial investment and slow return. A US federal tax break added an incentive for choosing solar power for the hot water. As the price, quality and availability of solar panels improves, their use will become more attractive.

The interior walls are plastered with clay from the property and treated with a lime wash for waterproofing. All of the paints and finishes used are low or zero VOC. (VOC: Volatile Organic Compounds are organic chemicals that have a high vapour pressure at room temperature conditions. They are numerous, varied and ubiquitous, and include both human-made and naturally occurring chemical compounds.)

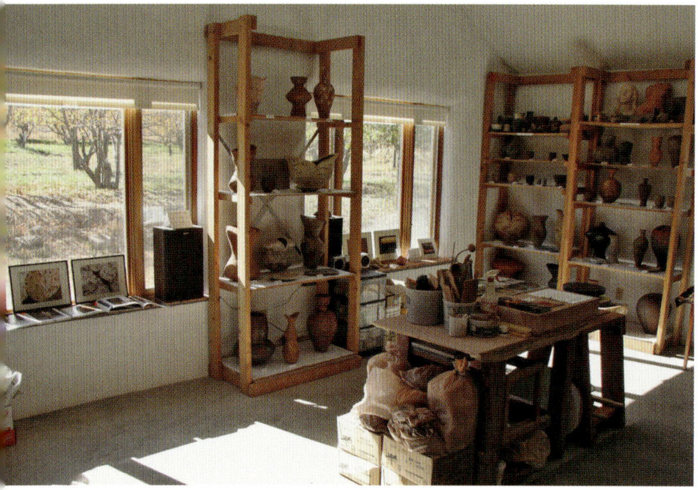

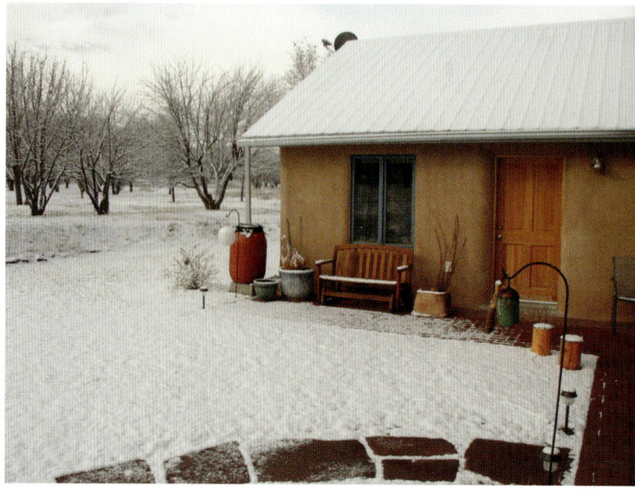

For those not able to build a new studio there are still many things that can be done to increase energy efficiency. One of the simplest things is to replace your HVAC (heating, ventilation and air conditioning) filter frequently. If you have a window unit, rinse out the foam filter often. In addition to increasing the unit's efficiency, it will also reduce dust.

Installing a programmable thermostat and shading windows with blinds and exterior plantings (especially on the west side) also reduces heating and cooling costs. Replacing older heating or cooling units with high-efficiency models will save energy and reduce costs over a relatively short time. Weather-stripping, caulking and adding to ceiling insulation all reduce the demand for both heating and cooling. Blowing in additional cellulose insulation into an existing attic space is an easy weekend project. The new choices in light bulbs, including CFLs, LEDs and cold cathodes, are all much more efficient than incandescent bulbs.

Starting with these small steps can help all of us reduce our carbon footprint and provide a better energy future for subsequent generations.

Building or rebuilding an energy-efficient studio is just one way to reduce your energy consumption and carbon footprint. Using the material resources in your own backyard is another way to apply sustainable principles to your practice, examples of which are discussed in the following section (and throughout the book in various ways).

LEFT: Finished studio interior, Ranchos de Taos, New Mexico, 2009.

RIGHT: Studio in the snow, Ranchos de Taos, New Mexico, 2010.
Photos: Lee Akins.

Treasured trash: ceramic waste mitigation practices

Kristin Schimik is a ceramic sculptor who lives and works in Seattle, Washington and writes about sustainable ceramic practices.

The ceramics programme at the University of Oregon in Eugene has a long history of engaging in environmentally responsible studio practice. Currently, the ceramics department has a system set up to capture glaze waste, including heavy metal colourants, and fire the materials up to cone 1 with recycled clay into paver blocks. Students in the ceramics programme at the university have been participating in the recycling of clay and glaze waste into usable paver bricks for over 10 years.

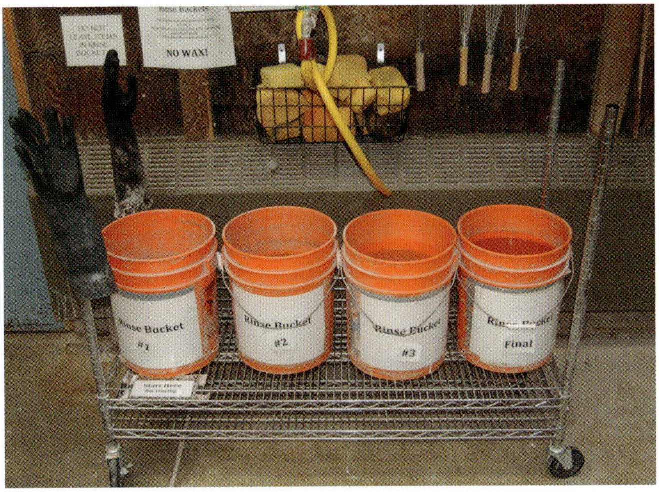

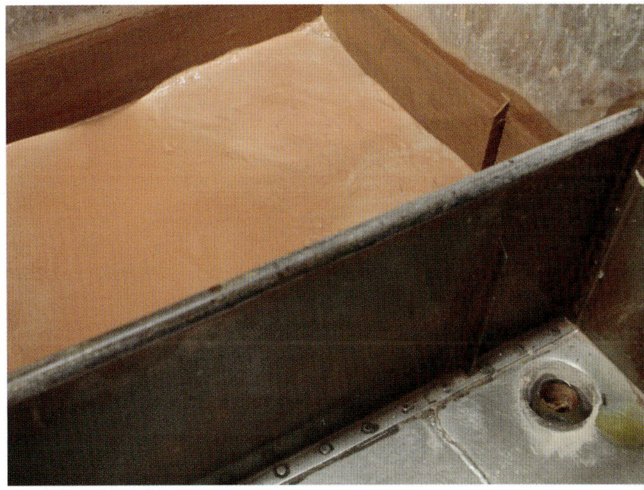

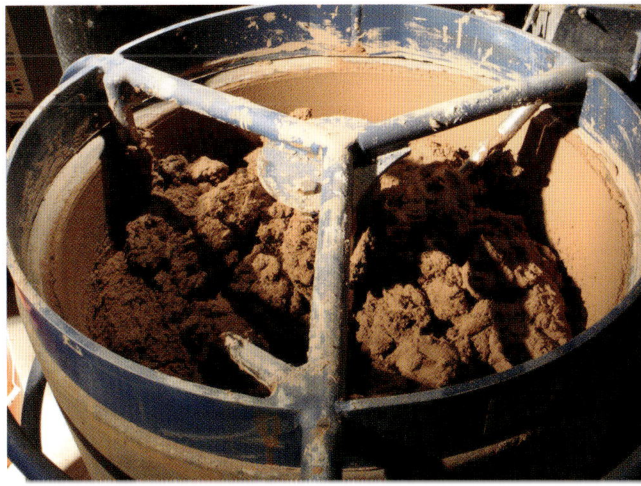

ABOVE: Kristin Schimik, Oregon four-bucket rinse system.

TOP RIGHT: Kristin Schimik, glaze waste slurry.

RIGHT: Kristin Schimik, Brick paver mix in Soldner mixer.
Photos: Kristin Schimik.

The University of Oregon glaze waste recycling system grew out of dialogue between faculty, staff, and the community about ways to reduce the environmental impacts of the art programme. The work began in the mid-1990s as a result of the efforts of Professor Sana Krusoe and then graduate student Nancy Frazier. Krusoe stated that she 'learned about waste conservation from Gordon Ward, a local potter, who used one glaze, kept all his rinse water, and converted it back to glaze'. Glaze waste was consolidated, tested, and donated for use in area public schools. However, an excess of glaze waste remained. When the task of recycling a backlog of glaze waste was given to Frazier, she began the process of making useable paver brick and recruited student volunteers to dehydrate, mix, shape and test fire different ratios of clay to glaze waste.

There is no running water in the glaze room at the University of Oregon. Instead, the students are required to wear gloves and to use a series of four rinse buckets, with each in the sequence cleaner than the last. There is a primary system set up to collect standard glaze materials and a secondary series of receptacles to collect the soluble

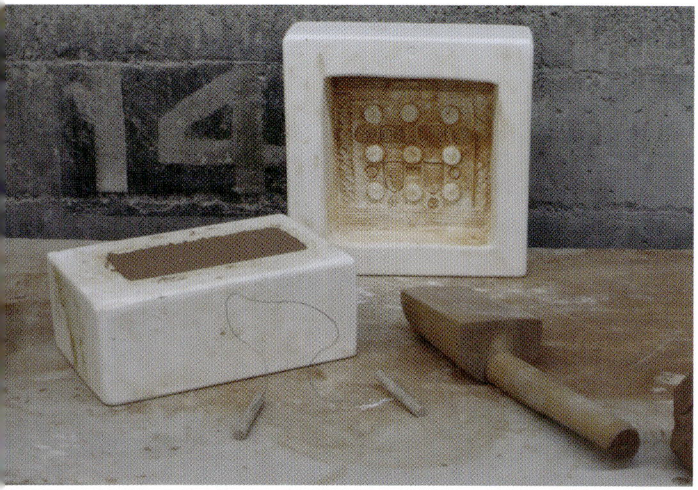

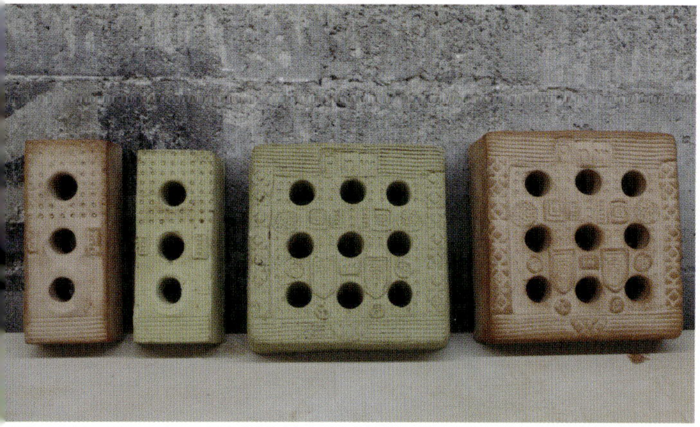

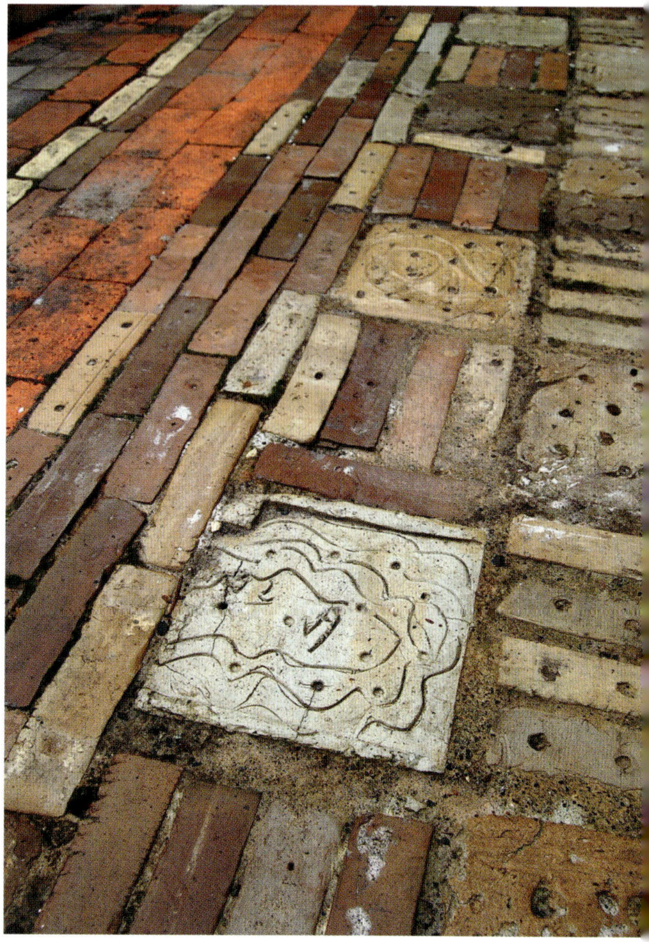

TOP LEFT: Paver brick moulds.

LEFT: Raw and fired brick pavers.

ABOVE: Oregon patio pavers installed. *Photos: Kristin Schimik.*

glaze materials. The insoluble glaze materials are allowed to settle, and then the water is siphoned off. The resulting glaze slurry is combined with waste clay at a 1:1 ratio and then mixed in a Soldner clay mixer. The smaller quantity of material collected in the soluble bins is allowed to dehydrate back into salts and then it is added to the mix. The *brick mix* is formed into perforated blocks and fired to cone 1 for use as pavers. The heavy rainfall common during Oregon valley winters makes the paver blocks highly desirable and the first blocks were immediately put to use around the ceramics facility. The pavers are about 10 inches square (25 cm) and two inches thick (5 cm) and usually fire out a strong apricot.

Krusoe's class in glaze chemistry participates in the waste reclamation process from start to finish. Often, the first objects that beginning ceramics students fire in the university programme are the paver blocks. The graduate studio technician and work-study students are also involved in processing the materials in order to maintain the efficiency of the system. To those interested in enacting a glaze waste recycling set up, Krusoe advises to remove or board over the sink and put up clear signage for the new recycling network. Users will adapt to the system.

Recycling ceramic waste: a methodology

Dave Binns is a maker and educator who is interested in pushing boundaries in researching new techniques and alternative uses of materials.

> The making of any ceramic artefact, be it functional, sculptural or architectural, inevitably involves detrimental environmental impacts – the inevitable generation of waste through making. As it is now universally acknowledged that we should strive to reduce negative environmental impact wherever possible, ceramic artists should be exploring ways of embedding a more sustainable and environmentally responsible approach within their practice.

Dave's research project (on the recycling of ceramic waste product, explained below) grew out of Dave's studio practice, and is relevant to clay artists wishing to adopt a more sustainable approach within their own studio. The project has involved the development of a new material made in part from studio waste. The material appears to have significant sustainable credentials and the potential to imbue a sense of place, whilst simultaneously offering a methodology for reducing the environmental impact of ceramic production and studio practice. The process for forming the material involves fusing varying proportions of ceramic and mineral waste with recycled waste glass.

While it presents many interesting creative opportunities for studio artists, architects and designers, the material does however have limitations in terms of workability. It cannot be worked like plastic clay, as the process involves moulds to constrain the material during fusing. In many ways it is closely allied to the glass kiln

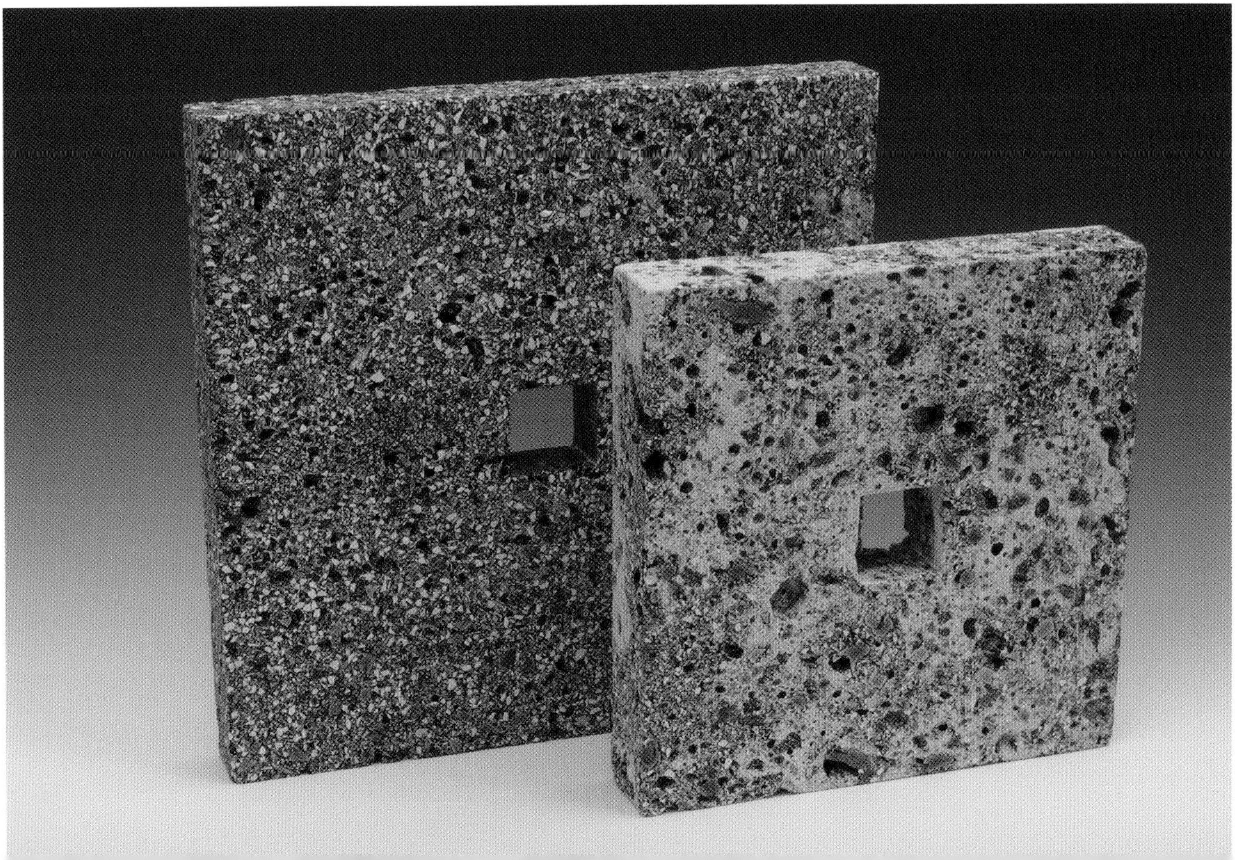

Pair of Square Pierced Forms, Dave Binns, 2011. 45 x 45 x 4 cm & 32 x 32 x 5 cm (17¾ x 17¾ x 1½ in & 12½ x 12½ x 2 in), kiln cast waste glass and recycled ceramic aggregates, ground and polished post firing. *Photo: courtesy of the artist.*

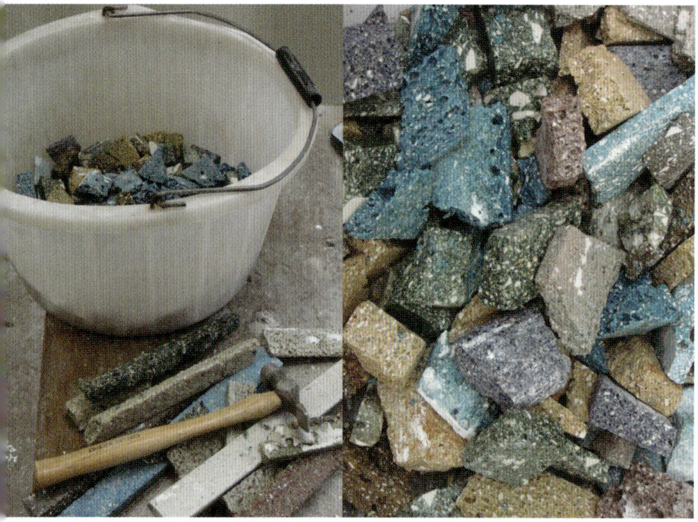

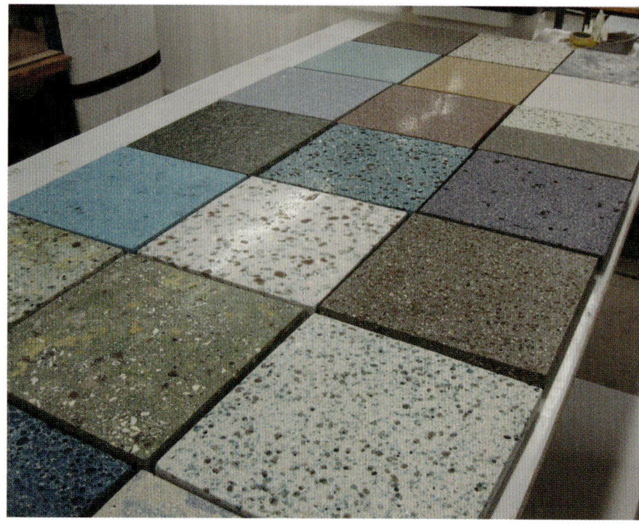

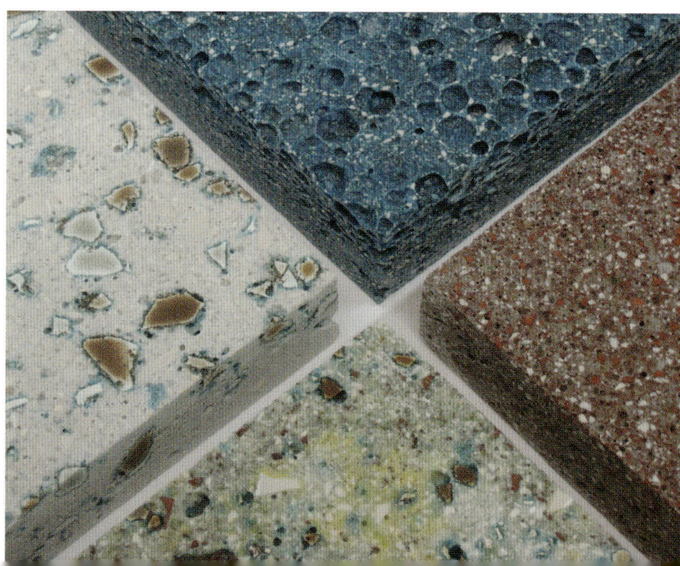

LEFT: Recycling the recycled: crushing trimming waste from cast tiles, kiln cast waste glass and recycled ceramic aggregates.

RIGHT: Prototype cast tiles: kiln cast waste glass and recycled ceramic aggregates, ground and polished post firing. Each tile: 30 x 30 x 3 cm (11¾ x 11¾ x 1 in).

BELOW: Detail of prototype cast tiles: kiln cast waste glass and recycled ceramic aggregates, ground and polished post firing. Each tile: 30 x 30 x 3 cm (11¾ x 11¾ x 1 in). *Photos: courtesy of the artist.*

casting process, therefore allowing a similar vocabulary of form to those found in cast glass. It is particularly appropriate for the making of architectural products such as tiles, bricks, cladding sheets, counter tops and shallow vessel forms. In contrast to using traditional non-replenishable virgin raw materials such as quarried clays or stone, which often damages ecological habitats when extracted and contributes to global warming when transported huge distances, this material can be produced from 97–100% locally sourced recycled waste. Further to its sustainability characteristics, the material is imbued with a number of unique aesthetic attributes, allowing colour and texture to be adapted to the artists or client's specific requirements.

The root of the research began through the making of ceramic sculpture within a craft studio environment, over time evolving into a systematic, scientific research project. The project's aims were to:

- identify appropriate sources of waste materials;
- explore how they might be combined within a kiln casting process for the development of material with unique aesthetic qualities;
- examine the creative potential of the material for architects, designers, artists and craft makers;
- explore how the process might lower the environmental impact of ceramic production.

The background to the research has been twofold. Dave writes:

> Firstly, within my own ceramic practice I have always been inquisitive about materials and their properties and interested in developing new techniques, whilst interested in challenging

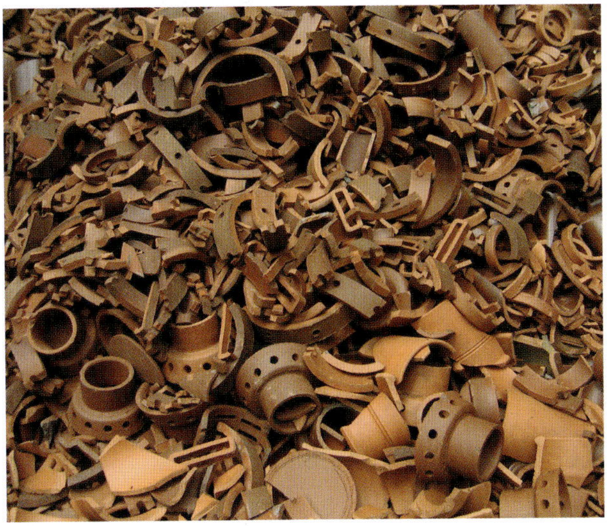

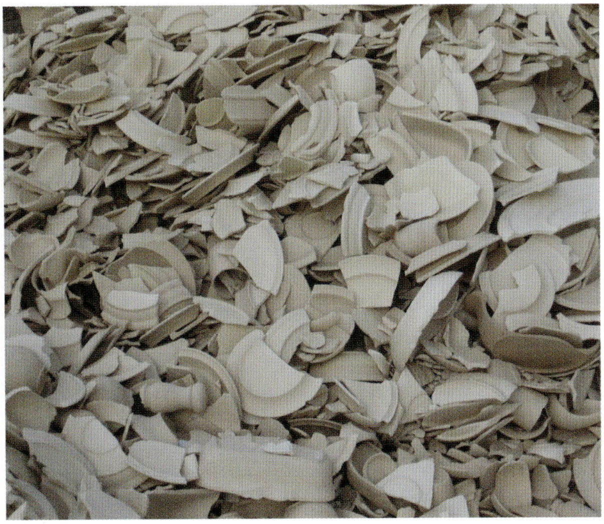

LEFT: Ceramic chimney pot and pipe waste, W. T. Knowles and Sons Ltd., Ash Grove Pipe Works, Elland, West Yorkshire, UK.

RIGHT: Bone china tableware waste, Furlong Mills Ltd., Burslem, Stoke-on-Trent, UK. *Photos: courtesy of the artist.*

conventional processes and practices. Secondly, as a ceramic practitioner, the potentially negative environmental impact of my practice has steadily risen in my consciousness as environmental responsibility has moved up the social and political agenda.

Introducing recycled waste

Designers, architects and artists continually strive for new forms of expression and innovative solutions to problems. A consequence of this is a hunger for new materials to sustain their creative aspirations. This relentless demand for new materials is, however, placing unsustainable demands on many finite mineral resources. Simultaneously, higher standards of living are creating ever-greater amounts of waste material that more often than not end life as landfill.

While the arguments for embedding sustainability throughout the construction and design industries are well established and firmly embedded in the consciousness of architects and designers, it often conflicts with their desire for materials that offer new aesthetic properties. It is, therefore, becoming increasingly important that alternative products are developed that both offer a new aesthetic and are environmentally sustainable – less reliant on virgin raw materials. As Wackernagel and Rees (2007) state:

> ... the Earth's ecosystems cannot sustain current levels of material consumption, let alone increased levels.

Concern over sustainability of resources is echoed in both UK government and European Union strategy, stating the need to increase the breadth of applications for recycled materials. Government strategy goes further, emphasising the importance of 'value added' opportunities from recycled materials; that is, high quality products that have a value beyond those already present in recovered materials.

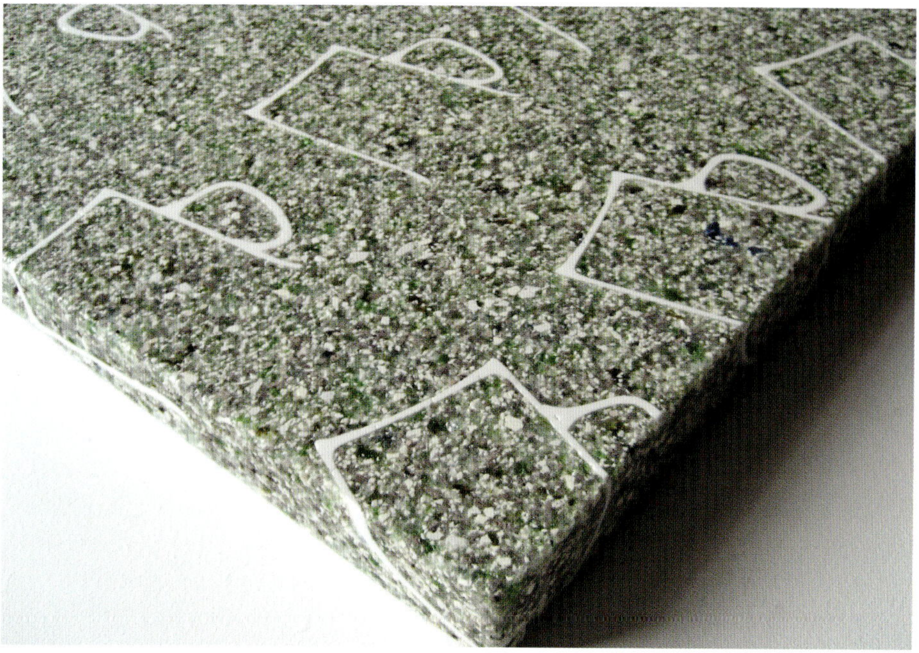

Large cast tile with cup fossils, Dave Binns. 65 x 65 x 4 cm (25½ x 25½ x 1½ in), kiln cast waste glass and recycled ceramic aggregates with bone china cups, ground and polished post firing. *Photo: courtesy of the artist.*

Recyclability

It has been found that any second-quality casts or waste from machining may be directly returned to the production process, avoiding any manufacturing waste, thus satisfying the desirable objective of 'closed-loop' manufacturing. At end of life, the product may itself be recycled. This would entail simply reintroducing it into the original manufacturing cycle as a raw material rather than the more common process of *downcycling* to less valuable products, further enhancing the eco-credentials of the materials.

Recycling waste within the ceramic studio

> As a studio artist producing ceramic sculptural forms over many years, I have grown increasingly concerned about the negative environmental impact of my practice – an awareness raised by the ever-increasing debates about global warming, consumption, reducing our carbon footprint and more generally, the need to start adopting a more environmentally responsible lifestyle. These thoughts neatly coincided with, and fuelled my evolving research.
>
> Whilst the research into using ceramic, glass and mineral waste had grown out of my art practice, it had moved into a broader arena, suggesting industrial production, with a focus on developing alternative architectural products – cladding, tiling, etc. It made sense therefore to apply the knowledge back into my art practice. Over the last two years therefore, my personal artwork has involved using a high proportion of recycled ceramic and mineral waste.

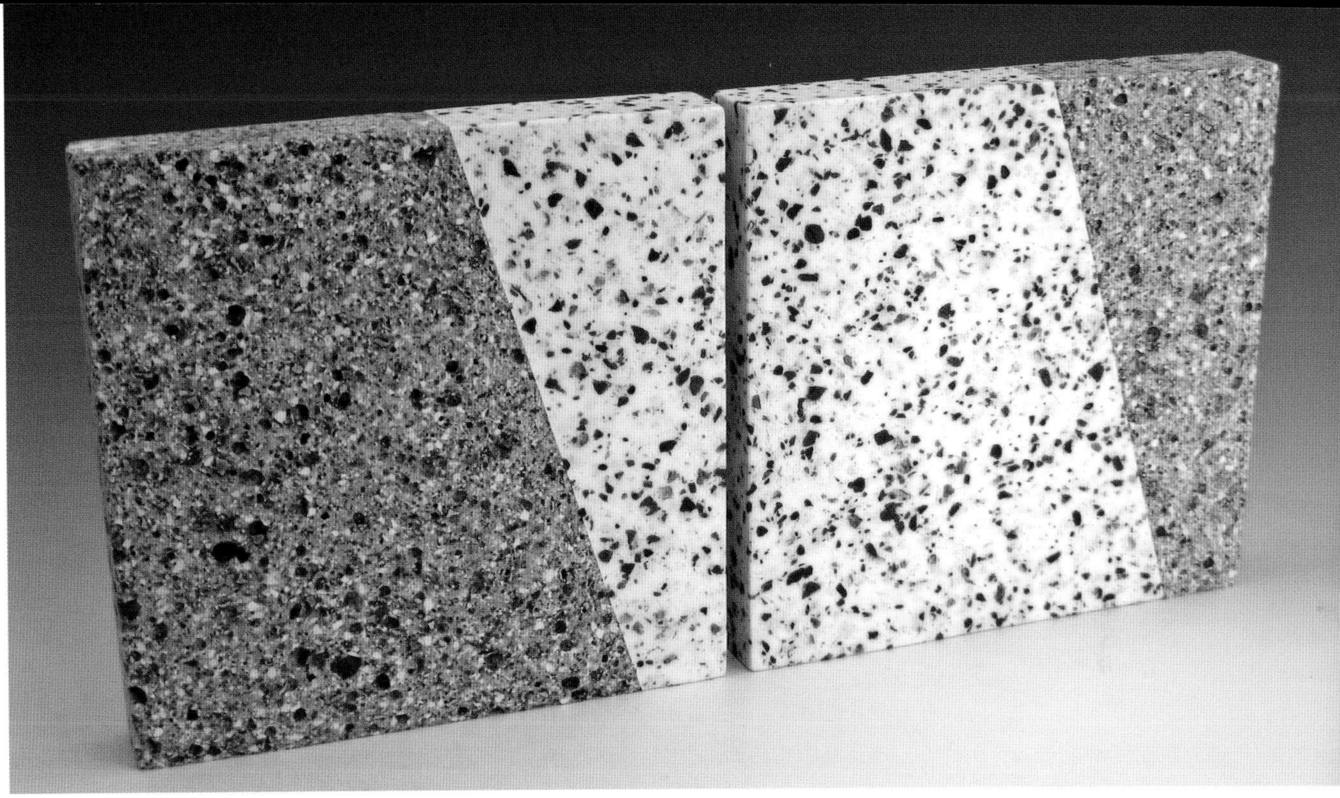

Two Piece Standing Form, Dave Binns. 34 x 68 x 6 cm (13½ x 26¾ x 2¾ in), porcelain combined with kiln cast waste glass and recycled ceramic aggregates, ground and polished post firing. *Photo: courtesy of the artist.*

Teaching in a large ceramics programme within an institution of Higher Education has meant I have access to significant amounts of waste materials – reject work, waste glaze slop, damaged kiln furniture, replaced kiln linings, etc. I am now able to make use of all this waste material within my artwork, meaning the department has reduced waste to almost zero. Reject work in particular, is crushed down to form varying sizes of grog, which is added to plastic clay when students required a courser textured body.

While not every ceramic studio or small ceramics department will generate enough waste to allow any meaningful commercial production, artists might consider developing small products from their studio waste. Alternatively waste could be gathered regularly from workshops within a relatively small geographic location; much akin to curbside collection of domestic waste. This could create a significant amount of waste, allowing the development of larger-scale projects.

The project highlights how research that started life within art practice, has led to a formalised systematic scientific method of investigation; taking the research from the familiar craft studio to the alien environment of the science laboratory. Furthermore, it presents a possible method by which studio-based ceramic artists and ceramic educational departments, can lower their waste output and reliance on non-replenishable sources of often imported raw materials.

It is my hope that this material may offer artists, architects and designers, the opportunity to use a durable, versatile, silicate-based material, with considerable eco-credentials, that has unique aesthetic properties, forges a strong link between material and place and contributes to a more sustainable society.

Eco & H_2O footprints

The *ecological footprint* is a measure of human demand on the Earth's ecosystems. It is a standardised measure of demand for natural capital that may be contrasted with the planet's ecological capacity to regenerate. It represents the amount of biologically productive land and sea area necessary to supply the resources a human population consumes, and to assimilate associated waste. Using this assessment, it is possible to estimate how much of the planet (or how many planet Earths) it would take to support humanity if everybody followed a given lifestyle. For 2007, humanity's total ecological footprint was estimated at 1.5 planet Earths – in other words, humanity uses ecological services 1.5 times as fast as Earth can renew them. Every year, this number is recalculated – with a three-year lag due to the time it takes for the UN to collect and publish all the underlying statistics.

Ecological footprint analysis is now widely used around the globe as an indicator of environmental sustainability. It can be used to measure and manage the use of resources throughout the economy. It can be used to explore the sustainability of individual lifestyles, goods and services, organisations, industry sectors, neighbourhoods, cities, regions and nations. Since 2006, a first set of ecological footprint standards have existed that detail both communication and calculation procedures. They are available at www.footprintstandards.org and were developed in a public process facilitated by Global Footprint Network and its partner organisations.

The *water footprint* of an individual, community or business is defined as the total volume of freshwater used to produce the goods and services consumed by the individual or community or produced by the business. Water use is measured in water volume consumed (evaporated) or polluted per unit of time. A water footprint can be calculated for any well-defined group of consumers (e.g. an individual, family, village, city, province, state or nation) or producers (e.g. a public organisation, private enterprise or economic sector). The water footprint is a geographically explicit indicator, not only showing volumes of water use and pollution, but also the locations. However, the water footprint does not provide information on how the embedded water negatively or positively affects local water resources, ecosystems and livelihoods.

Since 2009 there is a global calculation standard for the water footprint, maintained by the Water Footprint Network, an international network of governments, corporations, non-governmental organisations and UN bodies.

Save water; save the planet

The most important thing that an individual can do to save the planet is to save water.

This is especially true for potters and ceramic artists, schools with ceramics programmes and ceramic art centres that use water daily in their artistic pursuits. To quote former US vice president Al Gore: 'Water is the cutting edge of environmentalism.' Our planet, which has had almost the same amount of water on it since the dinosaurs roamed, is quickly running out of available freshwater. Current trends of overconsumption, pollution and climate change are leading us to predicted severe water shortages in the next decade and a half. Population growth has a lot to do with demands on the world's freshwater supply, but awareness and management of our limited resources will go a

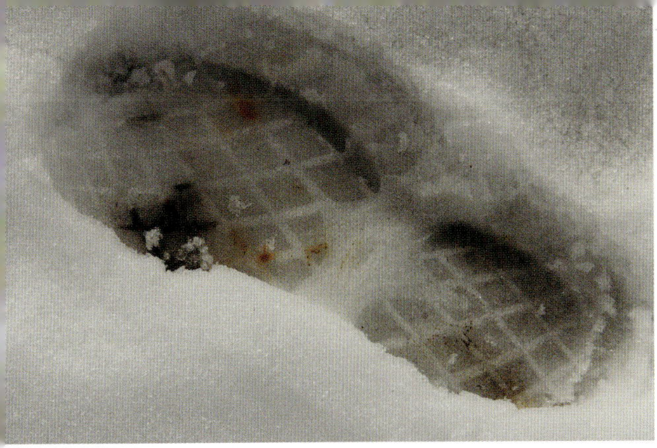

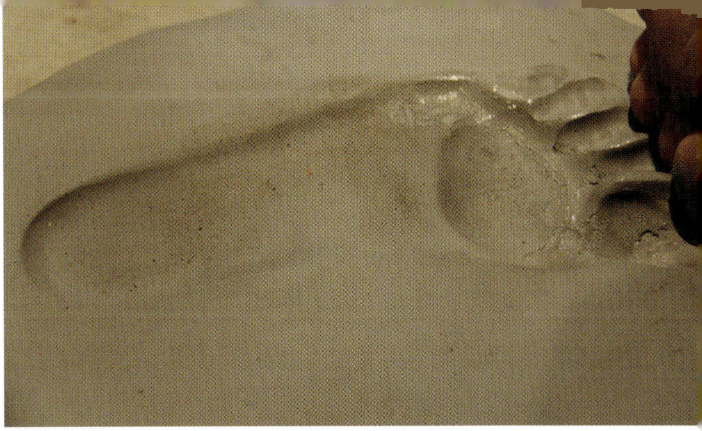

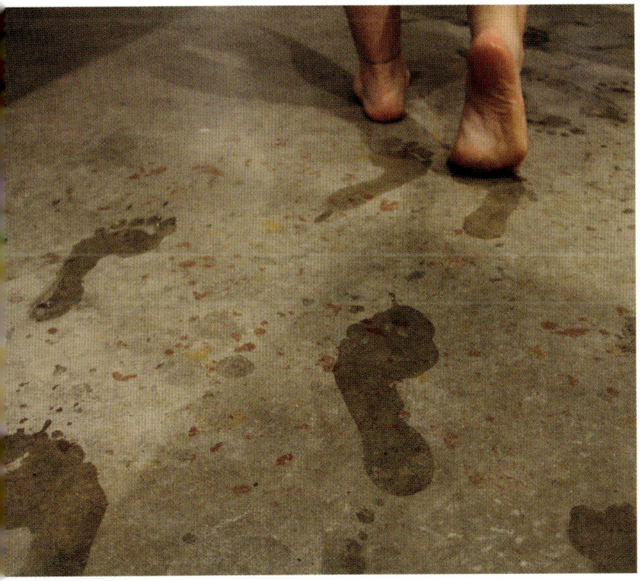

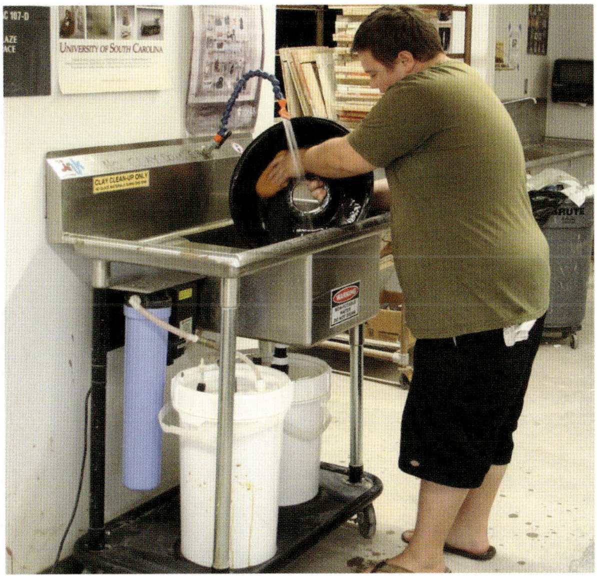

TOP LEFT: *My Eco Footprint (winter)*, Robert Harrison, Helena, Montana, 2012.

TOP RIGHT: *Ecological (clay) footprint*, Robert Harrison, HTH model, Helena, Montana, 2012.

BOTTOM LEFT: *Water footprint*, Robert Harrison, HTH model, Helena, Montana, 2012.

BOTTOM RIGHT: John Wood II using a CINK (portable, self-contained clay and water filtration system), Chaffey College ceramics studio, California, 2012. *Photo: Brian Kohl.*

long way to reducing waste and stress on the environment. Calculate your own water consumption/footprint by going to: www.waterfootprint.org.

Common-sense uses of our freshwater supplies, that is the water we use for domestic consumption along with water for a ceramics studio, can have dramatic immediate effects on our available resources. One specific product for ceramic studios is made by Creative Industries (CI), a manufacturer of ceramic products. CI has developed the Creative Industries CINK, a portable clay and water filtration system that captures clay for reuse and has a closed loop set up for water.

Consider water-saving approaches when building or upgrading homes and studios. Low-flush or duel-flush toilets, automatic or low-flow faucets along with faucet aerators which break water flow into fine droplets to maintain *wetting effectiveness* while using less water, and low-flow shower heads all make a difference. Wastewater reuse or recycling systems, allowing use of *greywater* for flushing toilets or watering gardens, along with high-efficiency appliances save water and energy. When landscaping, consider native and drought tolerant plants, drip irrigation along with *xeriscape* concepts for water efficiency. Another age-old practice is *rainwater harvesting* for reuse, either in the studio, or in domestic activities.

The sustainability of makers: the body

Ergonomics for sustaining the body

Christel Harrison, OTR, RHT, is a practising Occupational Therapist who lives and works in Helena, Montana.

Ergonomics by definition is the art and science of adjusting the work environment to meet the physical needs of the individual. The purpose of this section is to provide the individual with useful suggestions to sustain a healthy way of working in the studio. The ultimate goal is to minimise health issues such as back pain, tendinitis, carpel tunnel syndrome, to name a few, by maintaining good posture and decrease the stress strain on the muscles.

There are a few general principles that can be applied to any given work situation whether it is wedging clay, throwing, hand-building, loading a kiln, packing boxes, lifting glaze buckets or simply working on a computer that can decrease the potential for injury.

Work station heights

1. For greatest comfort, work in a sitting position as much as possible. The chair seat height should allow for feet to rest on the ground creating a 90-degree angle at the hips and knees. The work surface should be at waist height (29–30 inches/73–75.5 cm from the floor), which is 1–2 inches (2.5–5 cm) below elbow height.

a) Detailed work: Such as carving, china painting, applying decals, etc. it is recommended that the item be raised on a pedestal or banding wheel to decrease eye strain and once again avoid a hunched, shoulder posture.

b) Computer use: For a computer keyboard, the work surface should be at 26–27 inches (66–68.5 cm) from the floor to allow elbows to be at a 90-degree angle and a neutral or straight wrist position. The keyboard and mouse should be positioned on the same surface, which may include a computer keyboard tray. A wrist rest is very helpful in maintaining a neutral wrist position and avoiding resting your wrist on the sharp edge of the desk.

c) Chairs: When sitting for extended periods of time the chair should fit your stature properly for maximum support and thereby decrease fatigue. A good chair should include adjustable seat height, adjustable lumbar support, and armrests are recommended for extended, repetitive activities such as using the computer.

d) Throwing: Is typically done in a seated position and it is important to adjust the seat height so that by bending at the hips you can maintain the natural S-curve of the back and prevent low back pain.

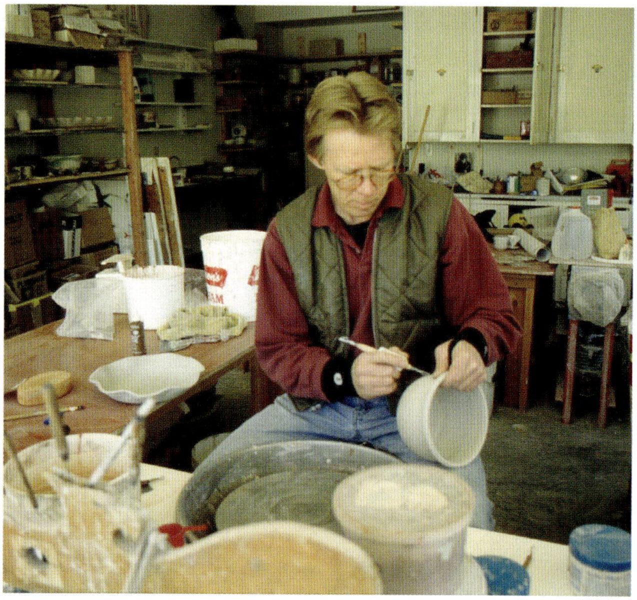

Richard Swanson working in the studio with 90 degree bend at his hips, knees, elbows and wrists in a neutral position, Helena, Montana. *Photo: Christel Harrison.*

2. These same principles generally apply to a standing station or workbench. When standing, the work surface should be 35–36 inches (90–92.5 cm) from the floor to allow elbows to be at a 90-degree angle and close to your side.

a) Detailed work: Raise the object to roughly chest height and arms supported on the work surface, but for extended periods of time it would be more beneficial to sit.
b) Packing: When completing heavy work such as packing boxes, the work surface should be at hip level (30 inches (73 cm) from the floor) to avoid shoulder and back strain.
c) Glazing: The work surface should be at waist height and glaze buckets within a 10-inch (25.5 cm) arm reach to avoid excessive twisting or reaching. Glazes should be at room temperature for ease in use as well as to prevent stiffness in the small joints of the hand.
d) Wedging: Use a solid worktable at a height of 30 inches (73 cm). Using smaller amounts of relatively soft clay will decrease the amount of force at the wrist as well as arm fatigue.

3. Regardless of the height of the standing station or the task being completed, it is *always* helpful when standing to have one leg propped on a short stool or footrest to decrease low back or hip pain. Anti-fatigue mats are also helpful to prevent slipping on a wet surface and allow for greater comfort when standing on hard surfaces like concrete for prolonged periods of time.

Richard Swanson lifting with hips and knee bent while maintaining natural 'S' curve of his spine, Helena, Montana. *Photo: Christel Harrison.*

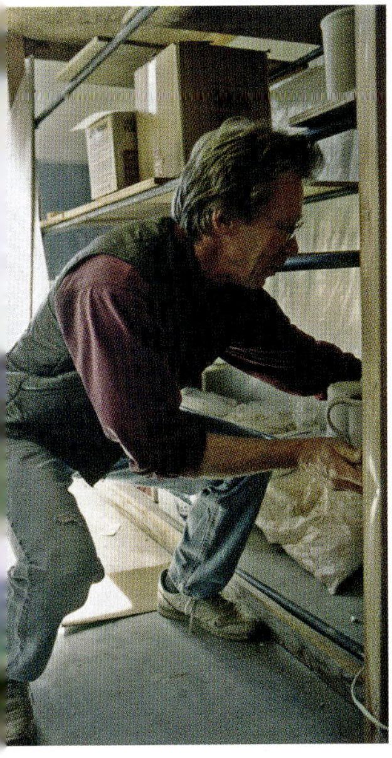

Lifting

1. When lifting it is important to avoid awkward bending positions, therefore the load should be close to the body with a straight back and knees/hips bent. The load should be no lower than knee height. Avoid rotating or twisting movements by maintaining the shoulders over the hips at all times.

a) Loading a top-loading kiln: Can be challenging as is it difficult to bend the knees and yet maintain the load close to the body, therefore it is recommended to use a *golfer's lift* which has you kick a leg back, bend at the hips while maintaining the natural S-curve of the back.
b) Front-loading kilns: Are inherently easier to load, but it is important to lift the shelves correctly with the shelf close to your body and bend with the knees. If the opening is small, requiring a crouched position, consider organising the objects close to you to avoid excessive twisting. Change your position every 10–15 minutes to stretch your muscles and have good circulation to your legs.
c) Boxes, buckets and crates: When possible use a wheeled handcart to move heavy, bulky boxes and crates. Ask for assistance when moving heavy, bulky objects (how heavy will depend on the individual's stature and capability). When carrying buckets have one in each hand to carry a balanced load and likewise, use two hands for heavy buckets.

Tools

1. Hand tools: Should have a large-barrelled handle to fit comfortably in your hand to allow for a comfortable grip when tools are being used for prolonged periods of time. Padding existing tools with insulating foam tubing is an inexpensive way to enlarge the handle of the tool.

2. Frequently used tools should be placed within a 10-inch (25.5 cm) arc of working position to avoid overreach. This would include water bowl close to the wheel and having your computer mouse next to your keyboard.

Vision and neck posture

1. To facilitate a relaxed neck and shoulder posture while avoiding eye fatigue when viewing a computer monitor it is recommended that the eye distance to computer monitor should be in the range of 18 to 30 inches (46 to 76 cm). This would be dependent on the size of the monitor, size of the font and the individual's visual acuity.

2. The height of the computer monitor should correspond to the top of the individual's forehead creating a slight downward tilt of the head to view the monitor.

3. Laptop computers are difficult to adjust to fit an individual's stature, therefore are not recommended for periods of prolonged use.

4. Beware of overhead lighting that may cause glare and thereby eye strain. Lighting is best if the source is natural and coming from the side of the viewer.

5. Task light is best for detailed work.

Preventive stretching exercises

Just as an athlete must maintain good condition of his/her body for a physically demanding activity so too does anyone performing demanding, repetitive tasks. *Therefore it is essential that artists working in the ceramics field should consider a regular exercise programme that includes stretching exercises for the upper extremities.*

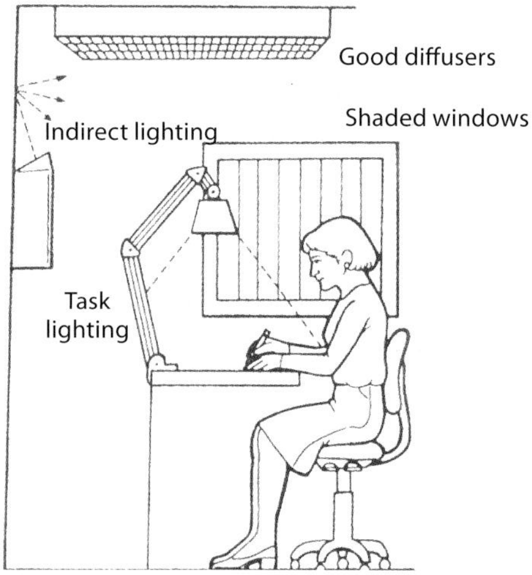

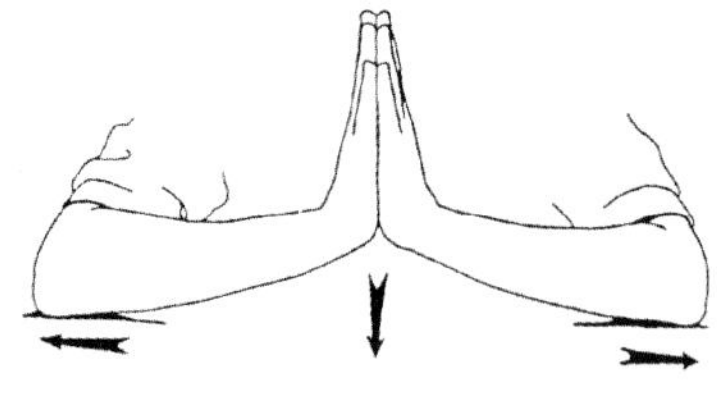

Sitting with elbows on table and palms together, slowly lower wrists to table until a stretch is felt. Be sure to keep palms together throughout the stretch.

LEFT: Ideal lighting and seated work position for computer or detailed work. *Photo: Christel Harrison.*

ABOVE: Stretching exercise for wrist and forearm muscles. This exercise should be done throughout the working day and comfortably held for a count of 3. *Photo: Christel Harrison.*

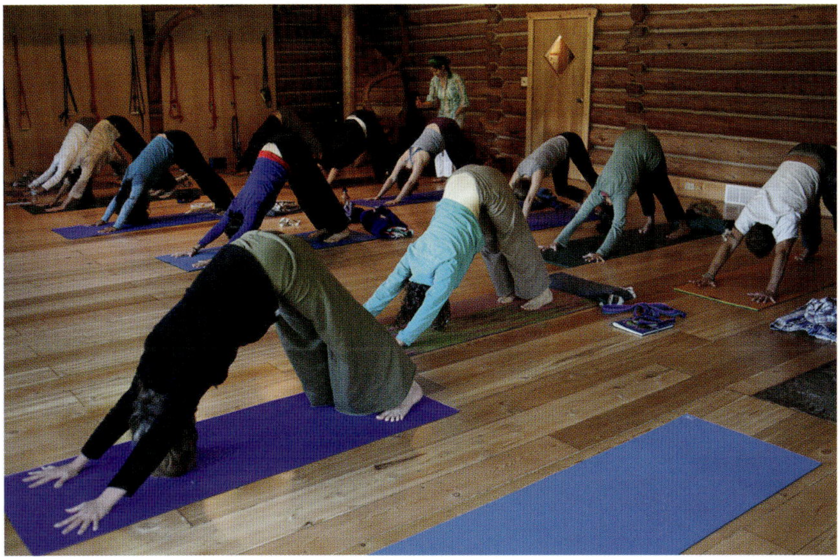

Elizabeth Sparks, *Yoga class*, 2011.

One with the clay: yoga and ceramic practice

A deeper awareness of the world's history, beauty and cultures came to many western cultures during the cultural revolution of the 1950s, 1960s and 1970s. One of the most beneficial aspects of this awareness was a greater understanding of the health benefits practised for millennia by eastern cultures. Ancient Indian Yoga and Chinese T'ai chi are just two of many forms of exercise meant to help sustain us as makers. Many makers have incorporated these practices into their daily routines to help sustain their bodies for the long term.

Liz Sparks is a potter and educator who has practised yoga for many years along with her ceramic practice. Liz believes that Yoga also helps her with her clay work. A yoga pose requires focus and intention, where distracting thoughts can lead to a loss of balance. Working in clay means tuning out thoughts, worries or things that can drain your energy in order to be *in the moment with the creative process.* For Liz, these two things are interconnected and help each other. There is a common understanding in yoga that if you are looking and comparing yourself to others, you are not in your practice. For Liz, this is also true in her work. When she goes within and allows the creative process to come out, without worries of how it may be received or viewed by others, then she is in her practice.

The healing arts and her clay work are tied together in the sense that she uses clay with an intention to heal, either through designing an object for a specific purpose, or using clay to create an enriching environment.

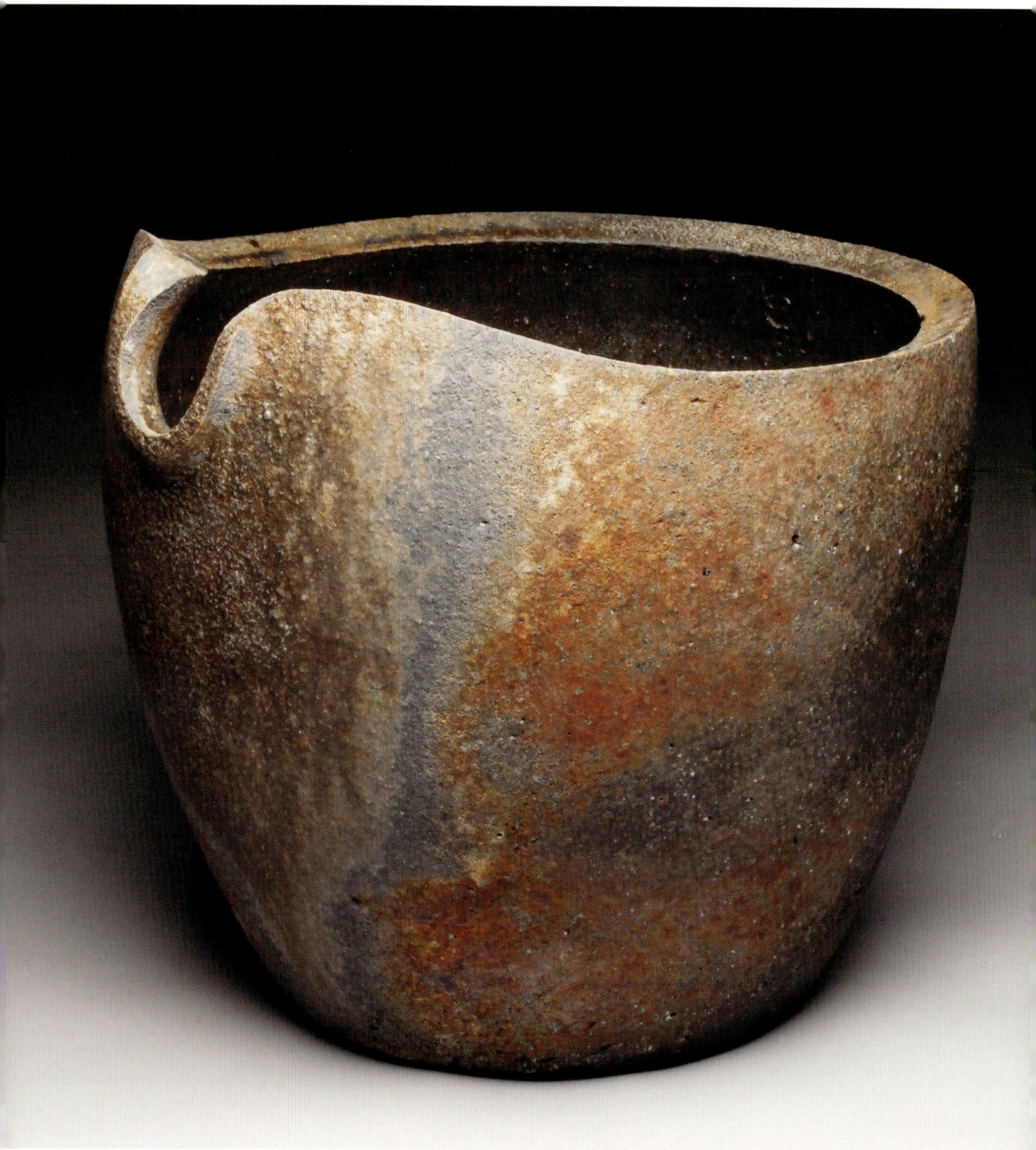

3

Ceramic artists working sustainably

I felt a chapter devoted to artists working sustainably was essential. Like so many aspects of the sustainability conundrum, the definitions are broad. I sought to profile artists/potters who made the commitment through their chosen lifestyle, as well as artists/potters whose work includes reclaimed, recycled and reused materials.

Many of the lines between the definitions of sustainable enterprise are *blurry*. I am convinced that the majority in our field are contributing in many ways to the sustainable effort. We are making and will continue to make a positive difference!

Out of necessity: art making with repurposed material

There is nothing new about repurposing discarded or found materials. This practice has been prevalent since the beginning of time. Human-made structures of every shape and description have been razed and the materials repurposed for millennia.

My own use of repurposed material came *out of necessity*. In the late 1970s I was working on my Master's degree in ceramics and transitioning from functional pottery to sculptural work. Intrigued by how the change of scale in my sculptural work would affect the viewer's perception of the work, I looked for materials for my research. The kiln yard had an abundance of discarded bricks languishing in piles and waiting to be taken to the landfill, or perhaps in my case awaiting reuse. And so my journey into large-scale site-specific indoor and outdoor installation activity began.

LEFT: *Crucible*, Dave Peters, 2011. Wood-fired local stoneware, 35.5 x 33 cm (14 x 13 in). *Photo: Dean Adams.*

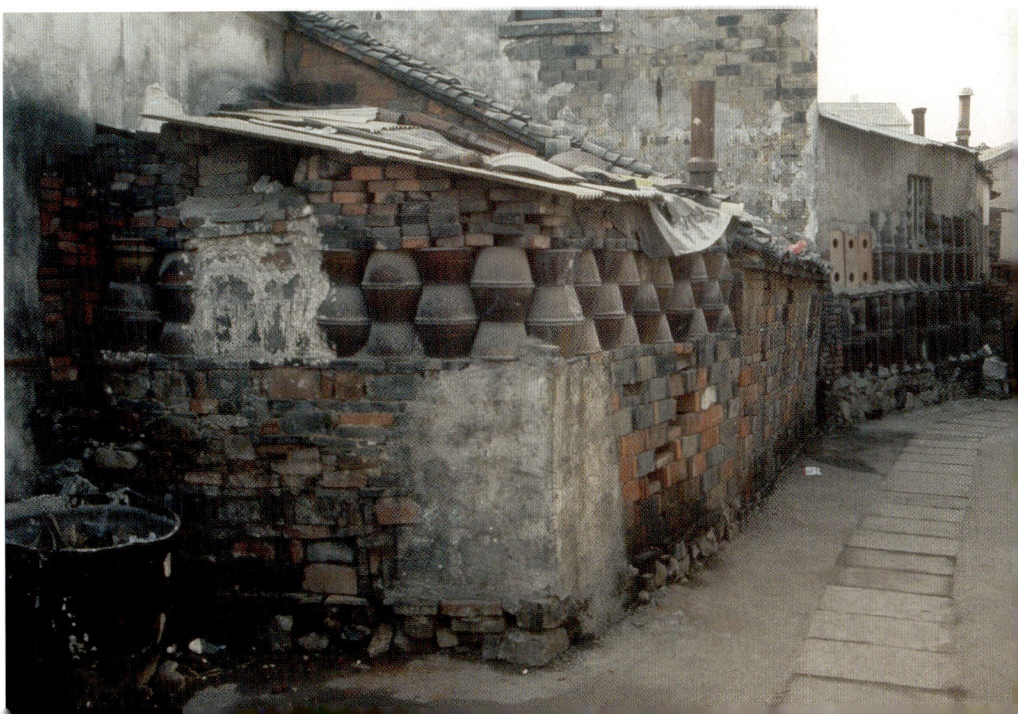

RIGHT: *Recycled Walls*, Dingshan (near Yixing), China, 1992. *Photo: Richard Notkin.*

In 1984 I was an artist-in-residence at the Archie Bray Foundation for the Ceramic Arts and found myself in the right place at the right time. The Archie Bray Foundation had just purchased the old Western Clay Manufacturing Company (a 19th-century brick factory on 26 acres of property) adjacent to the pottery. I was like a kid in a candy store with acres of brick and tile production, along with space to site large-scale work. I made a proposal to the then director of the Bray, Kurt Weiser, and was given the green light to proceed with an installation.

The details of my first installation, *Tilex*, are important because during the process of moving and handling the historic factory-produced extruded drain tile, I took the time to reflect on the repurposing aspect of creating new artwork from ageing, dormant

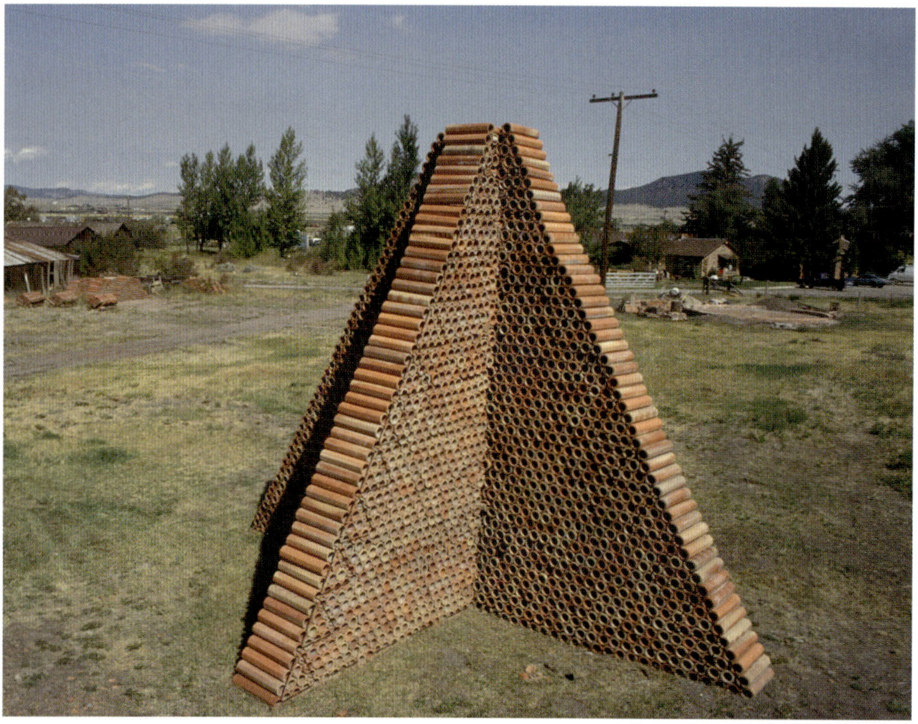

TileX, Robert Harrison, 1984–85. 6.7 x 7.6 x 7.6 m (22 x 25 x 25 ft), site-specific architectural sculpture, reclaimed/repurposed extruded clay drain tile, steel banding, Archie Bray Foundation for the Ceramic Arts, Helena, Montana. *Photo: Robert Harrison.*

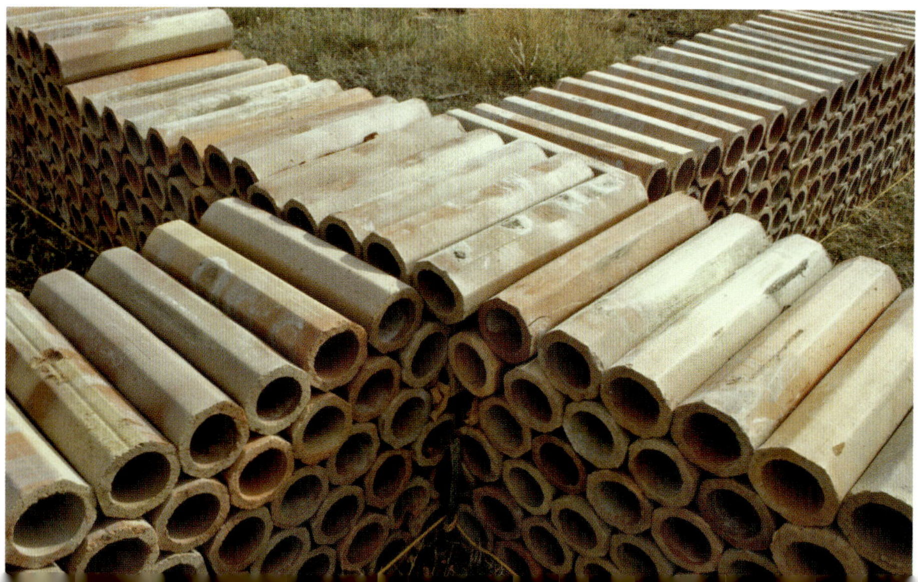

TileX, Robert Harrison, 1984–85 (construction detail). Site-specific architectural sculpture, reclaimed/repurposed extruded clay drain tile, steel banding, Archie Bray Foundation for the Ceramic Arts, Helena, Montana. *Photo: Robert Harrison.*

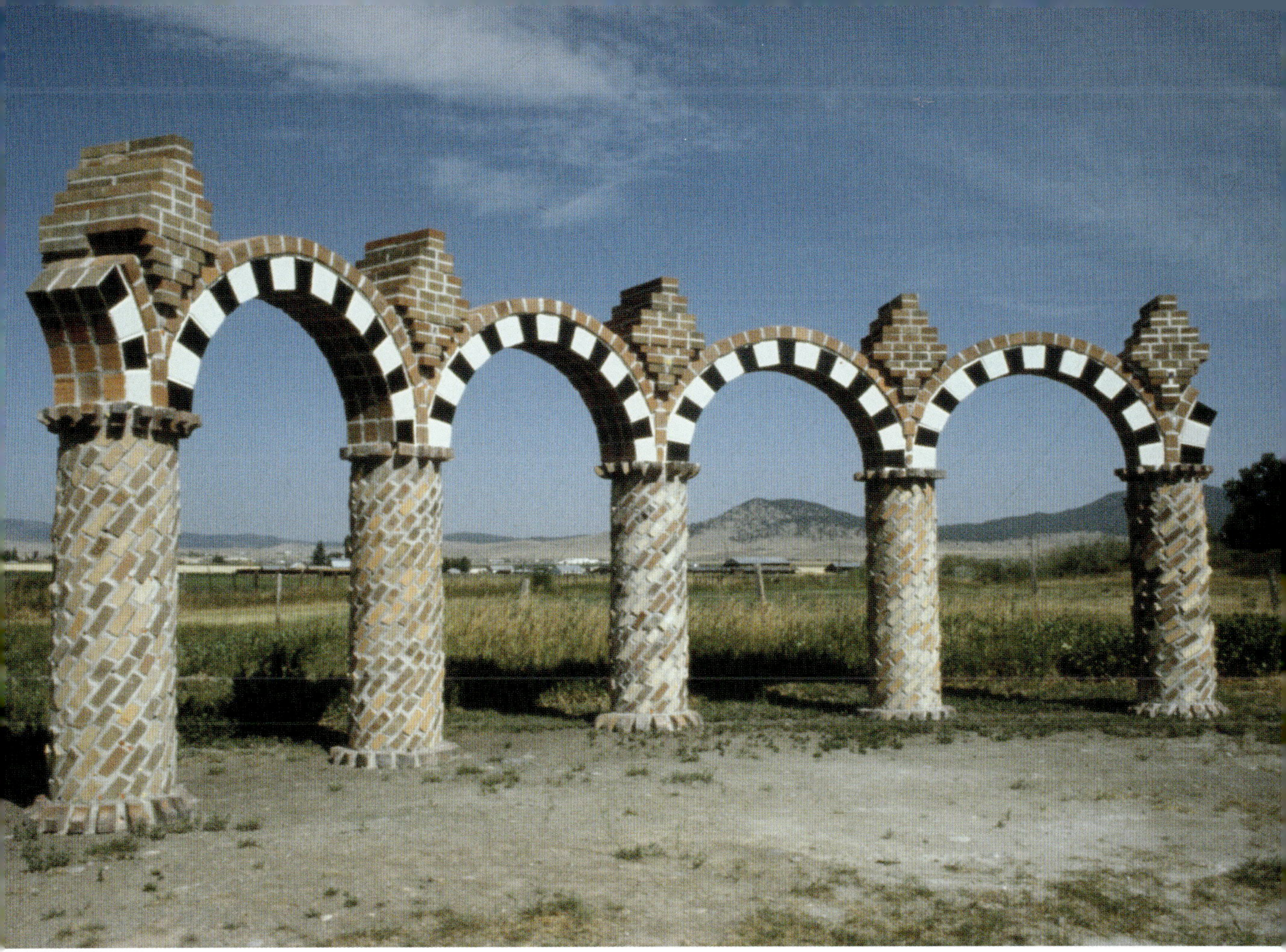

Aruina, Robert Harrison, 1988. 3.3 x 7.6 x 0.6 m (11 x 25 x 2 ft), site-specific architectural sculpture, reclaimed/repurposed brick and tile, mortar, cement, Archie Bray Foundation for the Ceramic Arts, Helena, Montana. *Photo: Robert Harrison.*

material. This project literally laid the foundation for a three-decade-plus career in the large-scale site-specific sculpture realm. The fact that the material had been made for another purpose and had historical significance certainly added a philosophical patina to the work.

Since that first experience on the grounds of the Bray Foundation, I continue to actively search for art-making materials *that have had another life*. I think incorporating materials that have a history and reference to *the place* makes the work that much more relevant to *that* place and *that* community.

The process of repurposing material for art making not only keeps the material out of the landfills, but brings a renewed appreciation for the particular material, perhaps to a new audience. One can look at this activity as a type of social activism, resurrecting the specific material to a higher order, now defined as *upcycling*.

I have chosen to work with primarily earth-based materials (ceramic, stone, wood, steel), which meshes with my aesthetics. I continue to be intrigued and inspired with industrially produced materials (brick and tile), and plan to keep juxtaposing the natural with human-designed and -produced materials. Reclaimed, recycled, and repurposed materials along with a sustainable philosophy will remain at the heart of my work.

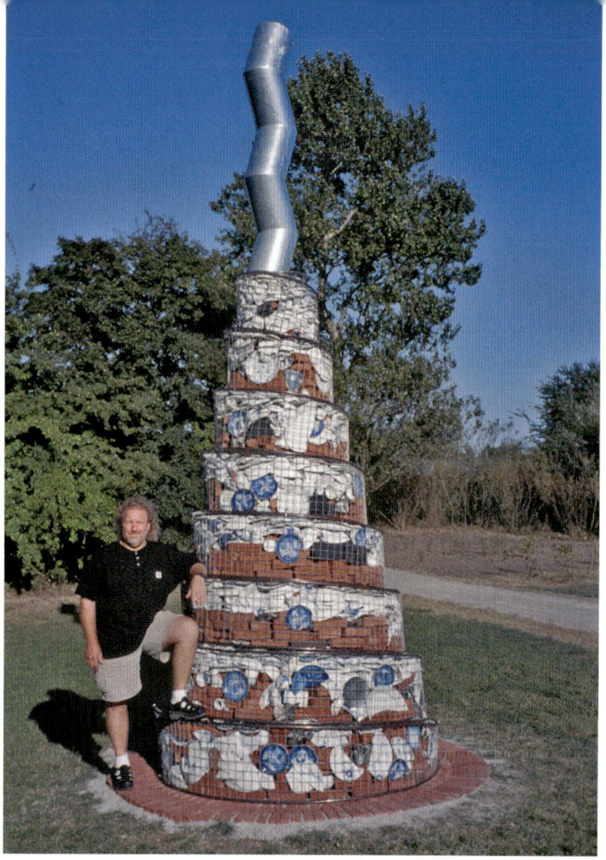

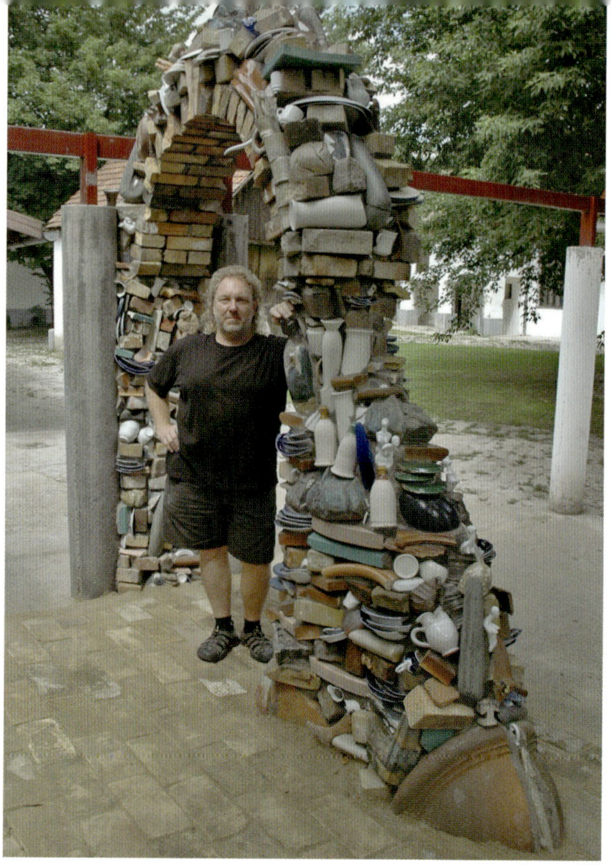

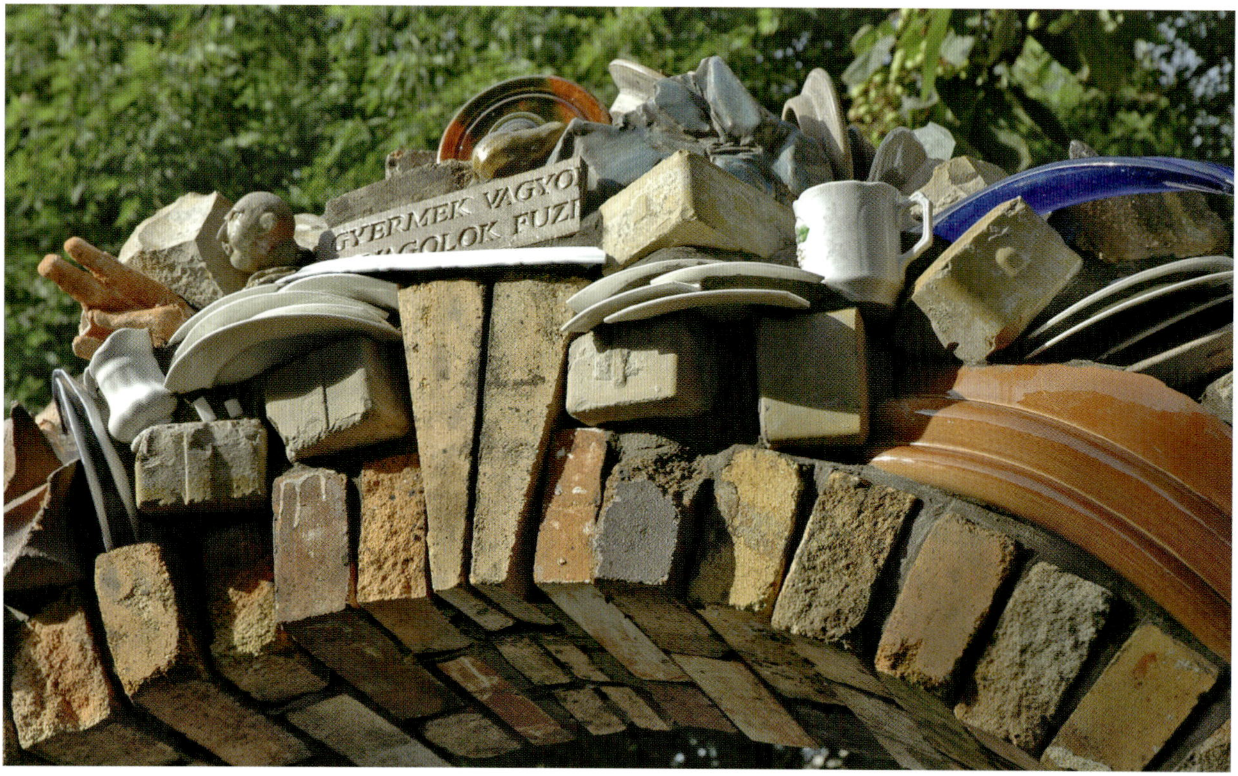
GYERMEK VAGYO
GOLOK FUZI

FAR LEFT: *Skaelskor Stack* (and artist), Robert Harrison, 2003. 4.5 x 1.8 m (15 x 6 ft), site-specific architectural sculpture, repurposed brick, Royal Copenhagen porcelain shards, galvanised steel mesh and fabricated steel pipe, copper tubing, Museum of International Ceramic Art, Guldagergaard, Skaelskor, Denmark. *Photo: Robert Harrison.*

LEFT: *Hungarian Arch* (and artist), Robert Harrison, 2006. 3.4 x 2.7 x 0.9 m (11 x 9 x 3 ft), site-specific architectural sculpture, reclaimed/repurposed brick industrial and handmade ceramic elements, mortar, cement, International Ceramics Studio, Kecskemet, Hungary. *Photo: Robert Harrison.*

LEFT: *Hungarian Arch* (detail), Robert Harrison, 2006. 3.4 x 2.7 x 0.9 m (11 x 9 x 3 ft), site-specific architectural sculpture, reclaimed/repurposed brick industrial and handmade ceramic elements, mortar, cement, International Ceramics Studio, Kecskemet, Hungary. *Photo: Robert Harrison.*

RIGHT: *Bray Arch*, Robert Harrison, 2011. 3 x 1.8 x 0.6 m (10 x 6 x 2 ft), site-specific architectural installation, reclaimed brick and shards from the Archie Bray Foundation, galvanised steel wire, aluminium tubing, aluminium, Holter Museum of Art, Helena, Montana. *Photo: Robert Harrison.*

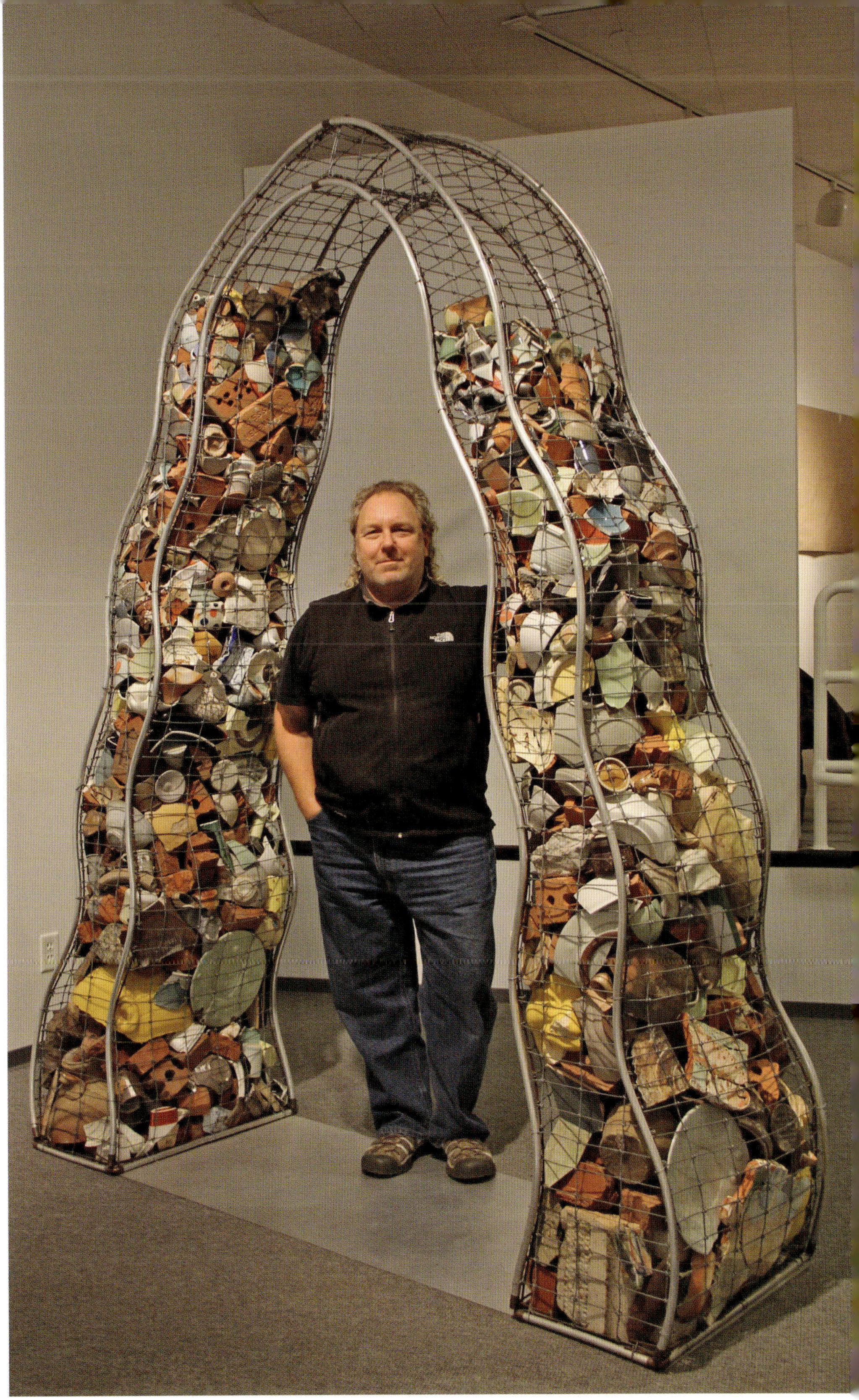

Sustainability in ceramics practice: a Down Under perspective

Janet DeBoos is a maker and educator, and has been dedicated to sustainable practices and lifestyle for decades. Janet writes:

> A sustainable practice is one that is economically viable over time, and which leaves the planet in such a state that there is not a net diminishing of resources – both environmental and social. It is hard when manufacturing, for that is what we do, to imagine not having a net diminution of resources, for we use materials to make things. But if one looks at a broader picture, one that includes social capital as well as natural and manufactured resources, it is possible to actively engage with ceramic manufacture in a way that moves towards sustainability.

There are several ways in which sustainability can be viewed in ceramics practice, and the considerations fall into a number of areas:

1. economic sustainability
2. a.) environmental sustainability: resources
   b.) environmental sustainability: waste and by-product
3. ethical/humanitarian sustainability
4. personal/intellectual sustainability.

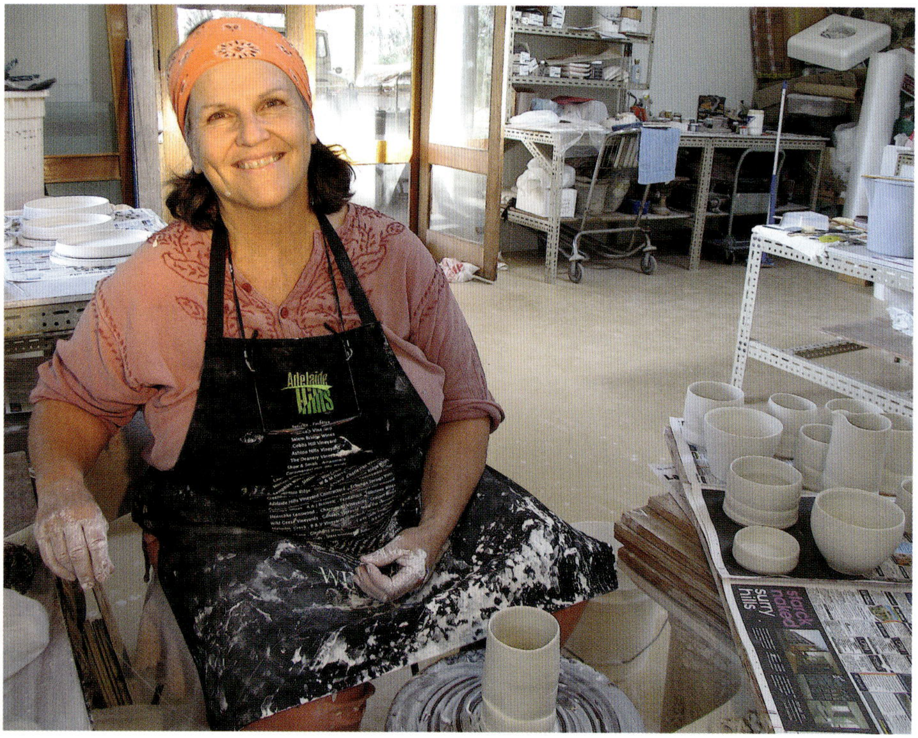

Janet DeBoos at work in her studio in National Territory, Australia, 2011. *Photo: courtesy of the artist.*

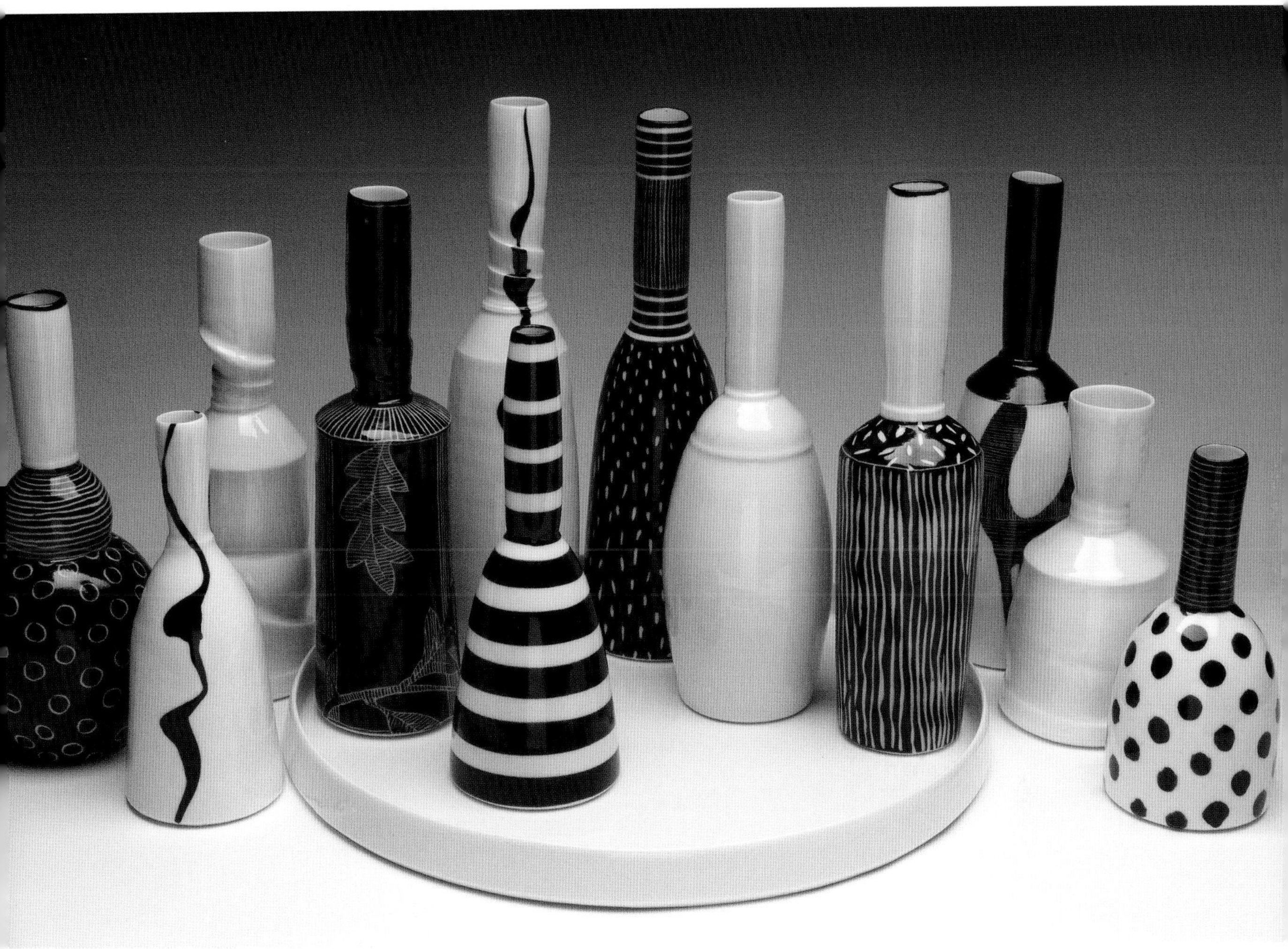

Expanded Korean Vase, Janet DeBoos, 2011. Porcelain. *Photo: courtesy of the artist.*

Although she has written each of these separately, so that she can cover them with her practice, and particularly her engagement with Chinese manufacture, they are all inextricably linked. Janet continues:

> If we separate them, then we fall into the 'silo'-thinking traps that have brought us to this point where sustainability is *the* issue in contemporary life.
>
> Starting with point 4: I believe that if we are intellectually honest with ourselves, it becomes easier to make decisions about our practice. I left a nascent career as a science teacher/botanist because the urge to 'do something with my hands' was so strong. This didn't make sense in any conventional approach to starting a career, but made much sense to me. I had already experienced the deep pleasure of making things well, and somehow wanted to turn this into what I might now call a career. It was the late sixties, and 'dropping out' was not uncommon, but I felt rather that I had 'dropped in' by going to art school.

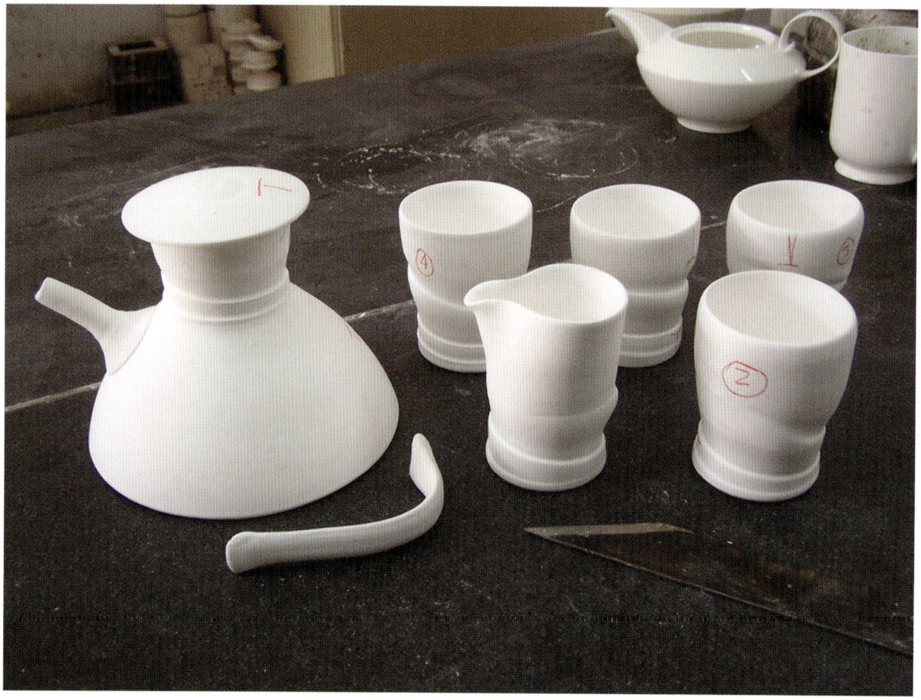

Bisqued models for collaboration set, Janet DeBoos, Huaguang Zibo Bone China factory, China, 2001. *Photo: courtesy of the artist.*

> I tell this story because I do think that we sometimes operate on the basis of what we are told, rather than what we work out for ourselves. If we were less malleable (and susceptible to advertising and media comment) and followed our gut feelings more, I think we would live in a very different world.
>
> As a science student in the sixties, I had been introduced to what was a comparatively new concept; the ecosystem. In fact, Ecology was a new undergraduate course being offered at Sydney University, and the most forward-looking graduate students were conducting studies of ecosystems, rather than individual species. The idea of the interconnectedness of everything made such sense.

Janet and her partner decided to build and run a production pottery on a block of land they had in the mountains near Canberra. The building was constructed as a studio (although they have lived in it since production was reduced) that had low energy needs, was self-sufficient with respect to water, and had a vegetable garden.

They started and ran the pottery, the first work being made available to other than a local audience at a craft fair in Sydney in 1983. Contrary to expectations, Janet found that many of the 'truisms' that she had been teaching about an economically sustainable practice (and that she had been taught) were unfounded.

> I learnt that cheap does not necessarily mean efficient, and the sole financial cost of any real consideration was my time, that financial costs were slight compared to the wealth of pleasure gained through making things, that employing other people didn't make sense in a small business with variable order and cash flow

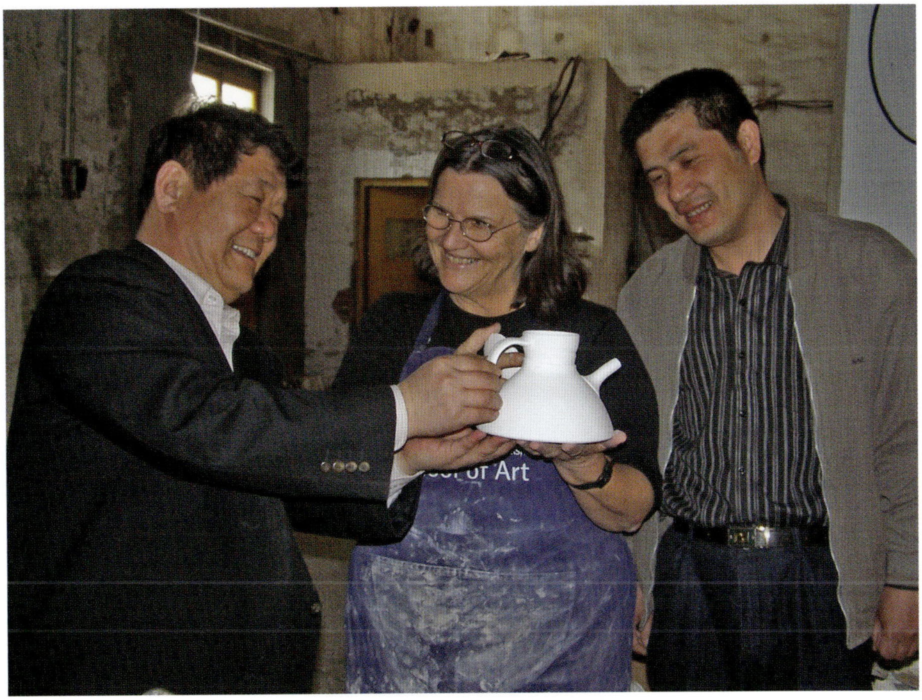

Janet DeBoos with her first-fired glazed *Harmony Teapot*, Huaguang Zibo Bone China factory, China, 2001. *Photo: courtesy of the artist.*

if you were going to pay them award wages and be ethical in your treatment of them (it also meant that you couldn't just take a holiday when you wanted to), that living away from towns/tourist centres allowed uninterrupted work that was more efficient, and that the work could be supplied at wholesale prices to outlets that were specialised sellers. The price reduction was more than made up for by the longer working periods, that despite what some outlets said, you could raise your prices above what was the market norm for domestic pottery items, that decorative ware was easier to make than domestic pottery, had fewer seconds, and returned higher prices, and that the decorative ware was production, every bit as much as the domestic ware.

I think it was an inkling of what we (ceramic practitioners) were doing bringing so much 'stuff' into the world that led me to decide in the late eighties to take a personal decision to make only useful, domestic, ceramics. I was not convinced that I could make sculptural work that had meaning, continuing value and integrity (as much of what was made did not) and I did not want to contribute to what I saw as an increasing amount of badly made, personally expressive indulgences that were filling the world. But I did know that I could make meaningful and beautiful pots that people could use, get pleasure from and might even pass on to the next generation. I also realised because of the history of ceramics, functional pottery is already rich with symbolism, and in exhibitions I could use the repetition that is part of studio practice as a way to talk about the whole process by which work gets made, used, and therefore remade in an endless iteration.

I write all the above, because I think that a sustainable practice is not something that one can put on like an overcoat that is part of this year's collection. I think that there needs to be a deep-seated understanding of one's practice to be able to even start to put in place sustainable methods and philosophies. The reason that I went to China was not because I wanted to 'have work made in China', but because there was a constant cry in the nineties that homogeneous design and cheap Chinese imports were destroying the market for handmade functional pottery; that potters 'couldn't compete'. Of course they couldn't if they had subscribed to a philosophy that devalued their labour in an industrialised and global economy.

Since the early nineties, I had been working almost exclusively in porcelain, which I started using in conjunction with work made from white stoneware because I wanted to talk about 'specialness'. The difficulty of working with porcelain (at first Limoges and subsequently Southern Ice) was such an engaging challenge, and its beauty was so seductive, that I have continued to this day to use it for tableware. I was also at this stage charging over AU$100 [£65] for a small cup. This reflected the work and the loss rate inherent in each one. I was often criticised for charging this much, but if I had made a small bowl with no handle, no one would have commented. The cost for a cup today is about the same (allowing for inflationary increases) because I have got better at making them, and have put in place some practices that reduce my loss rate.

I was told the last time I was in China, that the Yixing teapots 'were going through the roof' in price because the clay from which they are made has become scarce. This scarcity, and the resultant increase in cost will mean that we, and the master craftspeople using it, will value it more, and that which gets made from it, and fired, will be of a higher quality; fewer pots at higher prices is a good thing.

I think that in the end, we have to accept that we are not making things for the average low-income worker. But what can happen with well-conceived and well-run projects is that some workers can become more engaged in making products of this kind, and have working lives that are more meaningful as a result.

The actual environmental cost of most of our ceramic art practices is relatively small compared to our use of cars, having goods transported across countries and continents and the domestic rubbish we create through mindless consumption. It is this aspect of environmental impact that we need to urgently address.

I feel quite strongly that our practice has value in terms of its social meanings and its capacity to be an educational tool, and that if we are mindful that what we are creating will form part of the 'stuff' of consumption, the continuation of ceramic studio practice is justified.

True blue: Paul Scott's Cumbrian blues

Paul Scott is known for his use of printed blue and white imagery on glazed ceramic wares. Paul writes:

> Contemporary attitudes to the reuse of existent material are generally very positive – recycling wood in contemporary furniture has become commonplace, and the patina of age a prerequisite for selling much 'Country Living' type craft. If it does seem to be less acceptable with chipped or crazed ceramics then I'm not exactly sure why – perhaps it's because *Antiques Road Show* valuers frown upon the cracked or chipped.

Paul habitually collects glazed tableware – from eBay, junk and antique shops. Some of it may have crazed glazing, be chipped or the gold lustre worn from the edges. Paul continues:

> At first I was reluctant to use these pieces in work for sale, being aware that they are seen by some as flaws and devaluations ... but over time I have grown very fond

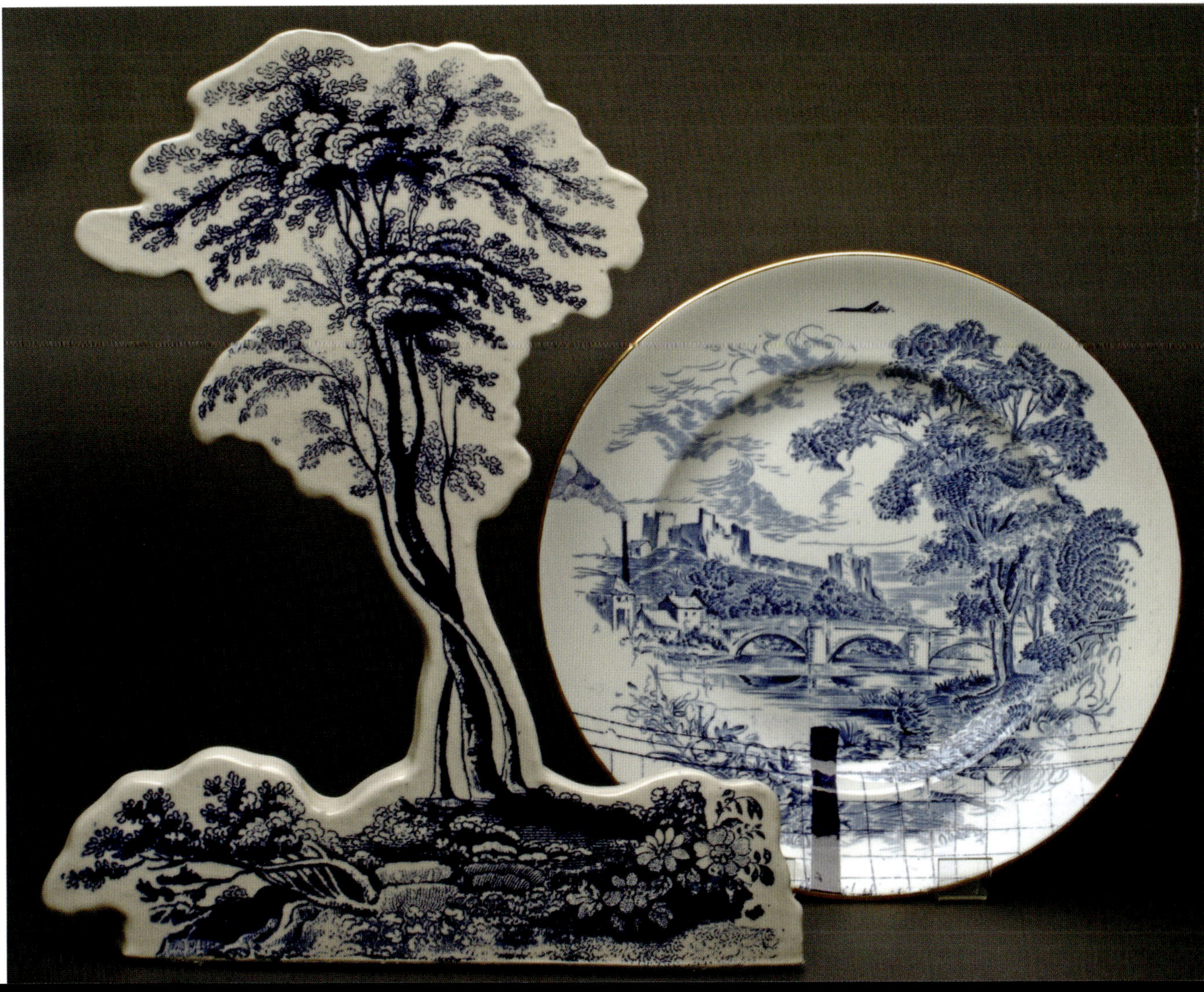

English Countryside Vignette, Paul Scott, 2011. In-glaze decals on hand built tin-glazed form. *Artisancam Tree* and *Enoch Wedgewood* earthenware plate. Plate: 34 x 27 x 8 cm (13½ x 10½ x 3 in). *Photo: courtesy of the artist.*

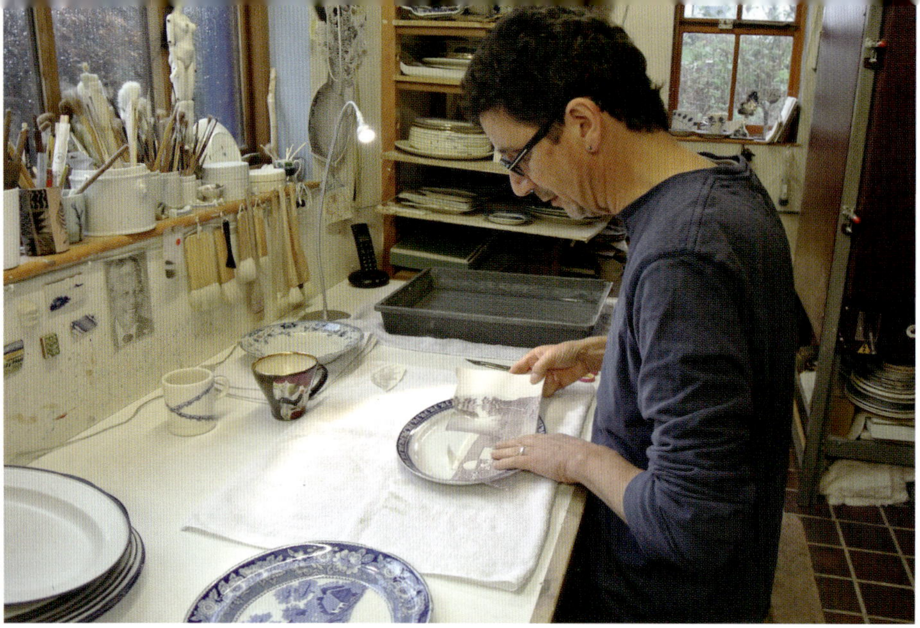

Paul Scott collaging decals in his Cumbrian Blue(s) Studio, Cumbria, UK. *Photo: courtesy of the artist.*

of these imperfections because they evidence the object's history. For me these characteristics are no longer flaws or reasons to reject the form – in fact quite the opposite; they allude to the object's previous life, it has already been used and handled, it already has a history. For me this evidence of wear is an enhancement to an object. When reworking the readymade I acknowledge and bring attention to the mark or chip, if it is on the rim of a plate or the lip of a jug, I will fill the chip with gold lustre so it is quite obvious. Crazed glaze and dirty cracks often fuse in the kiln with unexpected results, I really like these – a bloom of grey at the bottom of an earthenware soup dish adds to its richness. I enjoy objects where glued-together forms have the join marks accentuated in bright contrasting colours. I am currently working on a body of work which uses an old stapling method (with half round brass wire) to repair cracked tablewares. This used to be a common technology for restoring broken pottery before modern effective glues were developed.

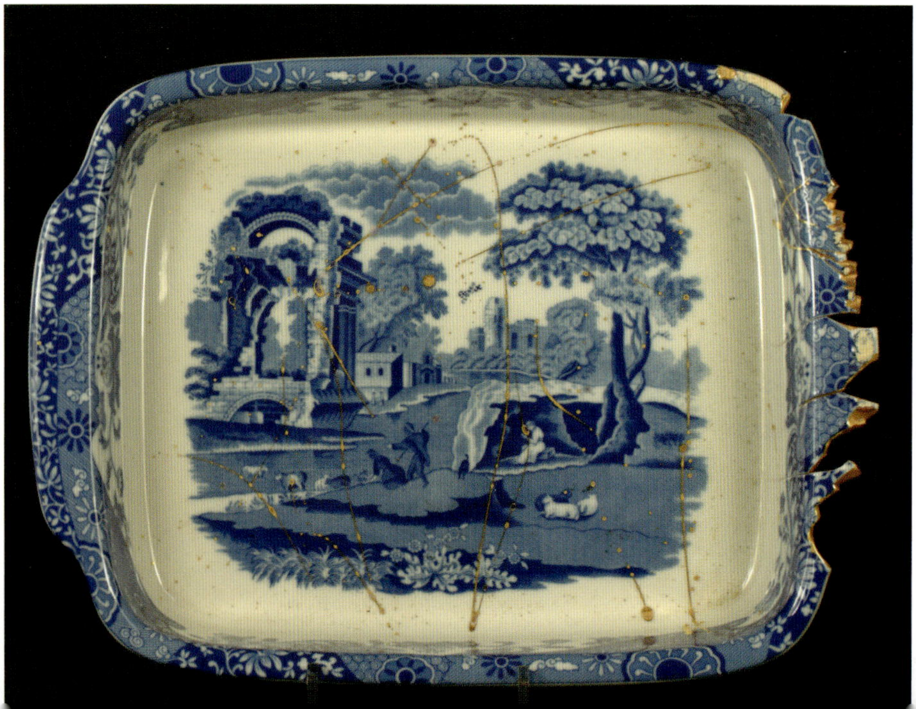

Spode Works Closed, Paul Scott, 2009. 30 x 23 x 7 cm (11¾ x 9 x 2¾ in), in-glaze decal and gold lustre on Spode's Italian porcelain casserole dish, salvaged from kiln area (marked 'Made in Czech Republic'), *Collection of the Victoria and Albert Museum. Photo: courtesy of the artist.*

Restoration regeneration: working with broken ceramic

Bouke de Vries was born in the Netherlands, and is London based. His career as one of the most respected ceramics conservators/restorers in London, led him to his exploration of making sculptures of broken china and porcelain, *upcycling* the reclaimed pieces into extraordinary sculptural works. In his daily work as a ceramics conservator/restorer Bouke was always faced with issues around perfection. Bouke writes:

> It's a world where a broken finger can sometimes render a once-valuable object practically worthless, literally not worth the cost of restoring. Although still imbued with all the artistry that made it, a piece can easily be consigned to the dustbin of history. The Venus de Milo is venerated despite being armless. Why not a Meissen muse? And even when an object is 'worth' restoring, many owners want to hide the damage, to deny the most dramatic episode in a piece's life. This is very much a western view; in Chinese/Japanese culture damage was accentuated by repairing it with gold lacquer, celebrating this part of its history.

His first series of artworks – the 'explosions' – tried reclaiming broken ceramic objects. Instead of being reconstructed, the objects are de-constructed. Bouke continues:

> Instead of hiding it, they highlight their new status, using the skills he developed as conservator/restorer (compare Ron Mueck's virtuosity as a model maker) to instil new virtues, and to move their stories forward. The spaces between the fragments become essential, sometimes giving objects a cubist quality. With some works it is hard to determine where the original makers stop and where my work begins. The object's damage is always the starting point; it's like I invite it to tell me a story, which I then try to interpret.

LEFT: Bouke de Vries working on an 'exploded' teapot, 2011. *Photo: Tim Higgins; © Bouke de Vries.*

RIGHT: *Exploded Armorial*, Bouke de Vries, 2011. 31 x 31 x 22 cm (12¼ x 12¼ x 8½ in), 18th-century Chinese armorial teapot and mixed media. *Photo: Tim Higgins; © Bouke de Vries.*

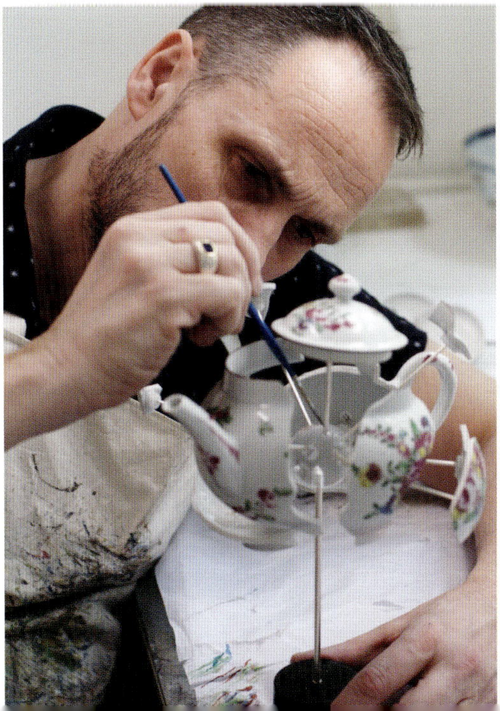

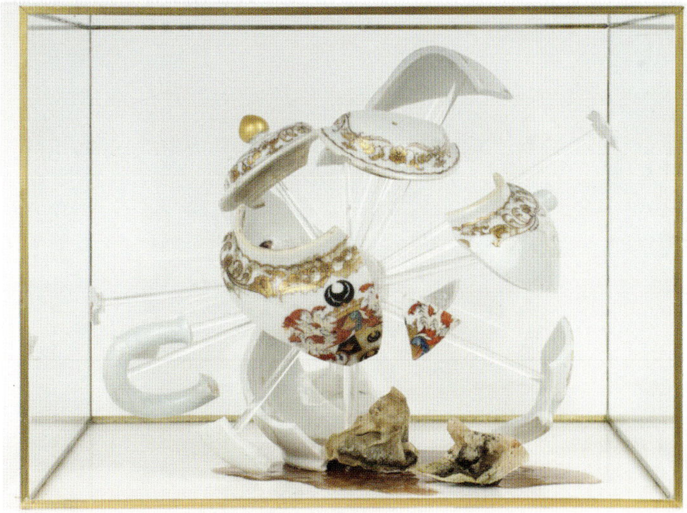

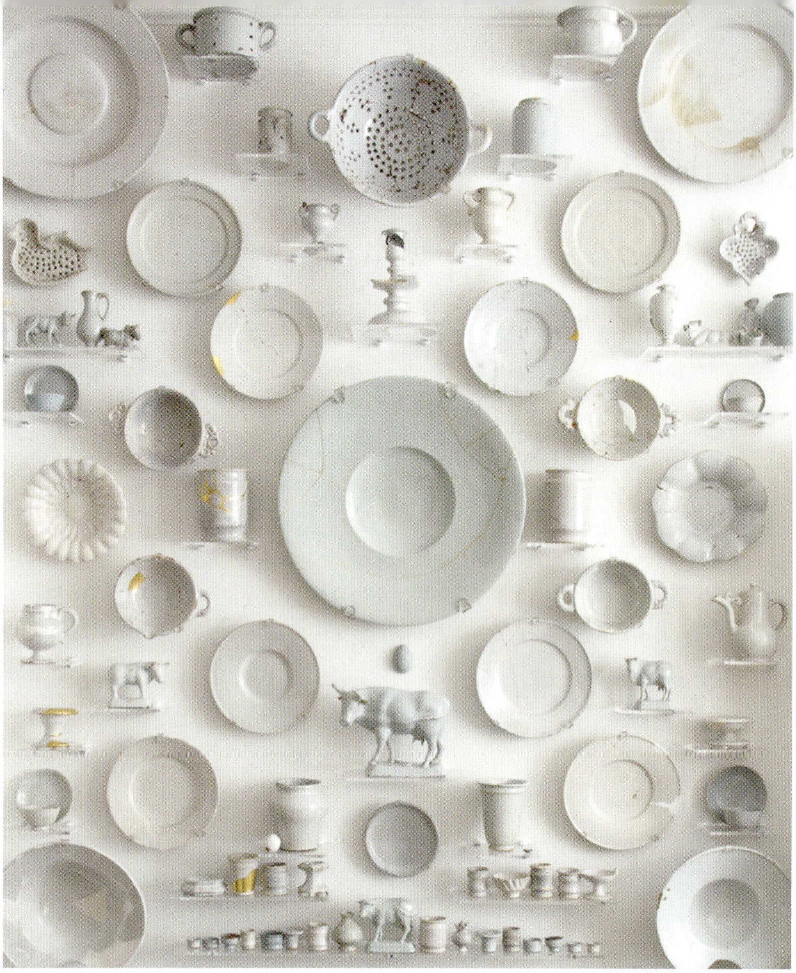

Wall, Bouke de Vries, 2007. 1.5 x 2.3 m (5 x 7½ ft), 17th- and 18th-century white Delftware, gilding and Perspex. *Photo: Tim Higgins; © Bouke de Vries.*

Another, more contemplative, series of works echoes his Dutch heritage, especially the flower painting of the Golden Age, a tradition in which his home town of Utrecht was steeped (de Heem, Kalf, van Alst, van Huysum, etc.). Everyday objects – milk jug, teapot, cress drainer – are imbued with references to the *vanitas* and *memento mori* paintings of the 17th and 18th centuries. An installation in his home in London is arranged in the manner of Daniel Marot with fragmented white Delft domestic pottery rescued from ancient middens and dredged canal bottoms.

> My figurative pieces address life today just as they addressed life at the time they were made, giving them a historical narrative. Subversion is never far away. The Meissen muse becomes a binge drinker, giving us the finger in a scene where Hogarth meets Asbo.
>
> The mounting of some of my works alludes to objects already in museums: archeological pots with missing areas often use Perspex rods (e.g. the Pre-Industrial Utensils collection at the Museum Boijmans-van Beuningen, Rotterdam); and classical sculptures, where missing sections of elbow or shin are replaced by metal dowels. Again my practice as a ceramics conservator continues to feed my art.

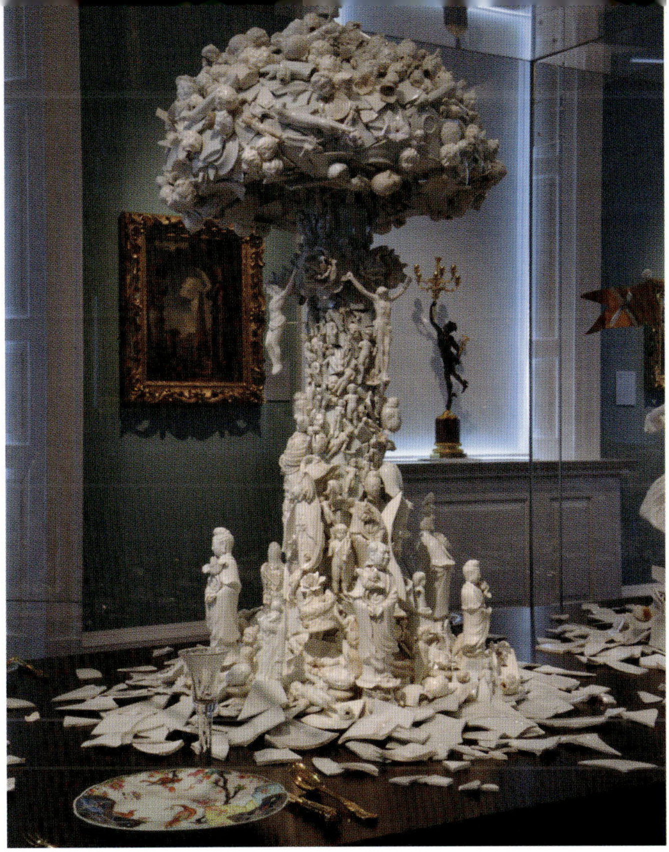

Cloud, Bouke de Vries, 2012. 0.6 x 1.15 m (2 x 3¾ ft), 19th–21st-century ceramics and mixed media. *Photo: Tim Higgins; © Bouke de Vries.*

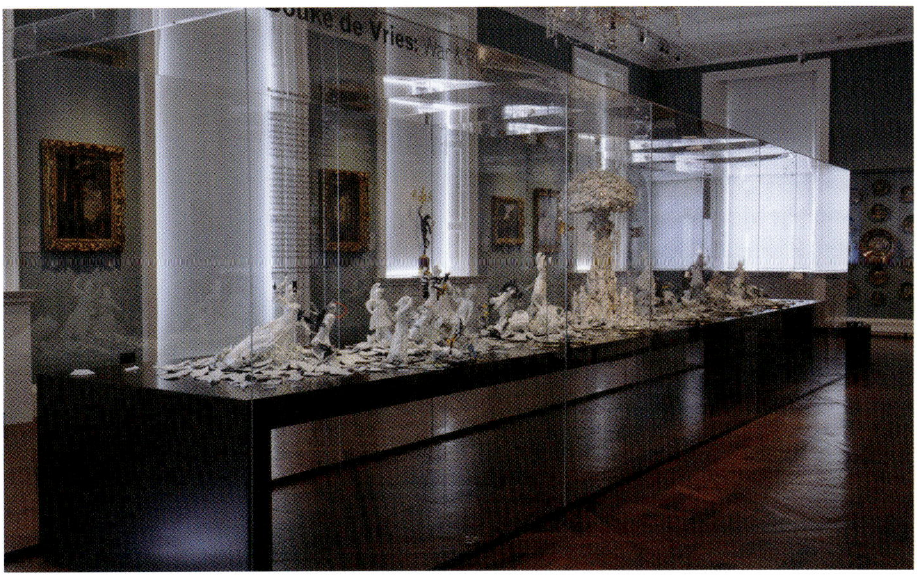

War and Pieces, Bouke de Vries, 2012. 8 x 1.5 x 2.06 m (26¼ x 5 x 6¾ ft), 19th–21st-century ceramics, jesmonite, sugar, plastic and mixed media. *Photo: Tim Higgins; © Bouke de Vries.*

Having started very much on a domestic scale, my art has now started to develop into more site-specific installations, such as the table commissioned in 2012 by the Arts Council for the Holburne Museum, Bath, which looked back at the sugar/porcelain table decorations of the 17th and 18th centuries, while looking forward to more contemporary, even futuristic, interpretations.

In defense of the imaginary object

Ilana Crispi is an artist and educator and confronts many complex issues in sustainability through her work. She writes:

> Ceramic artists are object makers. We get our hands dirty and work with real materials. We're engaged in a romantic endeavour. There is a visceral and physical experience of material that is surrounded by an aura of both history and sensuality. Some of this aura is imagined by people with faint memories of playing in the mud as children and slightly more recent associations of Patrick Swayze's ghost throwing in the movies. There is also a much longer history of clay that is grounded in geology and the very beginnings of human creation. The stories and myths associated with clay date back at least to the beginning of histories throughout the world. Along with some of the earliest-known fertility figures and architectural constructions are stories of an Egyptian god forming humans on the wheel or Helen of Troy's breast providing the ideal form for a ceramic cup. Clay may have always occupied the concrete realm of hyper-materiality, the ultimate grounding substance, and the much more ephemeral realm of imagination and storytelling. Perhaps the Sumerians chose the perfect substrate to record their stories: clay tablets marked with everything from inventories of livestock to fantastical stories of Gilgamesh searching for immortality.

Ilana poses provocative questions that attempt to get to the core issues confronting the Earth and its inhabitants. She continues:

> While clay may hold stories of immortality and creation, our use of it will not necessarily sustain us. The romance of the material does not absolve us from the responsibility of being object makers. Is the object even necessary? Our society is inundated with products and opportunities to consume and discard. One ceramic vessel is clearly better than a stream of plastic bottles and disposable cups. This green assertion immediately becomes more complicated: What is the origin of the clay? How was it mined? How far did it travel? What other materials were used in the clay or glaze? What happened to the excess materials? How much energy was used in the firing? How much pollution resulted from the creation of this ceramic cup? Would it have been a better choice to find and use a cup that already exists? I'm not advocating that we shrink our environmental footprint down to a state of creative paralysis. As object makers, however, we do need to be aware of the full trajectory and ramifications of the objects we make.

So how can we make objects responsibly in a world that already has too much stuff? One answer to this challenge that Ilana has explored in her own practice is to focus on the idea. While she still fires clay and makes ceramic objects, much of what she makes is more ephemeral. Ilana has used clay to create temporary and sometimes jarring environments that may change and evolve throughout the duration of an exhibition. In other works the ceramic element is completely contained in the process and what

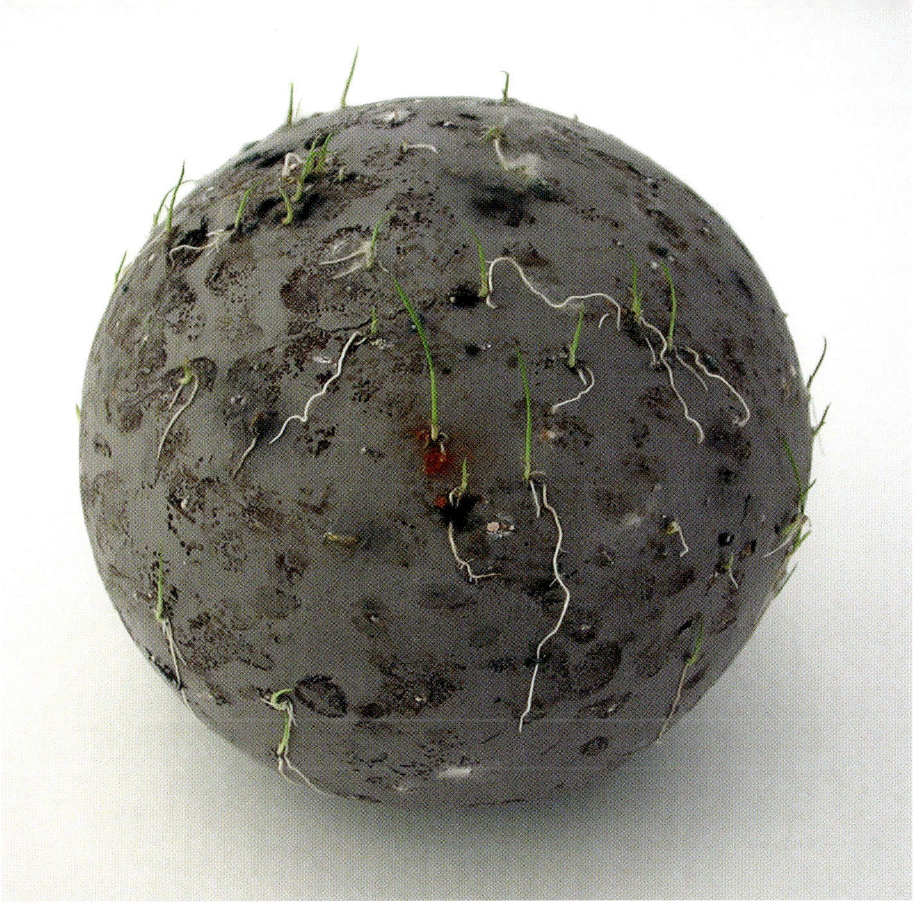

All Sides of a Sphere, Ilana Crispi, 2006. 46 cm (18 in) x 46 cm (18 in), archival digital print, 1 of 28 different images. *Photo: courtesy of the artist.*

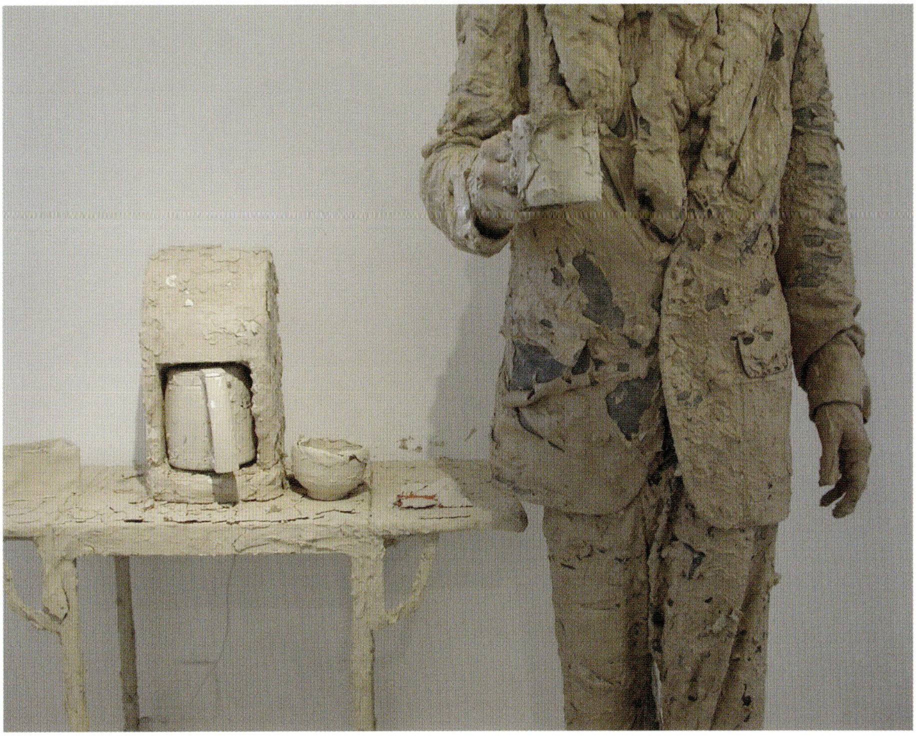

Green Room, Ilana Crispi, 2011. Video still, 3m 10s video. *Photo: courtesy of the artist.*

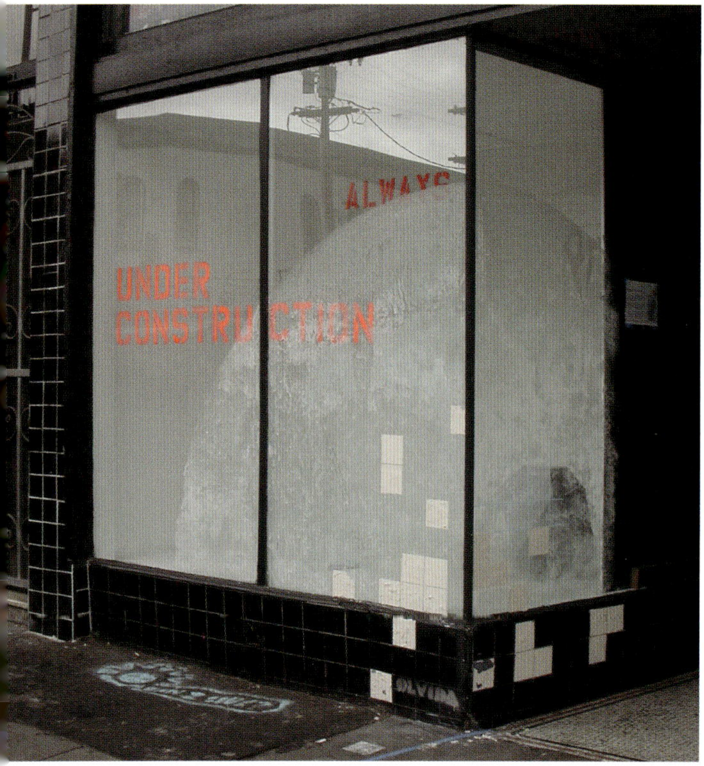

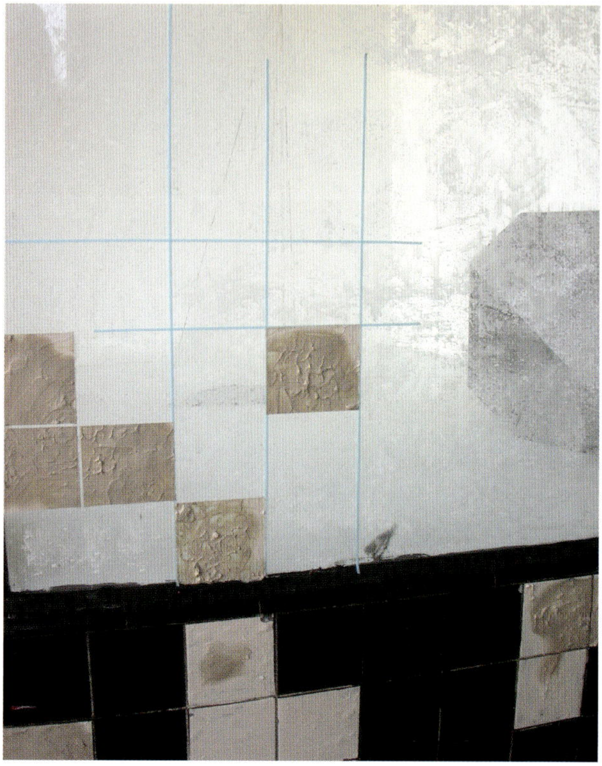

LEFT: *Always Under Construction*, Ilana Crispi, 2009. Mixed media installation. *Photo: courtesy of the artist.*

RIGHT: *Always Under Construction* (detail), Ilana Crispi, 2009. Mixed media installation. *Photo: courtesy of the artist.*

is shown as finished product is a photographic image or video: *All Sides of a Sphere*, is an example of this.

In other works, architecture and art history have been more of a focus. Ilana says:

> I've covered ceramic facades of buildings with temporary layers of wet clay that dry and crack and eventually expose the ceramic material underneath. While temporary installations and video and photography of clay forms can be an effective tool for communicating ideas, this type of practice is not necessarily a free green ride. Incorporating technology and photography is no less problematic in terms of environmental impact. Being aware of the contradictions between the intentions and implementations of a creative practice is necessary in order to maintain any kind of balance. As ceramic artists we are object makers, but we are also contributing to a much larger story. Instead of romanticising the histories and traditions of our material, we must also examine the ramifications of making objects in a world that already has too much stuff. I don't suggest that we stop making objects to play chess. Instead of abandoning the object entirely, we must challenge ourselves in our use of resources and re-examine the romantic aura of making stuff. For some of us, however, the work we make can be all about the narrative and aura of the medium. We can create work that is more lasting in the imagination than as vitrified and archival forms.

Design, artistry and sustainability

Roderick Bamford is a ceramic artist/designer and educator. Rod and his partner Janine Brody operate their Cone 9 Studios north of Sydney, Australia. Rod writes:

> Creative engagement with sustainability has, outside the sciences, been significantly influenced by recent developments in design, where methods of thinking and practice have provided models for ways that capitalism can incorporate strategies for sustainable development. The capacity of capitalism to meet this challenge is yet to be really tested, however it is within this economic structure that ceramics, indeed any creative practice currently operates. Barring some radical alien intervention, sustainable change built with motivated individual visions, and supported by collective agreement will hopefully transform mainstream practices. Whether this is sufficient to avoid forecast environmental and social catastrophes remains to be seen, but *all individuals have the opportunity to participate in the common cause of sustainability.*
>
> These ideas inspire both the conceptual content of artwork and design ideas, and their material realisation through studio practice. A key focus in my educational role, the notion of 'sustainable culture' forms a core ethical benchmark to reflect on my own practice and a continual challenge to innovate. The experiences, and the project summaries written here, reflect aspects of my own integration of these ideas, including practical strategies used in studio practice that contribute to my broad understanding of 'sustainable' studio practice, one that cannot be separated from other aspects of life, and the notion that sustainability is indeed an evolving, pluralistic concept.
>
> I have long nurtured a keen interest in cycles of culture expressed through the attributes of materials and the experiences of people engaged in their transformation into objects of common or exclusive significance. Ceramic objects, and their key role in prehistory, collectively capture the substance of culture told through fired fragments of the stuff under our feet, a beacon of longevity and persistence. My own short ceramic history includes working experiences with ceramics created in villages, my own studio and large factories.
>
> For a number of years my sculptural work has been concerned with the aesthetics of materiality, especially tangible tensions between development, redundancy and waste. But it was almost 20 years ago during a residency at the Kohler Company in Wisconsin, USA that the sheer magnitude of contemporary material cycles first really struck me. Huge piles of stuff in, huge piles of stuff out, and huge piles of waste. I recall plaster and clay being delivered not in bags, but by bobcat scoop via a car on a railway siding and five-metre [16 ½ ft] high piles of iron ingot. At Kohler, 'Fordist' notions of the human 'inside' the machine collided with a new material aesthetic that conjured hybrid notions of a tortured William Morris tooling the potential for Buckminster Fuller's utopian future.

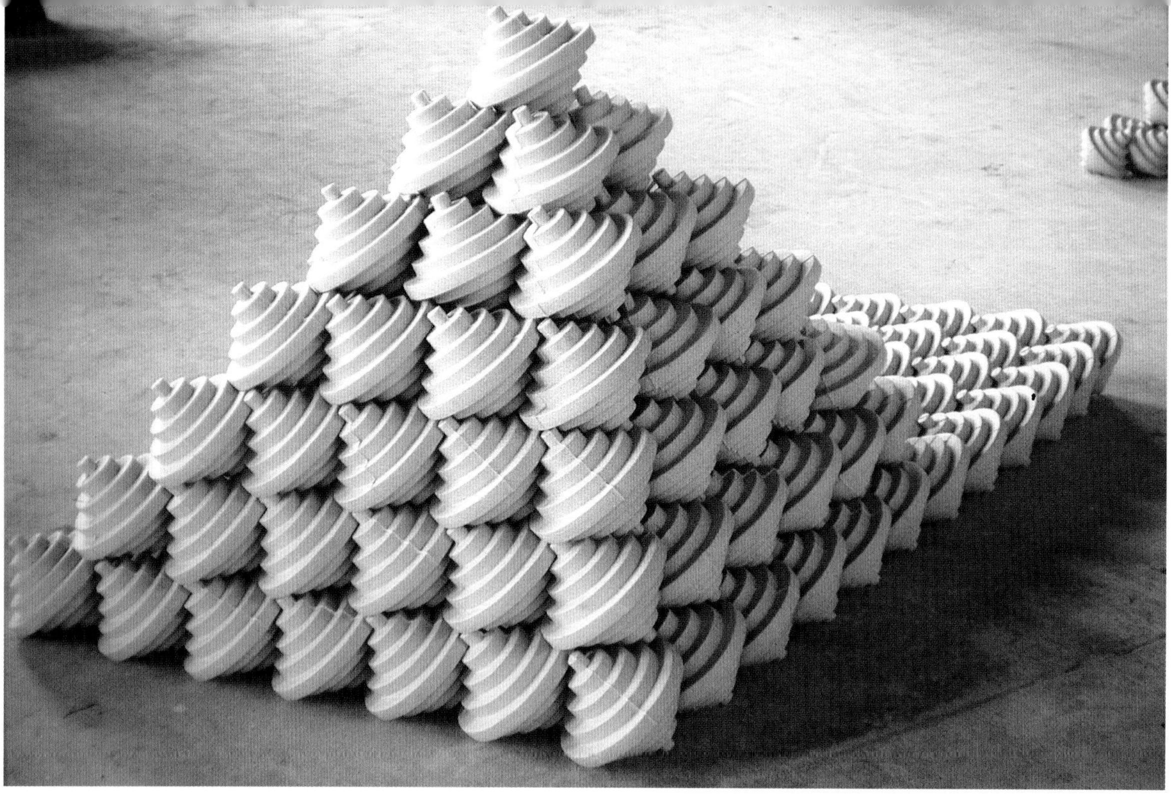

Insensible Order, Rod Bamford, 1989. Kohler Company Artist-in-Industry Program, Kohler, Wisconsin. *Photo: courtesy of the artist.*

The experience inspired a series of slip cast installations including 'Insensible Order' a work based on the interaction between states of science, technology and play, designed, engineered and produced in the factory. Kohler spurred my interest in a creative application of industrial technology and its relationship to design, yet most significantly, the legacy heightened my concern for the place of humans and humanity within the global ecology.

The Kohler experience both reinforced and challenged an education where anything produced by machine constituted 'devil's work', had me questioning the value of my own practice and the destiny of studio waste, particularly kiln failures. Back in Australia there was a practical angle to be explored, and some of the industrial strategies I discovered at Kohler were adapted to production during a period where Cone 9 Studios produced a range of architectural tiles and commissions.

The bakery industry became a source of equipment that was modified for studio purposes. Stainless steel benches, rack systems and tools drastically reduced rust contamination. Energy was reduced by using kitchen exhaust hoods mounted on kilns as heat exchangers to dry moulds. Systems for tile production used the pressure of stacked porous boards to prevent warping and dry tiles. Hand-operated gravity-fed slip dispensers replaced buckets and pumps. More scientific laboratory procedures maintained clay slips and moulds at predictable levels of performance, and helped manage irregularities in supplied materials. The convergence of traditional pottery craft practices and industrial processes formed an unusual balance in the studio, yet was surprisingly effective, not only saving time and enhancing flexibility, but reducing production failure rates. Waste too, was significantly reduced.

> As my interest in eco design has grown, I continue to look for ways to apply 'dematerialising' strategies in the studio. Informed by a carbon audit, the three Rs of sustainable practice (Reduce, Reuse, Recycle) can offer an attractive formula for savings accompanying environmental benefits, providing a longer-term outlook is maintained. On some occasions these may be small adaptations or changes, such as moving to low-energy, high-efficiency lighting, doing business wherever possible with other companies that have a green focus, or sourcing local materials to reduce carbon miles.
>
> In one example, we designed and fabricated a custom polypropylene sink filtration system from available storage containers and plumbing parts to collect clay and glaze materials before they enter the municipal drainage system. A percentage of waste is either recycled into low-fire clay bodies, with the remainder disposed of more appropriately. Perhaps the most challenging studio initiative, however, has been developing an effective 'once firing' system to eliminate the energy used in bisque firing, with the accompanying advantage of saving labour and time associated with loading and unloading the kiln.

Over recent years, a great deal of research has been directed towards durable, lower-firing porcelain and stoneware clay bodies. Many tableware and sanitary ware industries have lowered firing temperatures from 1300°C (2372°F) or higher to the low 1200s (2192°F) without loss of strength, whiteness or translucency.

> After some initial research setbacks we have developed a 1200°C [2192°F] porcelain body that is super white, translucent, and can be once fired. *Using this combination we anticipate reducing energy consumption by more than 40% per firing cycle and extending the kiln element life considerably.* As natural gas is not available to the studio neighbourhood, we have also endeavoured to install

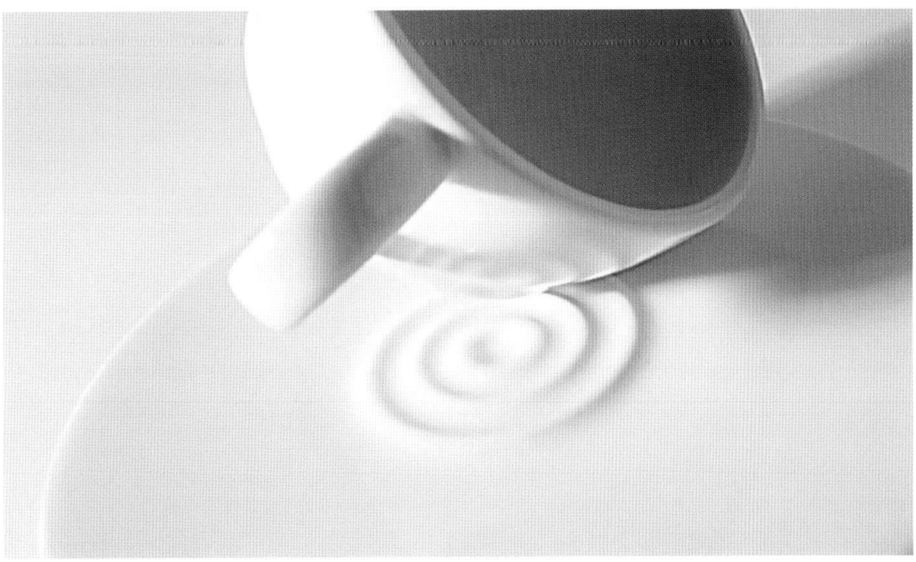

The Cup Suite (detail), Rod Bamford, 2001. *Photo: courtesy of the artist.*

a solar farm on the studio roof. Unfortunately, frustrated by infrastructure costs required to link the installation to the grid and difficult regulatory requirements, the project was recently abandoned. Some strategies are simple yet require not technical, but behavioural adaptations. For example, as Cone 9 Studio production uses handmade, machine-assisted production techniques, a degree of customer understanding of the time required to create the work has always been necessary. As we endeavour to reduce carbon emissions, this understanding has actually assisted in negotiating deadlines on the basis of rescheduled production sequences to better integrate natural drying cycles and associated energy savings. All of these initiatives help keep the studio alert and competitive, creating a unique identity that is valuable in a very niche market.

It is possible for many of these strategies to be adapted for studio use in the educational environment, where much work remains to be done to keep pace with energy savings strategies adopted by the ceramics industry. At the College of Fine Arts (Cofa), my studio research is being extended to develop low-firing porcelain and related technologies for the school ceramics studio. The results will be made publicly available in the hope that ceramic suppliers, clay and glaze manufacturers may be encouraged to adopt 'cone 10 alternatives'.

GM Fruitbowl, Rod Bamford, 2003. 67 x 20 x 13 cm (26¾ x 8 x 5 in). *Photo: courtesy of the artist.*

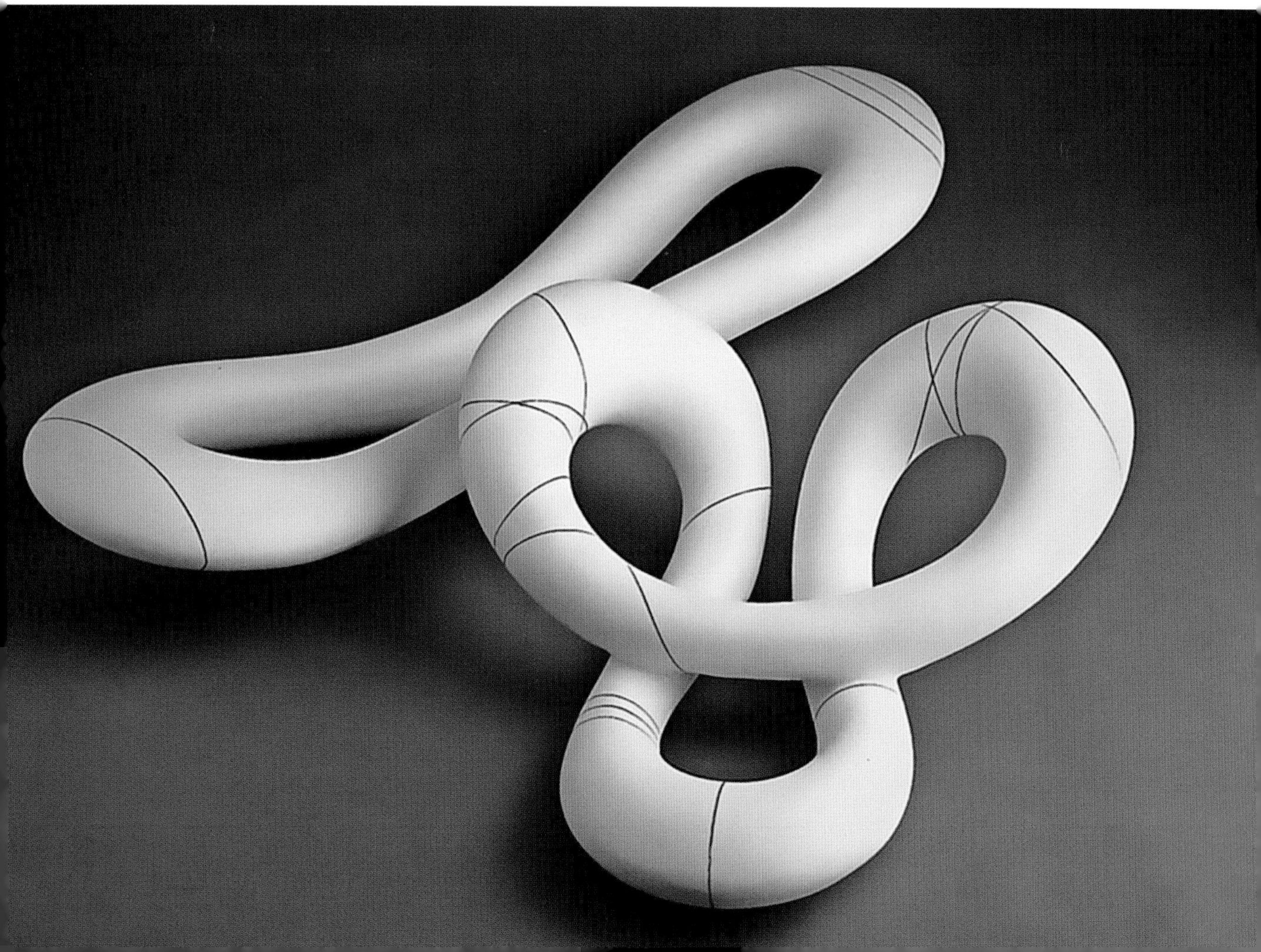

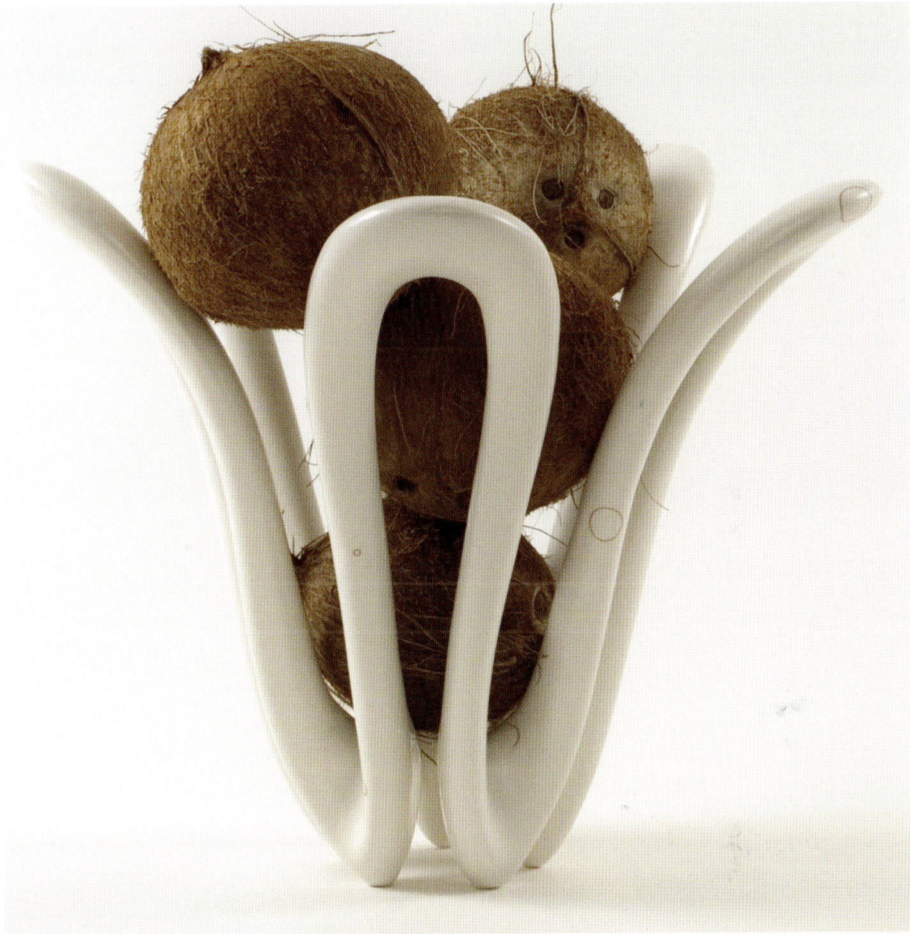

Sonic Loop Coconut, Rod Bamford. *Photo: courtesy of the artist.*

Waste is uneconomical, unproductive and bad business – especially toxic waste. This concept is elegantly brought to our attention by the architect William McDonough and organic chemist Michael Braungart in their maxim Waste = Food (*Cradle to Cradle* McDonough, W and Braungart, M, North Point Press, New York, 2002).

In response to this broader framework, there is significant recent growth in the notion of social sustainability. Businesses and public organisations are beginning to subscribe to the notion of being good corporate or global citizens. Although some of these actions are justifiably dismissed as simply spin (particularly *greenwashing* seen in politics and advertising), there are many examples of positive changes being achieved. In 1981 a damaging crisis with its Billy Bookcase product prompted Ikea's concern, both for its business and its impact on the environment. In 1991 the company adopted the 'Natural Step' framework to develop social and environmental policies.

Sustaining healthy communities and a diversity of traditions, where thriftier ways of living are often embodied, is critically important if we are to challenge the increasingly wasteful trajectory of contemporary material culture. Anthropology, it appears, is the key to understanding what constitutes a sustainable culture.

To repurpose/reuse existing material: a life-long commitment to sustainable practices

To build his world, humans created myths and bricks.

Alexandra Lewy Gazeau
(From Jacques Kaufmann's catalogue 'No Where, Now Here', 1995)

If your mind can see the beauty in mud, and mine in stone, then your mind is more awake than mine.

Zen-Wabi Sabi

Reuse, or repurpose existing materials can be added to the definitions of art, when the role of art is seen as a way to reveal the invisible part of what already exists, a reality since it's very beginning. There are different levels to perceive the materials: at least physically, and metaphysically.

Jacques Kauffman first encountered bricks in 1984, when he was leading a ceramic project in Rwanda, Africa. The purpose of the project was about minimising transportation of building materials, valuing locally produced materials and utilising local resources as related to the local skills. How to employ people, with non-agricultural works, in rural areas, using local materials, with the goal of providing better living conditions? The answer was with ceramic activities.

In 1972, the Club of Rome (a global think tank), together with the Massachusetts Institute of Technology published the book *Limits to Growth*, describing the world as *globalised*. It spoke about African debt and the limitations of resources, materials, energy, quality of water, air, living conditions, currency exchange rules, fair trade and so on. When rereading the text, it is easy to see that since the mid-1970s so much time has been lost, as humanity has followed a path going in the opposite direction than the one that should have been followed. How can we not feel responsible?

Working in Rwanda – not in the art realm, but in a field of intercultural and technical exchange – fed Jacques' attitude and sense of responsibility. Making art is not the only way to be creative and the experience was certainly not a waste of time, in fact it was just the opposite; the two and a half years oriented his vision, mind, and work. It was there that he discovered the *brick*, as both a material and an object that had the potential to rebuild his own art world.

A single brick does not exist by itself. A brick is related to the earth; it speaks of the earth, and establishes a relationship with a space, the space where humans exist. A brick is made for the long term, for generations. The life of a brick is at the same time modest, and ambitious; it has a long-term outlook.

To borrow and then return

Returning from Rwanda, Jacques came back with the feeling of a unique and global world, and with the understanding of large-scale ceramics at an architectural or landscape scale. He has explored this experience through his work, some years after his

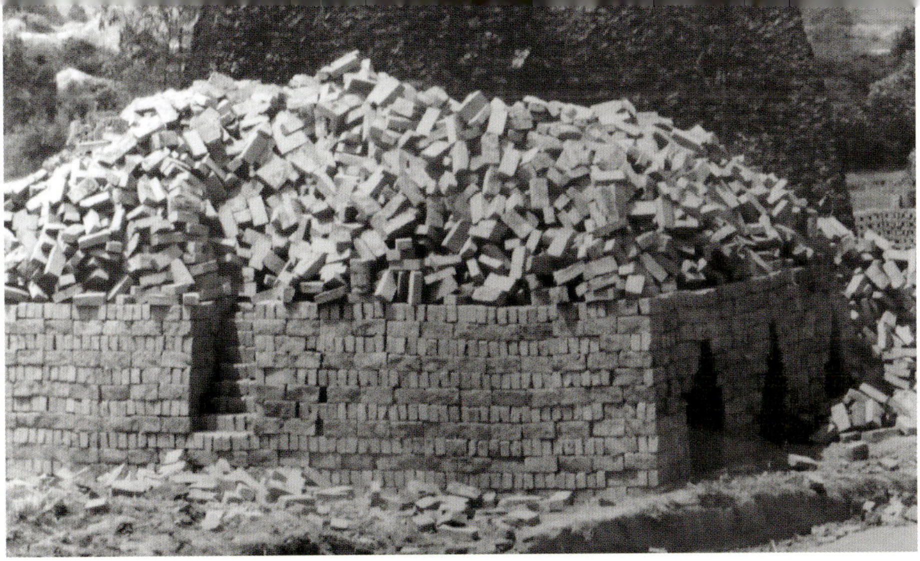

Found Object, Jacques Kaufmann. Fired handmade brick kiln, Rwanda, Africa, 1984. *Photo: Jacques Kaufmann.*

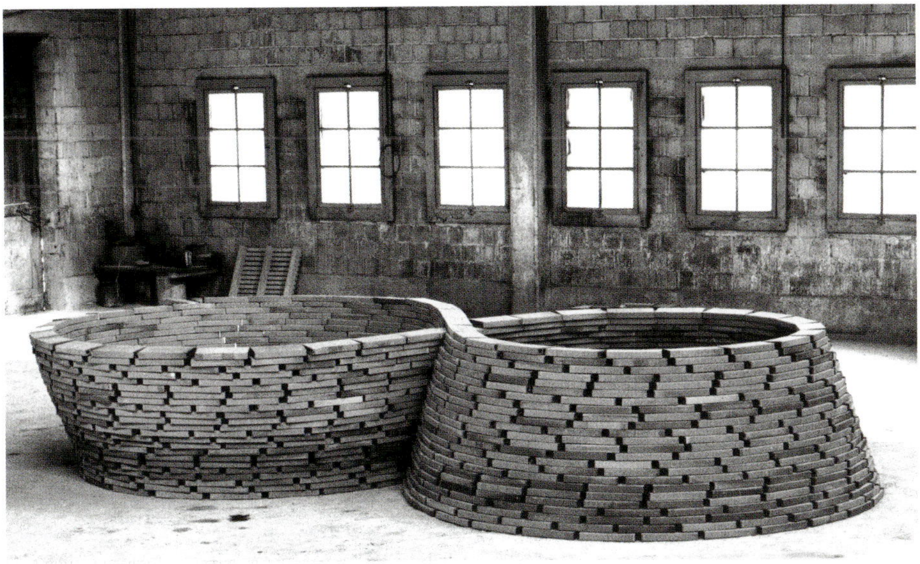

RIGHT: *A Form for Infinity*, Jacques Kaufmann, 1994. 4.8 x 2.4 x 1.2 m (16 x 8 x 4 ft), repurposed brick installation. *Photo: courtesy of the artist.*

BELOW: *The Flight of the Fly*, Jacques Kaufmann, 1994. 7.6 x 6.1 x 1.7 m (25 x 20 x 5½ ft), repurposed brick installation. *Photo: courtesy of the artist.*

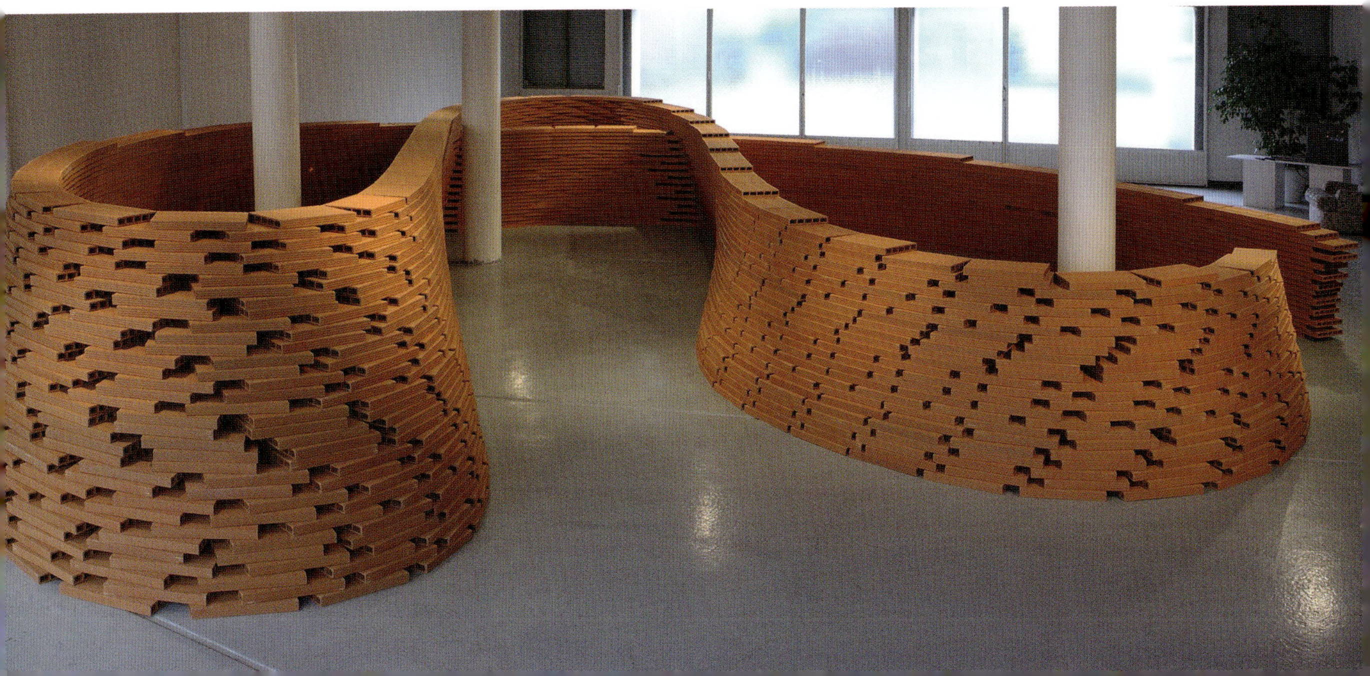

'return from Africa' (for example *Opening Night* and *A Form for Infinity* series). Usually his sculptural materials come from the nearest local tile or brick factory. By borrowing his art-making materials, and then returning them after his onsite installations, he is exploring a way to deal with space, at nominal cost and energy. He is experimenting with the collaboration of hands and eyes at 1:1 scale of the space, in a sort of meditative-action process, where body and mind are clearly connected. In these works, a brick is like a fragment of a coil, and the repetition and the accumulation of bricks or tiles, allow Jacques to experience time, material and space through the process.

Reuse: divert (détourner)

Reusing, recycling or repurposing materials became an art practice when Marcel Duchamp challenged traditional art attitudes in the early 20th century. Repurposing can change the meaning of the physical product (the *Fountain*), or by any reuse or accumulation of existing materials. Jacques is not only interested in reuse or diverting existing materials, but is also interested in working with a factory's production line and actually recycling existing skills and tools.

A simple approach to sustainability: keep it small

Richard Notkin has long been recognised for his small-scale sculpture and teapots, which are densely packed with highly detailed imagery. Aside from the social and political commentary expressed in his work, the very act of working on such a scale is an easily attainable means to sustainability in the ceramic arts, or any art media for that matter. In Richard's own words, from his statement as a demonstrating artist in the 1979 NCECA/Supermud Conference at Pennsylvania State University:

> I view society as an integral part of my art, as opposed to maintaining a detachment from it ... My past, current and future works have and will continue to explore the complex environmental, economic and aesthetic impact of contemporary human civilisation upon the quality of life ... on our planet.
>
> My intention is to stimulate viewers to examine their own personal values by manipulating and juxtaposing various objects, images and symbols in a manner similar to that by which a poet fashions his or her particular craft. And, as the poet economises words, I have found a power in the conservation of material: I believe the aesthetic impact of a work of art is not proportional to its size alone, but to its content.
>
> Rather than requiring the viewer to step back and 'take it all in', my work invites the viewer to lean forward, enter and examine its microcosmic terrain of richly textured minutiae and pinprick detail. This close inspection promotes introspection. It is in this perspective that I pursue my creative endeavours, for it is not the objects created in themselves which are of prime importance, but the people who are touched, in some way, by them.

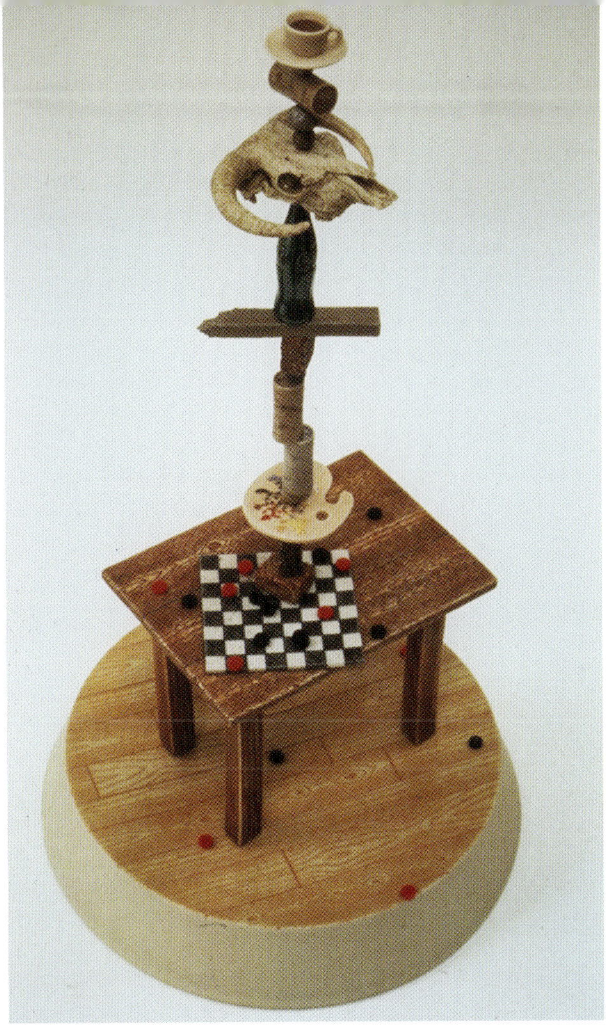

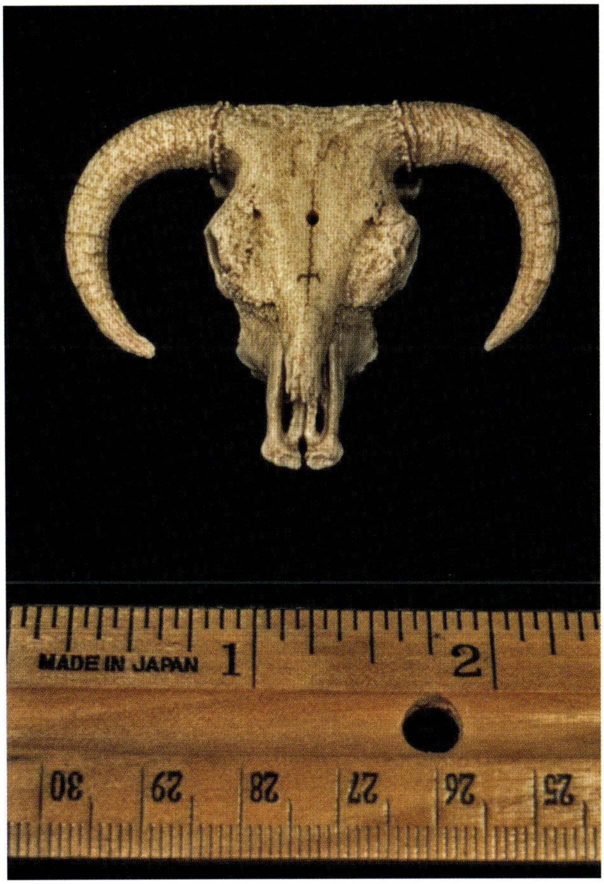

LEFT: *Endangered Species #2*, Richard Notkin, 1978. 28 x 16 x 16 cm (11 x 6¼ x 6¼ in), porcelain, glaze. *Photo: courtesy of the artist.*

RIGHT: Study of Skull for *Endangered Species #1*, Richard Notkin, 1978. 5 x 5 cm (2 x 2 in), porcelain, hand-carved, glaze. *Photo: courtesy of the artist.*

Richard's predilection for small scale came early. His father was an immigration lawyer in Chicago, and, following the Second World War, helped many refugees from China to settle in the burgeoning Chinatown just south of downtown. His family home was filled with gifts of Chinese arts and craft, highly detailed works in ivory, cloisonné, enamelled porcelain and so forth. Becoming fascinated with these intricately crafted objects, Richard has explored the challenge of capturing an incredible amount of information in a small amount of space. But he doesn't see this as a mission. During workshops and lectures he often states:

> I am not trying to be the Billy Graham of small-scale ceramics; every concept for a work of art has an appropriate scale.

Since the late 1990s, Notkin has produced a number of large ceramic murals consisting of several hundred to over a thousand individual relief tiles, all modelled in his intricately detailed style. But the concept of these pieces, in which the shading of the individual tiles compose a larger overall image, requires this macro/micro juxtapositioning of scales.

Richard feels that the sustainable aspects of working on a small scale are obvious: less impact on the planet; a smaller carbon footprint through the use of a minimal amount

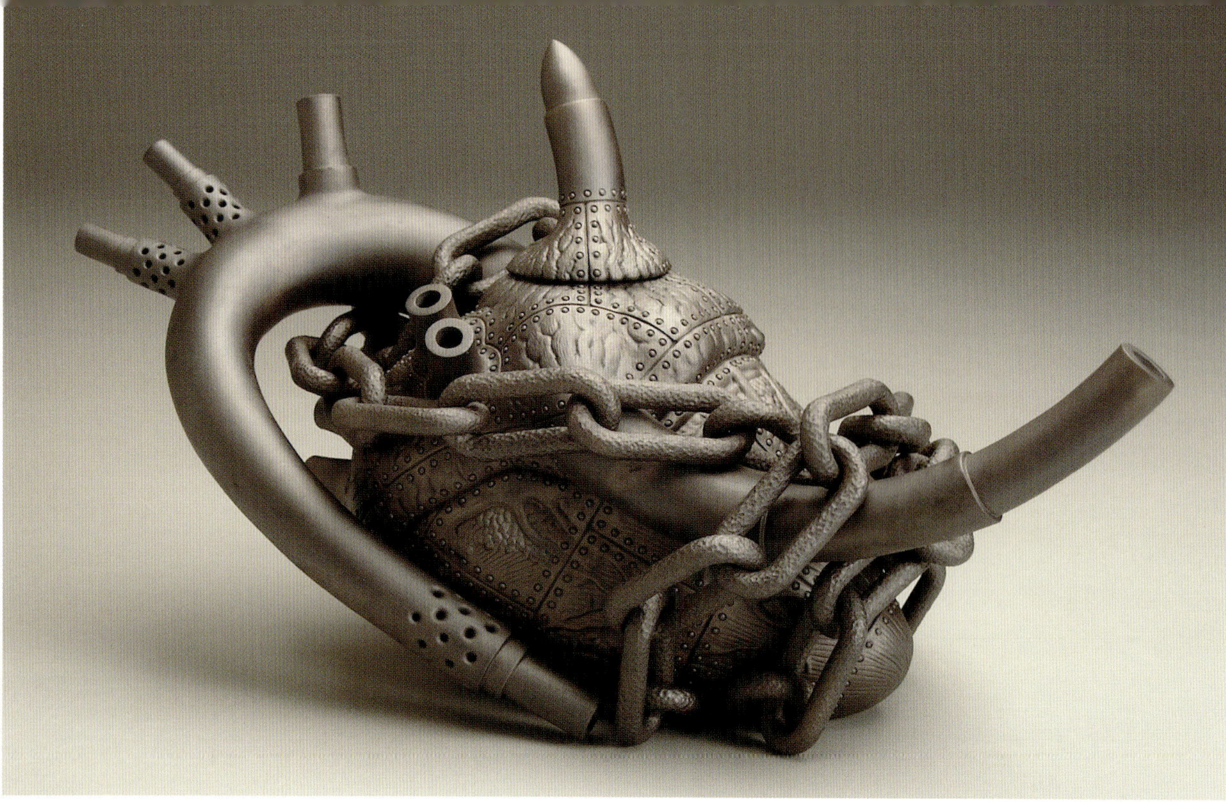

Heart Teapot: Hostage/ Metamorphosis IV-Yixing Series, Richard Notkin, 2006. 18 x 31 x 15 cm (7 x 12¼ x 6 in), stoneware, lustre, collection of the Holter Museum of Art, Heblena, Montana. *Photo: courtesy of the artist.*

of material; less consumption of energy (in both firing and shipping of artwork); and less space required for production, exhibition and storage. His first electric kiln used only 110 volts, with interior measurements of 13 x 11 x 11 inches (33 x 28 x 28 cm). The time element in detailing his carved pieces soon required about two to three months of labour to fill this small kiln. In 1974, Notkin transported about a dozen small-scale ceramic sculptures to a group exhibition on a flight from Sacramento to New York in his checked and carry-on luggage. Obviously, the costs of producing small-scale work are considerably less, making such work attainable even with limited studio space or resources.

To introduce other ceramic artists to the 'small-scale experience', Richard created an exercise titled 'A Cubic Inch of Clay', challenging participants in over 250 workshops since it was first introduced in 1978. Students are provided with approximately one cubic inch of fine low-fire white clay, and given one hour in which to manipulate it in any way that they choose. The stipulations include: you will not receive additional clay; the piece cannot be finished in less than an hour; you must spend the entire 60 minutes continuing to work on it. Aesthetics are left wide open, as are the techniques used. To promote a complete and focused immersion for the hour, silence is enforced: there is no talking allowed, and all cell/mobile phones and personal music systems must be turned off.

At the end of the exercise, Richard has each of the participants place their small pieces on a table, and, after a few minutes of silently viewing the work, queries the group about their experiences. As each is uniquely individual in terms of aesthetic philosophy, manual dexterity, patience and stamina, it is stressed that there are no right or wrong answers, only honest responses filtered through the mindset of personal subjectivity. Students are first asked about their general perceptions of the past hour. Did the time pass more quickly than at first anticipated? Did you have enough time to finish what you had

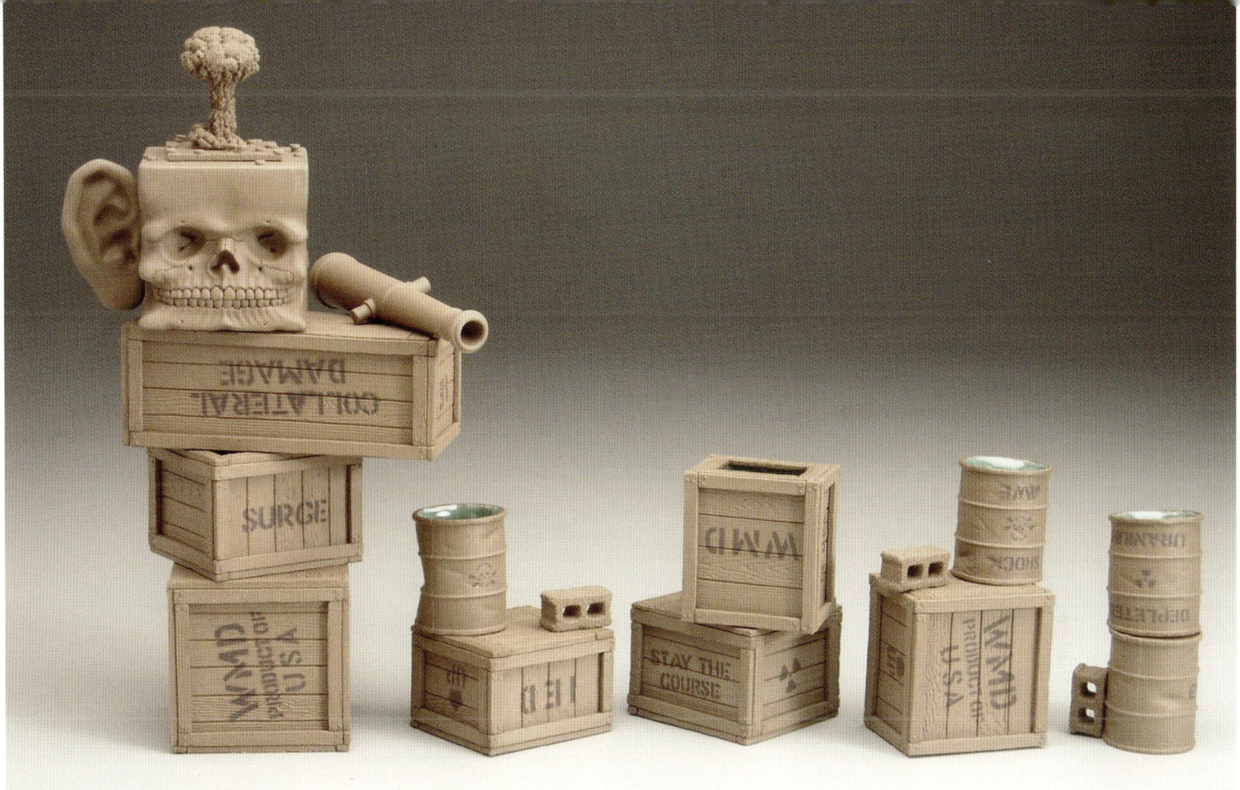

Teaset – Iraq 2007, Richard Notkin, 2007. Teapot: 29 x 18 x 11 cm (11½ x 7 x 4¼ in); Cups: heights vary, approx. 10 to 14 cm (4 to 5½ in), stoneware, glaze. *Photo: courtesy of the artist.*

intended, or would you have wanted more time? Did the scale of the clay 'expand' as you continued to explore your piece? Did this exercise open new possibilities of approaching clay for you? Any surprises? Would you do it again, and for what reasons? Finally, Notkin tells the group, 'If you absolutely hated this past hour, if you found it excruciating or just plain boring, you have also learned something valuable.'

After more than four decades creating small-format sculpture and vessels, Notkin feels that there is a long-standing prejudice against small-scale works in contemporary art, particularly in western cultures, with such pieces designated as 'minor works'. But throughout the history of the ceramic arts, there are many examples of diminutive works, which have achieved high regard and valuation. Well-known examples would include Qing Dynasty fine-enamelled porcelains, Yixing teapots, Sevres porcelains, and Imari ware, and contemporary ceramicists Ken Price, Ron Nagle, Adrian Saxe, Marilyn Levine, Jack Earl, Richard Shaw, Charles Simmonds, Kathy Butterly and numerous others. In its myriad of connections to functional vessels, the ceramic arts seem almost naturally suited to fitting a small-scale format.

Surely the small-scale approach to sustainability is viable, and another part of the solution to our efforts to continue the practice of the ceramic arts in a world where materials are becoming increasingly more precious and scarce, and massive consumption of energy threatens our planet's ecosystems and prospects for the survival of our species.

Richard Notkin lives and works in Helena, Montana. He is widely respected for his innovations in small-scale work and his work is collected globally.

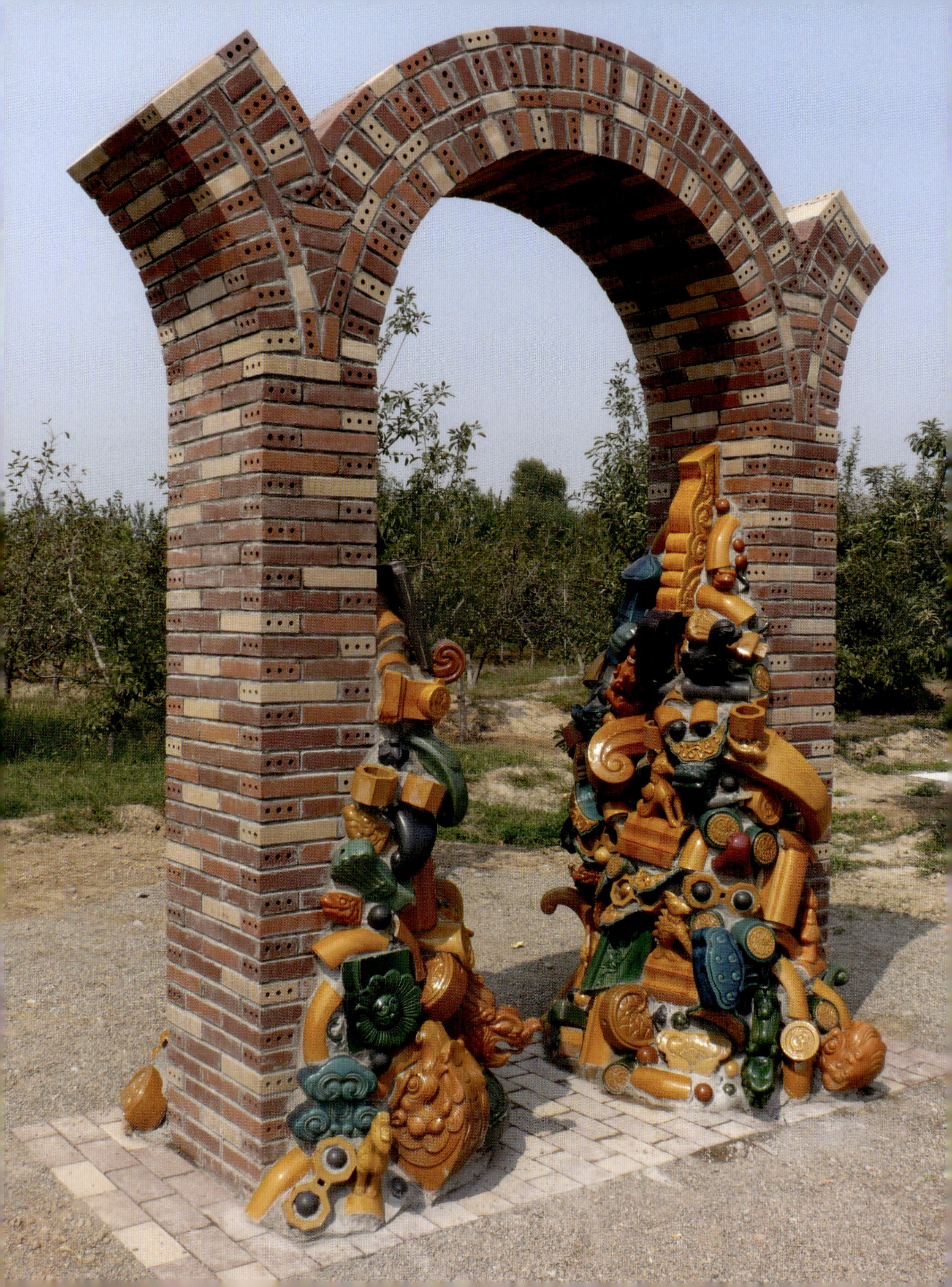

4

Working with industry

Working large scale: Robert Harrison, IAC, RCA, NCECA Fellow

My large-scale architectural works are inspired by industry. During my tenure as an artist-in-residence at the Archie Bray Foundation for the Ceramic Arts in the 1980s I was given access to industrially produced brick and tile. The opportunity and subsequent works essentially gave me a backdoor pass into industrial facilities. I feel fortunate to have been able to work in ceramic factories in North America and internationally. From bricks to sanitary ware and from tiles to teacups, industrial products and facilities can offer tremendous opportunities for an artist. My work continues to be informed by these opportunities and collaborations.

Industry is generally receptive to artists with new ideas for their products. The Kohler Company in Wisconsin, USA, makers of sanitary ware worldwide, has run an artist-in-industry programme for decades, occasionally introducing artist-designed work into their product line. Dave Binns has introduced his perspective on waste mitigation for industry, and Jacques Kauffman is working with architects on designing 'growing bricks' to cool modern buildings. Individual makers through their creative process of discovery are on the cutting edge of innovation.

In my experience, the ceramic and brick industry is perpetually looking for ways to maintain or reduce costs while maintaining or improving the quality of their product.

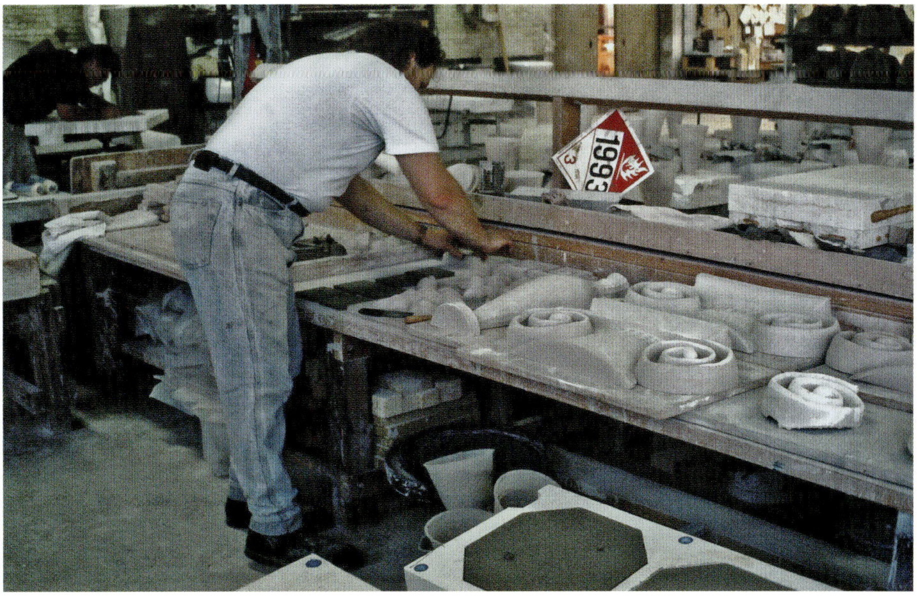

LEFT: *Fuping Gateway,* Robert Harrison, 2006. 3 x 1.8 x 0.9 m (10 x 6 x 3 ft), factory-produced brick and repurposed traditional Chinese temple, glazed ceramic roof tile, mortar, concrete, Fule International Ceramic Art Museums Complex, Fuping, China. *Photo: Robert Harrison.*

RIGHT: Robert Harrison working in the factory, Kohler Artist-in-Industry Program, Kohler, Wisconsin, 1989. *Photo: Robert Harrison.*

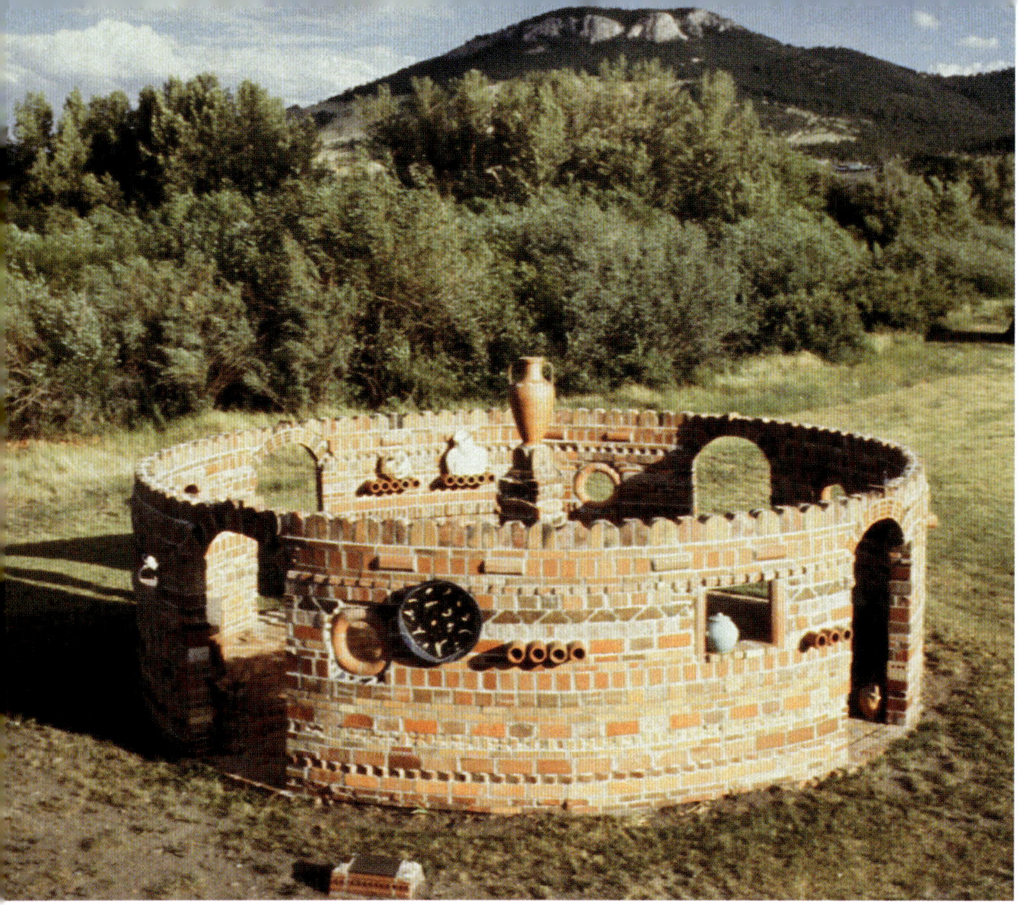

LEFT: *Potters Shrine*, Robert Harrison, 1985–87. 3.4 x 7.6 m (11 x 25 ft), site-specific architectural sculpture, reclaimed/repurposed brick, tile and pipe, (some dating to the early 20th century), ceramic objects, mortar, cement, Archie Bray Foundation for the Ceramic Arts, Helena, Montana. *Photo: Robert Harrison.*

BELOW: *Cullumned Spiral*, Robert Harrison, 1989. 2.7 x 7.6 m (9 x 25 ft), site-specific architectural sculpture, reclaimed sanitaryware shards, repurposed marble sink tops, mortar, concrete, Kohler Arboretum, Kohler, Wisconsin. *Photo: Robert Harrison.*

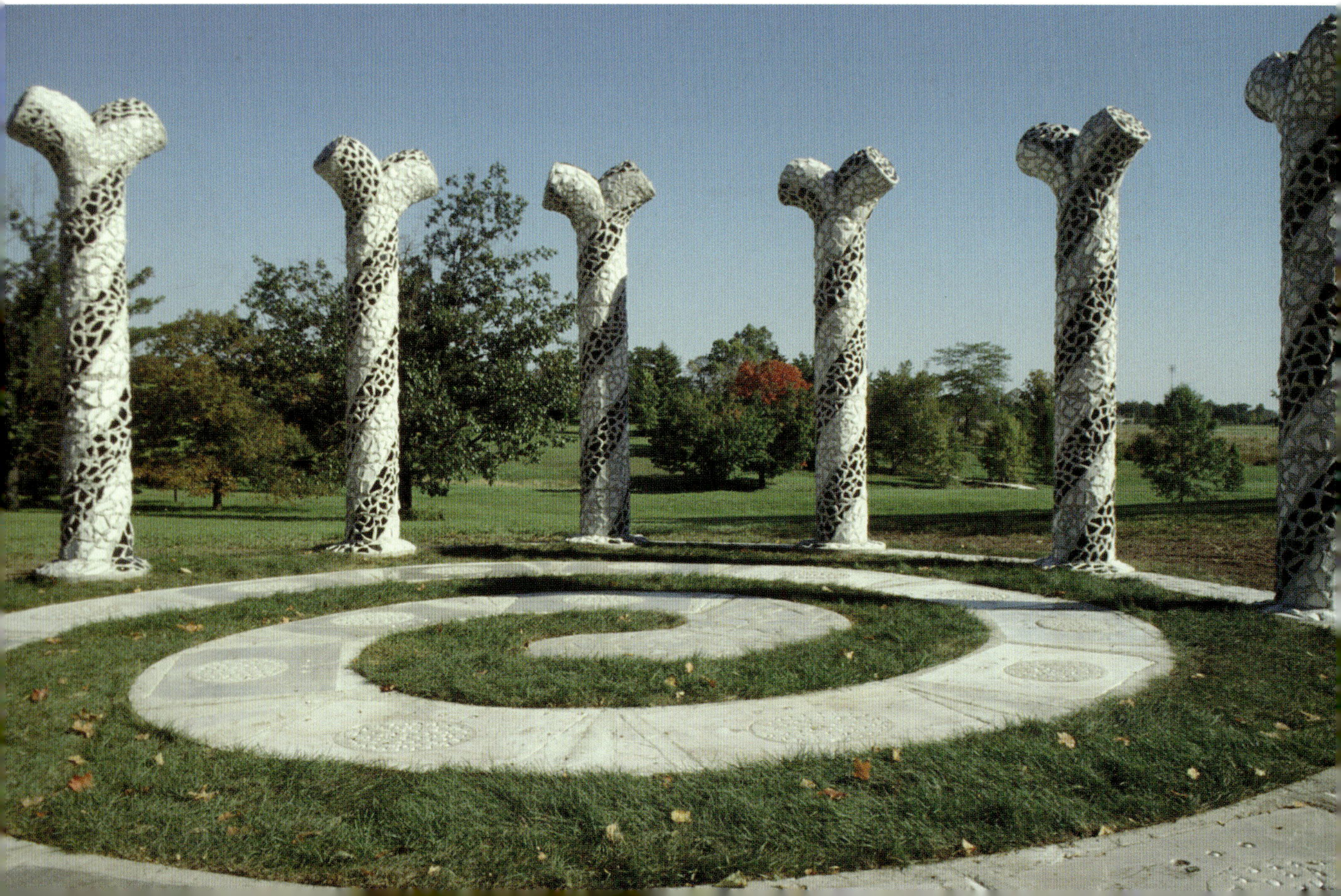

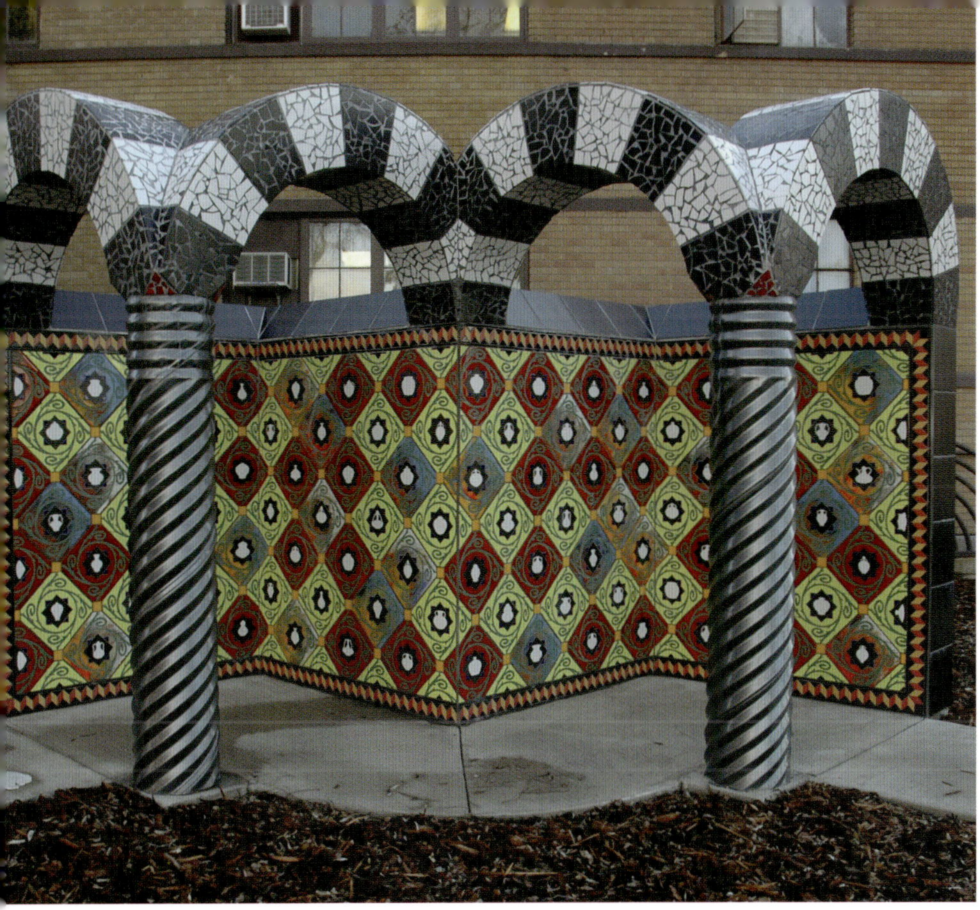

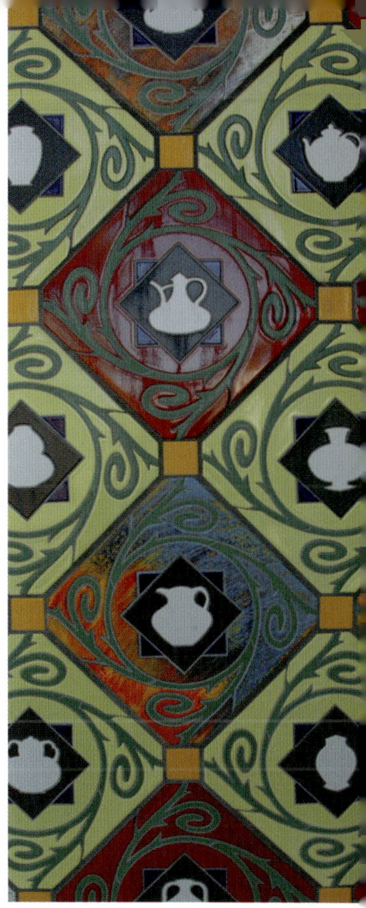

ABOVE: *Quarry Tile Gateway,* Robert Harrison, 2004–06. 3 x 4.9 x 1.8 m (10 x 16 x 6 ft), site-specific architectural sculpture, factory-produced, artist-altered ceramic tile, some water-jet cut, powder-coated steel culvert pipe, concrete, Quarry Tile Company, Spokane, Washington. *Photo: Robert Harrison.*

ABOVE RIGHT: *Quarry Tile Gateway* (tile detail), Robert Harrison, 2004–06. *Photo: Robert Harrison.*

They build their factories near the raw material source; they invest in energy-efficient kilns and equipment and examine ways to optimise their production process. Industry has the ability to take on leadership roles in sustainable efforts, and many have.

I felt it was important to include a section on large-scale projects that keep sustainability at the core. Whether a potter or artist works independently on small-scale work or engages in a much larger scale of working with industry, sustainable practices should be a part of the scheme. Clay as brick, a module capable of large-scale endeavours, has enabled the human species to create architectural edifices along with sculptural projects.

The lowly brick

A brick is a block, or a single unit of a ceramic material used in masonry construction, usually stacked together, or laid using various kinds of mortar to hold the bricks together and make a permanent structure. They have been regarded as one of the longest lasting and strongest building materials used throughout history.

The oldest discovered bricks, originally made from shaped mud and dating to before 7500 BC were found in the Middle East at Tell Aswad (modern-day Syria). Additional findings of early brick, dated between 7000 and 6395 BC, come from Jericho (a Palestinian city near the Jordan River in the West Bank). Ceramic bricks were used as early as 4500 BCE in early Indus Valley (modern-day Pakistan) cities.

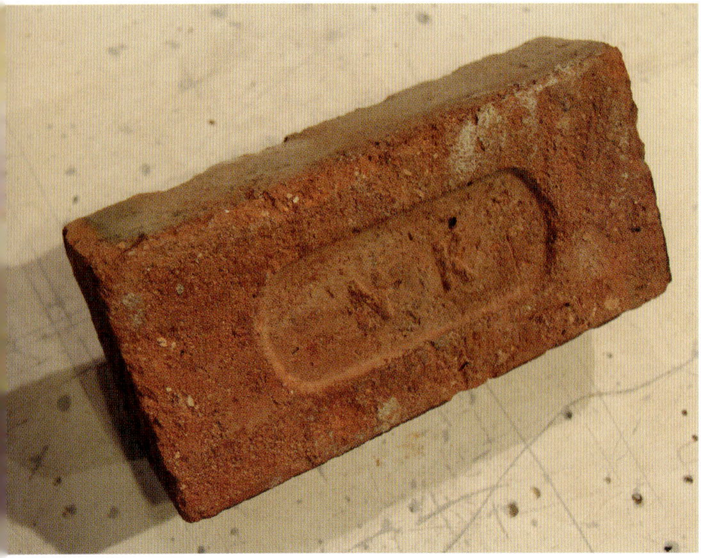

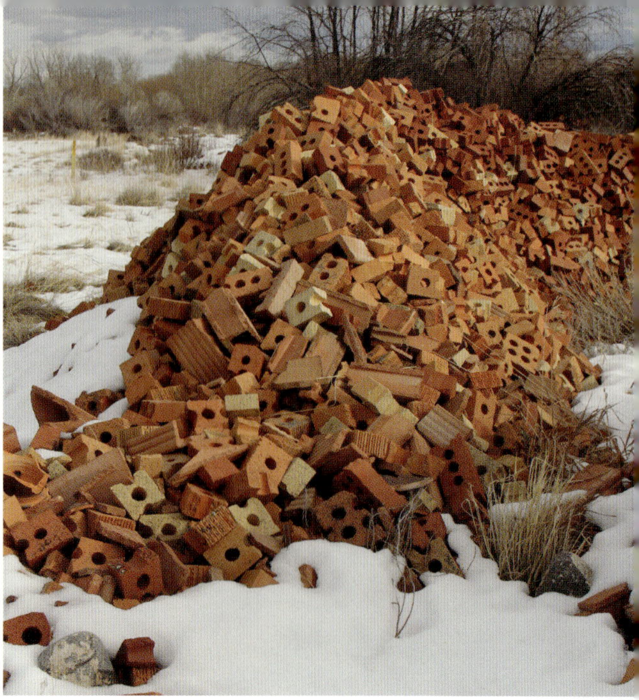

The first sun-dried bricks were made in Mesopotamia (now Iraq), in the ancient city of Ur in about 4000 BC, although the arch used for drying the bricks was not actually found. The Romans made use of fired bricks, and the Roman legions, which operated mobile kilns, introduced bricks to many parts of the empire. Roman bricks are often stamped with the mark of the legion that supervised their production. The use of bricks in southern and western Germany, for example, can be traced back to traditions already described by the Roman architect Vitruvius.

TOP LEFT: Studio brick, Robert Harrison, Granitewood Studio, Helena, Montana, 2013. *Photo: Robert Harrison.*

TOP RIGHT: Brick piles at the Archie Bray Foundation for the Ceramic Arts, Helena, Montana, 2012. *Photo: Robert Harrison.*

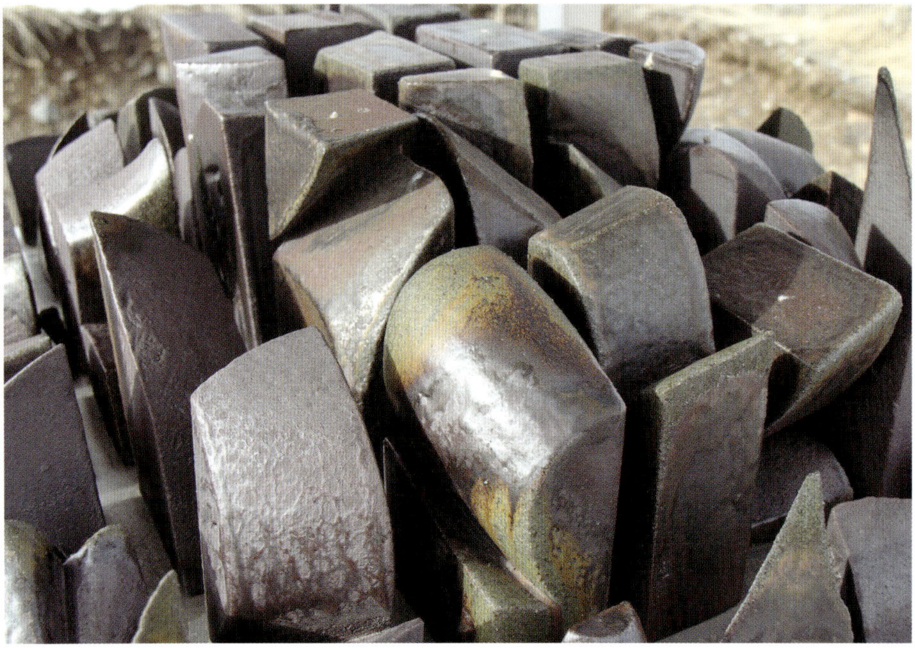

LEFT: *Gwen's bricks*, Archie Bray Foundation for the Ceramic Arts, Helena, Montana, 2012. *Photo: Robert Harrison.*

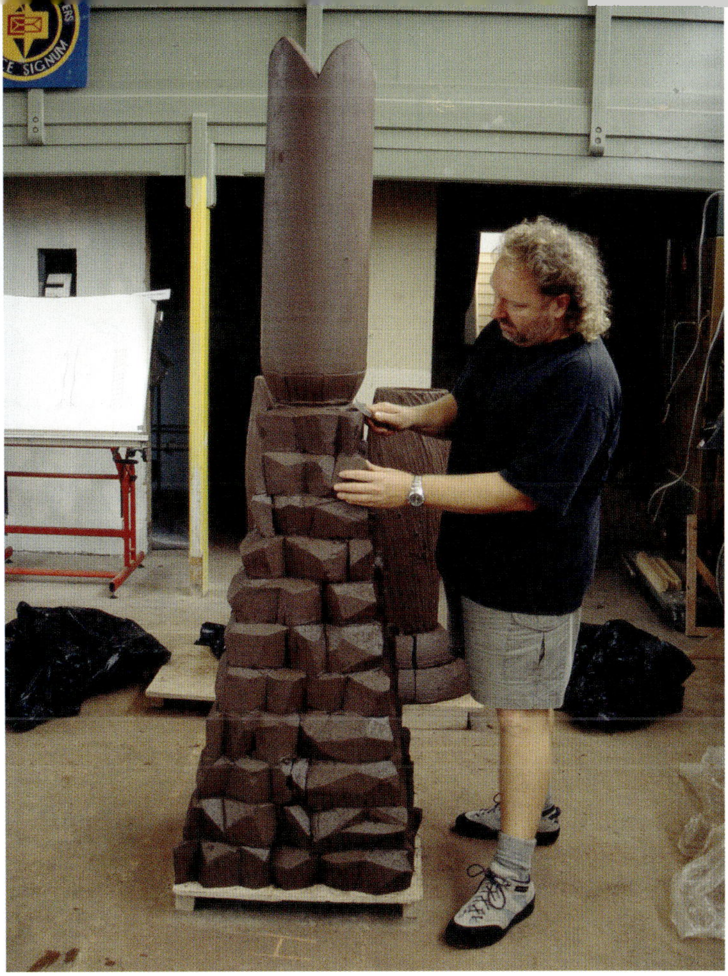

RIGHT: Robert Harrison working on carved brick stack at 'Creating the Yellow Brick Road' International Conference and Symposium, University of Wolverhampton, UK, 1999.

BELOW: *Ironbridge Archway*, Robert Harrison, 2000. Carved/altered brick and pipe, Rufford Craft Centre, Newark, Nottinghamshire, UK. *Photos: Robert Harrison.*

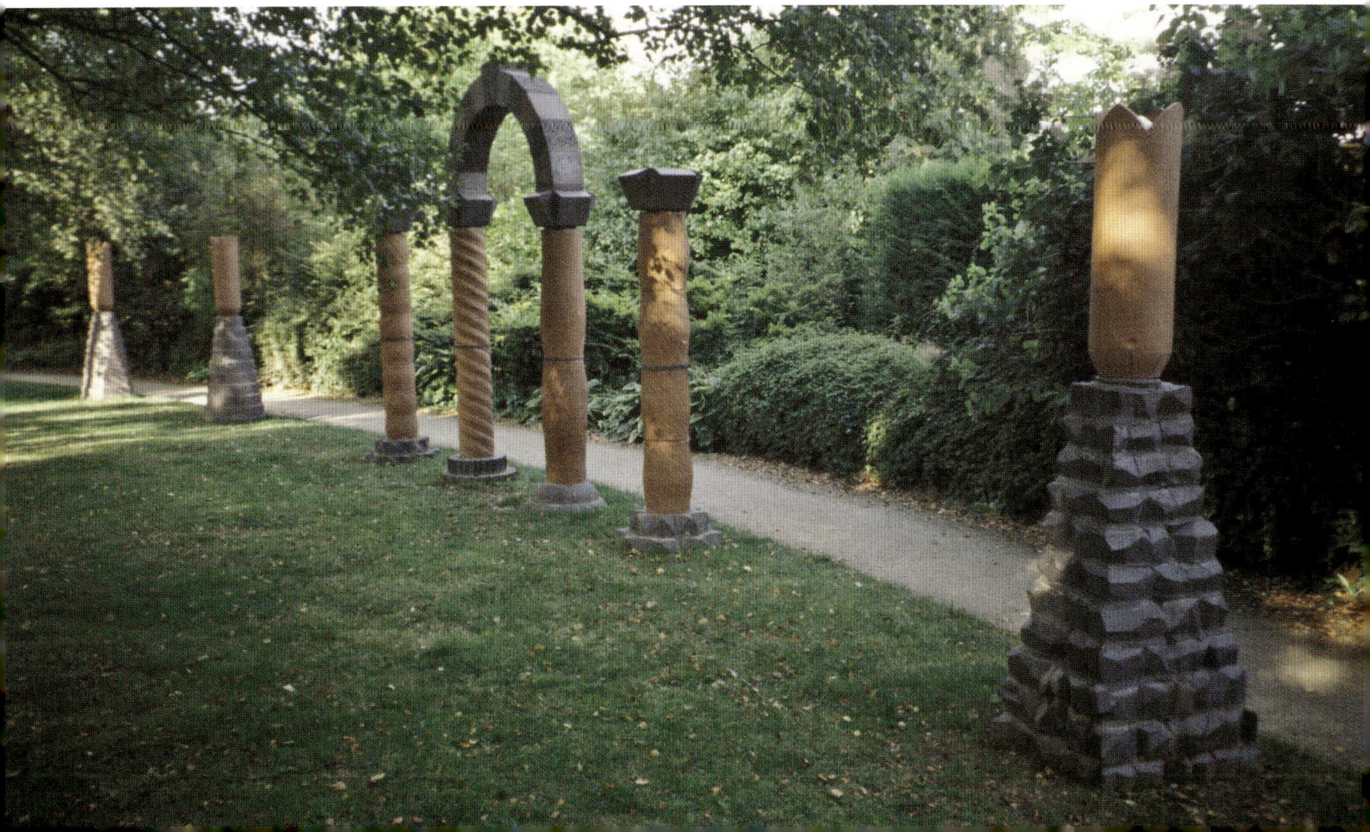

The Yellow Brick Road and its legacy

In the summer of 1999, **Gwen Heeney** organised a conference and symposium at the University of Wolverhampton in the UK called *Creating the Yellow Brick Road*. The concept of this groundbreaking event was to bring together artists, architects and brick producers to focus on the contemporary applications and uses of brick in the 21st century.

The event was a great success and an exhibition at the Rufford Craft Centre in Nottinghamshire, UK, along with the publication *Shaping Earth* documenting the conference and symposium, was subsequently produced. The wealth of documentation and information gathered inspired Gwen to write her seminal book *Brickworks*, which was published by A&C Black in 2003.

Creating the Yellow Brick Road also produced a wealth of passionate discussion among the attending artists who resolved to meet and work together again. It has taken some time, but after numerous conversations the concept of a world body of brick artists or the World Association of Brick Artists (WABA) was born. The founding members, are all members of the International Academy of Ceramics (IAC) and are artists who use and are passionate about brick as a sculptural medium.

In August 2011 WABA held its first symposium in southern Denmark with the generous support of Christian Petersen of the Petersen Tegl brick factory. During this meeting the founding principles of the organisation were developed and sustainable, ecological brick practices were identified as one of the ideals of WABA. As with any of the other facets of working with clay, using brick provides a forum to educate and promote sustainable practices. Artists working with brick engage manufacturers, architects, builders and the public and have an opportunity to espouse the benefits of sustainable practices and open doors to new possibilities with the material.

OPPOSITE, TOP LEFT: Gwen Heeney (UK) carving a brick sculpture, WABA International Brick Sculpture Symposium, Petersen Tegl, Broager, Denmark, 2011. *Photo: Robert Harrison.*

TOP RIGHT: *Sonderborg House*, Robert Harrison, 2011. 1.2 x 0.9 x 0.9 m (4 x 3 x 3 ft), salvaged Danish brick 'jewels', Danish flint stones, fabricated galvanised steel, concrete, WABA International Brick Sculpture Symposium, Petersen Tegl, Broager, Denmark. *Photo: Robert Harrison.*

BOTTOM LEFT: Ulla Viotti (Sweden) composing a brick sculpture, WABA International Brick Sculpture Symposium, Petersen Tegl, Broager, Denmark, 2011. *Photo: Robert Harrison.*

BOTTOM RIGHT: Fritz Vehring (Germany) assembling brick sculptures, WABA International Brick Sculpture Symposium, Petersen Tegl, Broager, Denmark, 2011. *Photo: Robert Harrison.*

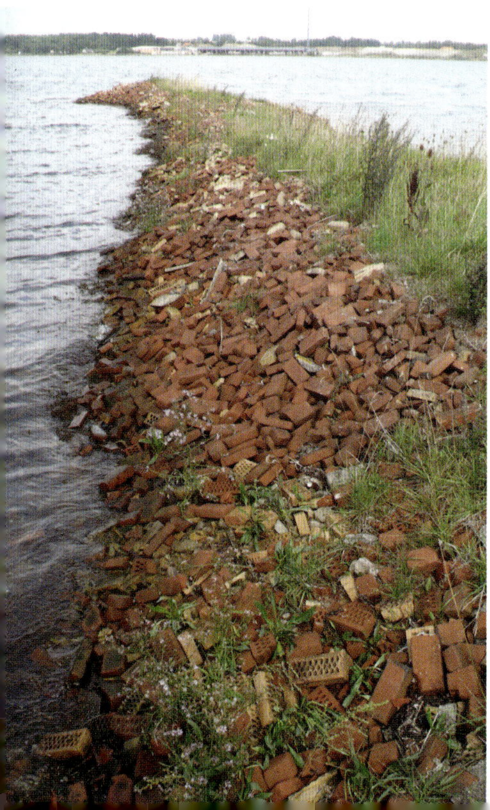

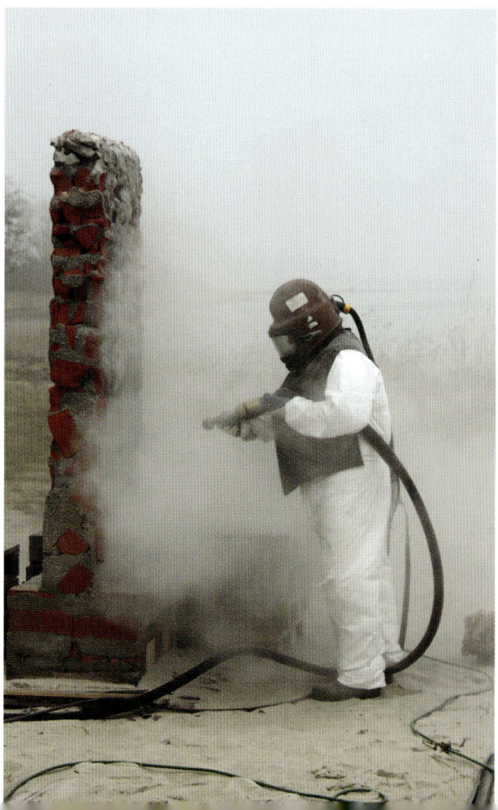

FAR LEFT: Denmark's Nybol Nor at Petersen Tegl (brick) Factory with brick jetty, near Broager, Denmark, 2011. *Photo: Robert Harrison.*

LEFT: Jacques Kaufmann (France/Switzerland) sandblasting brick sculpture, WABA International Brick Sculpture Symposium, Petersen Tegl, Broager, Denmark, 2011. *Photo: courtesy of the artist.*

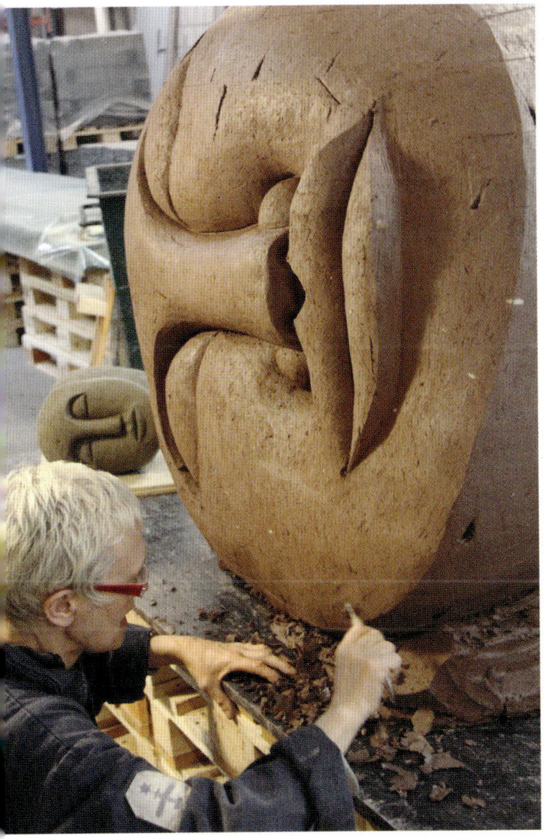

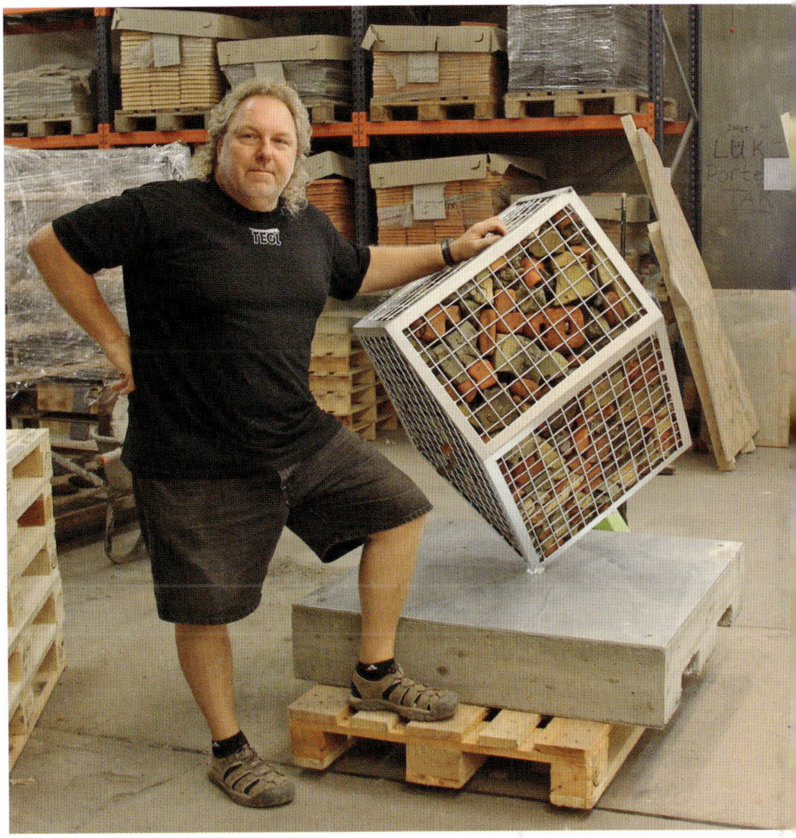
TEGL

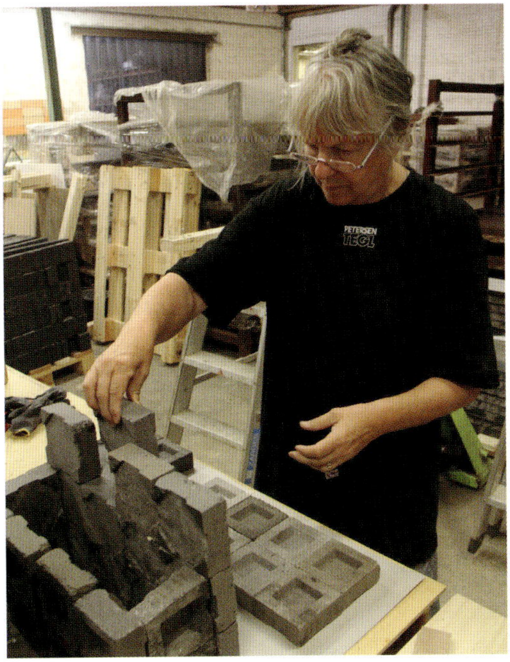
PETERSEN
TEGL

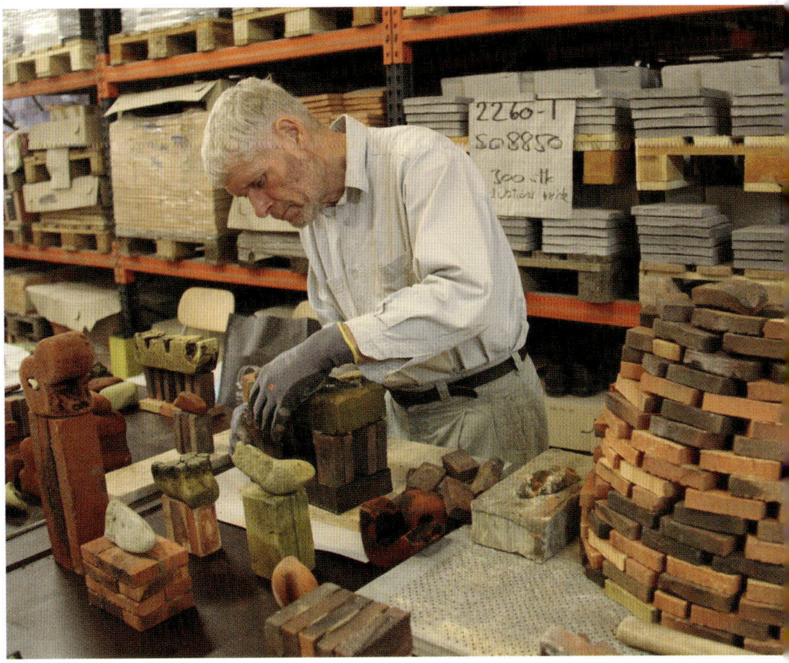
2260-1

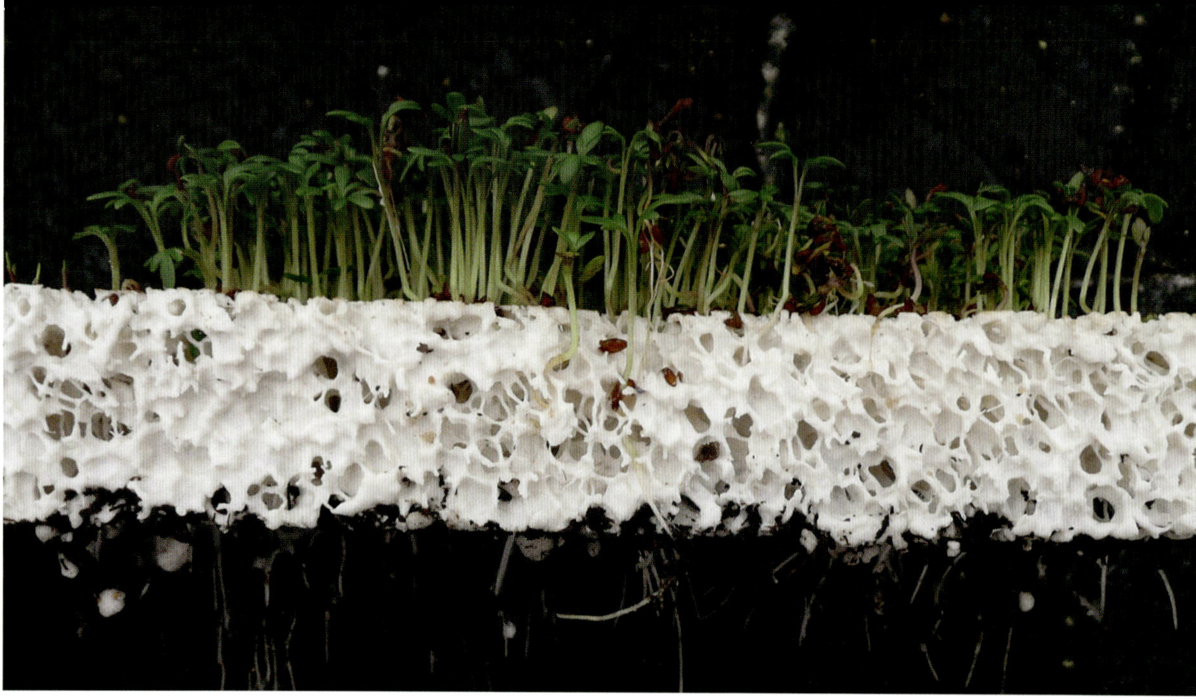

Growing Bricks, Jacques Kaufmann. Prototype research for 21st-century architecture, Jacques Kaufmann and colleagues at Hepia University, Geneva, Switzerland, 2012. *Photo: Jacques Kaufmann.*

The green walls: growing bricks

In 2010, **Jacques Kaufmann** became associated with an existing research group at Hepia University in Geneva, Switzerland and its schools of architecture and landscape architecture, where urban climate specialists, plants and soil specialists, architects and landscape architects are collaborating to develop a 'sustainable planted wall'. The challenge faced by the group was which material to use to fit the specifications and needs of the research? Jacques, of course, suggested they develop some unique bricks.

The goal of this project is to promote the idea of real *green* walls, versus the current fashion of decorating urban buildings with walls that *look green*, but have so many ecological issues, like requiring a great deal of water, physical care for the plants and all the related costs.

The fact is that a specific urban climate actually exists. During the summer months in large cities, it's not uncommon to see an 8 to 10°C (46 to 50°F) temperature difference between the city centre and the peripheral areas. Due to land values in city centres and the limitation of green spaces, there is no chance for additional water transpiration that could cool the urban climates. City centres are in a vicious circle, they are heat sinks, where summer temperatures can remain high for months. There is now a need to think about having plants in a vertical instead of a horizontal position.

Scientific studies conclude that by reducing the climate temperature by 1°C, cities could cut the number of deaths by 50% among the most vulnerable in the population. Not only would the *growing walls* contribute to cooling the building in the summer (and reduce the need for air conditioning), but consequently by increasing insulation values, these walls reduce heating needs during the winter months.

Water for the walls would come from precipitation and water storage, but it might be possible to imagine that the required water also comes from the grey water produced

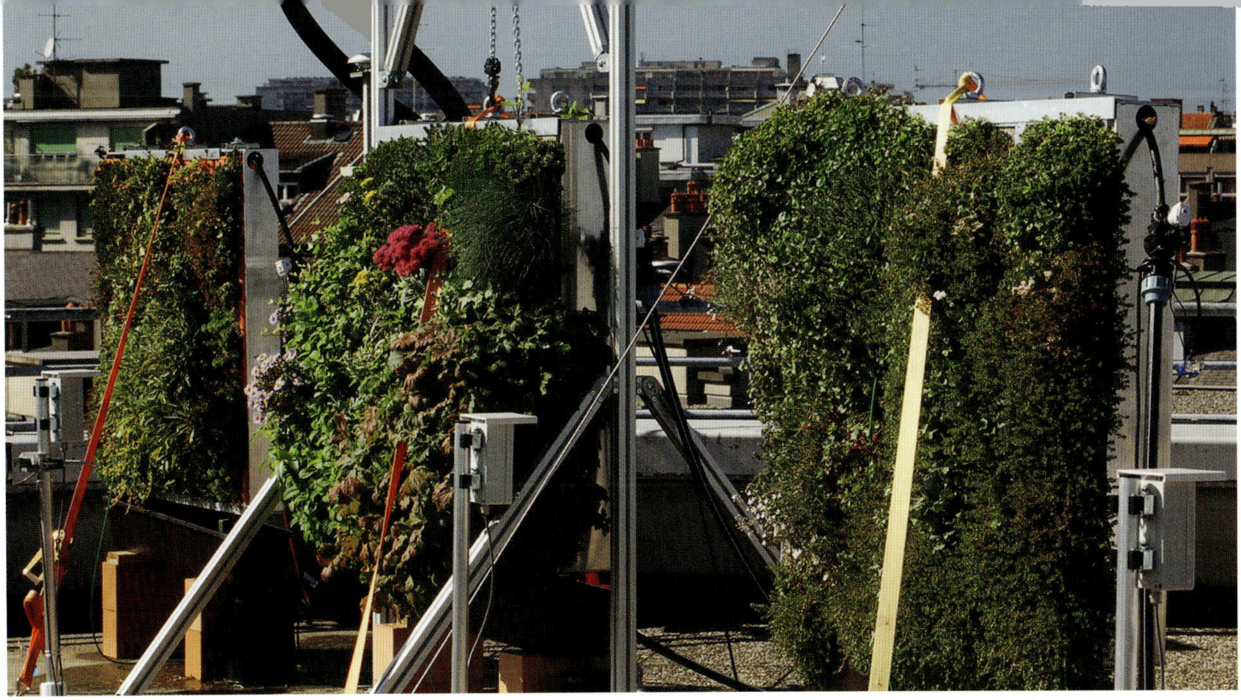

ABOVE: *Prototypes*, Jacques Kaufmann. Prototype research for 21st-century architecture, Jacques Kaufmann and colleagues at Hepia University, Geneva, Switzerland, 2012. *Photo: Jacques Kaufmann.*

RIGHT: *Growing Walls*, Jacques Kaufmann. Prototype research for 21st-century architecture, Jacques Kaufmann and colleagues at Hepia University, Geneva, Switzerland, 2012. *Photo: Jacques Kaufmann.*

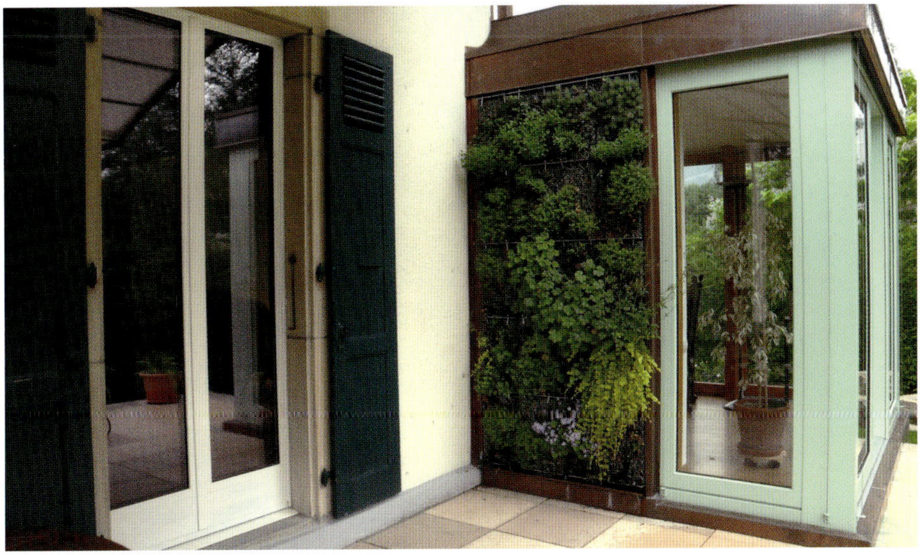

by the buildings (your shower for example), with the plants taking on the role of transforming and purifying the water. There is ongoing research into proving that plants can purify the air, and consequently bring back biodiversity in territories that have lost it.[1]

Alongside this large-scale project, where studies show a great potential, Jacques Kaufmann has tested on a small scale a *green wall* using bricks, produced in his studio. A villa under renovation in Geneva has welcomed this test, increasing comfort and aesthetics in a private living situation.

[1] Work in the scope of the research group: 'façades végétalisées', Switzerland. Project developed by Hepia/ Haute Ecole du Paysage d'Ingénierie et d'Architecture in Geneva. The Ingeneer School in Changins, Nyon, CREABETON Matériaux in Lyss, and Jacques Kaufmann.

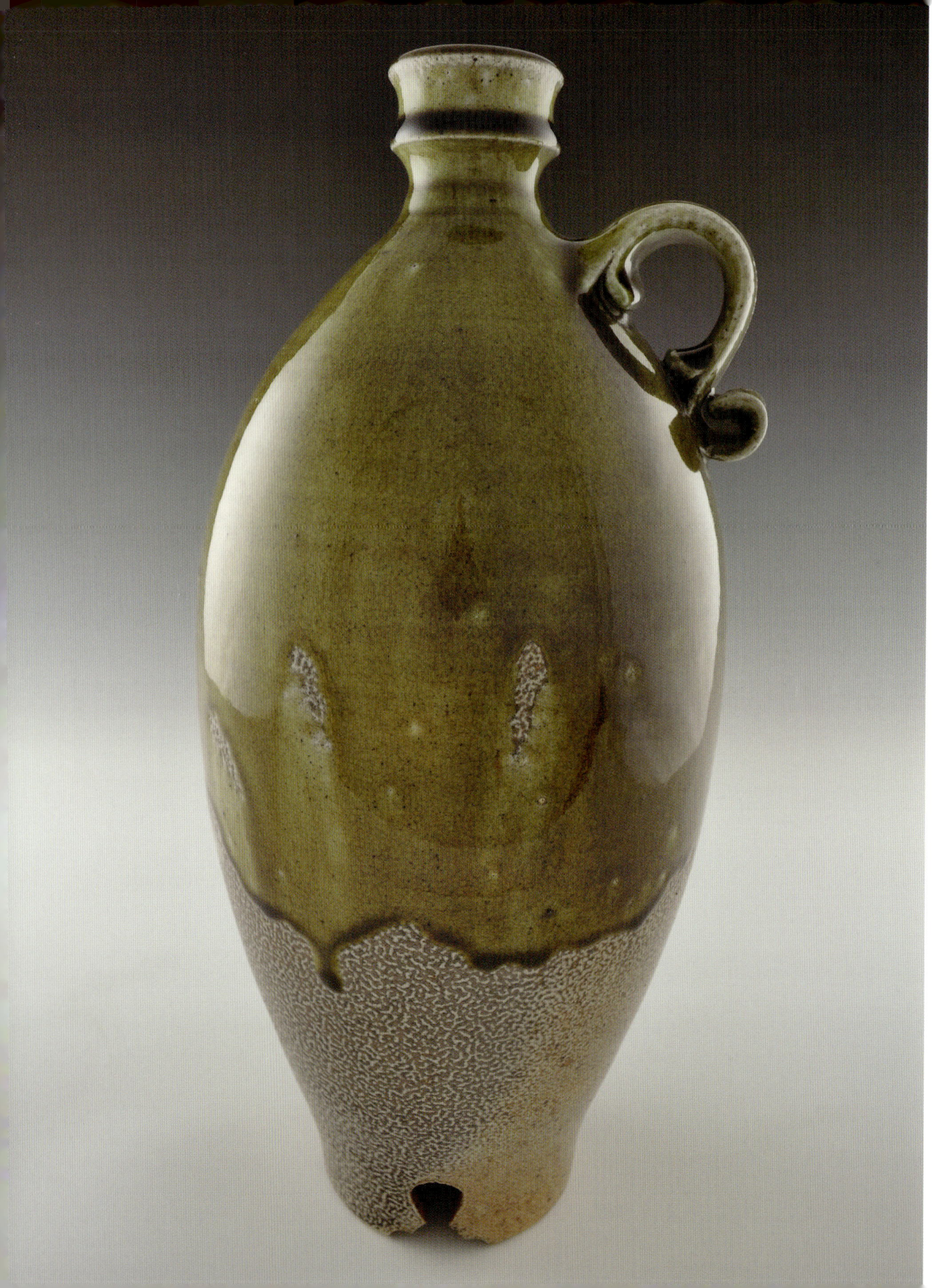

5 Sustainable endeavours: education and networks

Institutions of higher learning, art centres and organisations of various types and sizes have an opportunity to reach a larger audience with attainable goals in reducing carbon footprints and sustainable education. I have been fortunate to have been involved with several organisations that have made a commitment to sustainability through their programming and endeavours. A commitment to sustainable practices begins with the individual, but in order to reach a larger audience, schools, centres and organisations take leadership roles by setting an example of what can be done to ensure a better world for generations to come.

Applying sustainable principles to organisations

During my tenure (2004–2010) as president of the National Council on Education for the Ceramic Arts (NCECA) I took the opportunity to shepherd sustainable ideas and responsibilities to the organisation. The NCECA board of directors endorsed the concept of a Green Task Force (GTF) that continues to promote sustainable concepts and programming. Brian Kohl, NCECA communications director, board member and GTF chair writes:

> The National Council on Education for the Ceramic Arts (NCECA) formed the Green Task Force (GTF) to focus on the increasingly popular green/sustainability movement and how it relates to the field of ceramics. Initial meetings focused on what it was the Green Task Force could do to bring issues of sustainability to the international community that makes up the membership of NCECA. The GTF mission states:
>
> *NCECA's Green Task Force (GTF) is committed to environmental stewardship in all venues; from administrative work to conference gatherings and further extending to educate NCECA's members about important environmental issues affecting the ceramic arts. Creative solutions to issues will be shared and it is the GTF that will provide a forum for progressive discussion on green studio practices. The GTF will bring members the tools and information to help facilitate change, however a sustainable future in ceramics necessitates a community effort. We understand that it is not entirely feasible to make ceramics totally green, however it is possible to make small changes in our studio practices that will have lasting effects on minimizing global impact. In addition to educating our members, NCECA and members of the GTF will demonstrate, by our own policies and practices, that we are good*

Salt-glazed Bottle, Wil Shynkaruk, 2012. 33 x 14 cm (13 x 5½ in), stoneware. *Photo: courtesy of the artist.*

environmental stewards. Sustainability practices will be in place for the management and operations in NCECA's home office, and the annual conference. This will include but is not limited to: recycling of waste, handling of printed documentation, communication with members, and future site considerations. NCECA and the GTF have the future of ceramics in our sights; together we will discover additional ways to work in sympathy with our planet.

The Green Task Force maintains a booth at the annual NCECA conference, inviting individuals, manufacturers and organisations that promote sustainable practices to participate. A survey initiative has helped guide NCECA in what they do as an organisation to address environmental and sustainability issues, and how we can better serve our members in these regards.

Since 2008, the NCECA conference site deliberation and decision process includes reviewing sustainability commitments of prospective convention centres. Chosen sites include: LEED gold and silver certification, extensive recycling programmes, water reclamation and reduction strategies, sustainable and natural lighting and commitments to using local food and beverage services. These initiatives remain important to NCECA for all future site decisions, and continue to be shared with the NCECA membership.

In 2011, important changes were made to the call for future programme proposals. These changes appear in the *Education* and *Technology* categories and allow for proposals that 'advance knowledge and awareness of environmental concerns' and 'mitigate adverse environmental impact through innovations in sustainable systems and practices'.

LEFT: NCECA Green Task Force booth, Seattle, Washington, 2012. *Photo: Brian Kohl.*

RIGHT: NCECA Green Task Force. Left to right: Ben Culbertson, Laurie Popeck, Brian Kohl, Ben Hunter, Tampa, Florida, 2011. *Photo: Brian Kohl.*

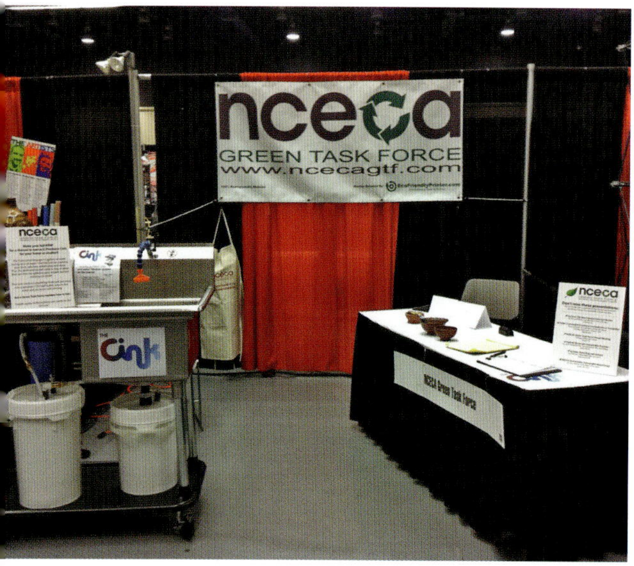

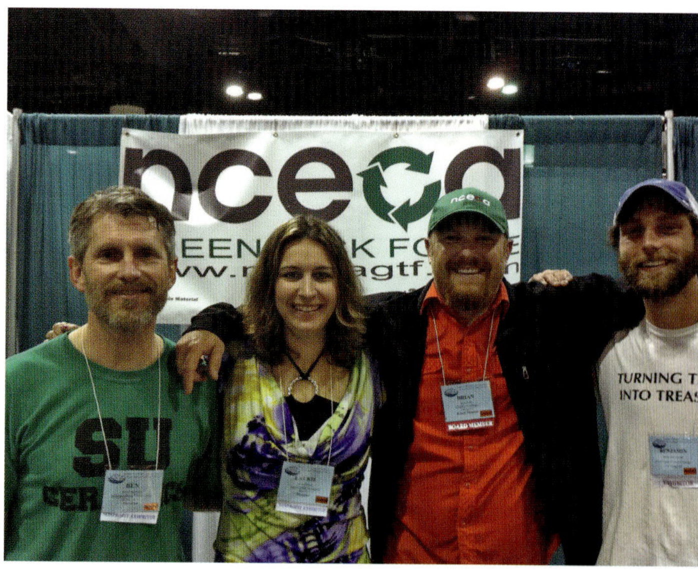

Educating with a sustainable perspective: efforts to 'pass the torch'

I believe makers are also educators, whether we teach formally or informally. Over the past 30 years, I have been teaching and involved in organisations that advocate ceramic education and firmly believe it is a responsibility we embrace without reservation. I made a point of asking contributors to this publication to reflect on their role as educators and what emphasis they place on sustainable practices when teaching. **Ilana Crispi** responds:

> As an educator I emphasise process and practice over finished pieces. This is especially useful for students new to clay. Instead of coming away with an early collection of doorstops or exceptionally bottom-heavy vessels that will ultimately end up in a landfill, I encourage my students to abandon the preciousness of the finished object. If a form isn't what was intended, or even a happy accident, then it's best to examine what happened and then wedge it up and start again. I don't require a specific number of fired and glazed forms; instead I expect a solid engagement with practice and a finished best example. For all of my students I provide historical context and an understanding of the environmental impact of working with clay in addition to technique and craftsmanship. I present them with examples of contemporary ceramic artists who are engaged with green practices, artists who use local clays and glazes and energy-efficient firing techniques. I also present less conventional ceramic artists who work with clay as a conceptual medium; artists who make ephemeral ceramic work or use clay to communicate ideas of social change or environmental solutions.

Brian Kohl writes:

> As an undergraduate student under Vincent Suez at California State University, Fullerton firing to cone 3 was the norm. In the 1970s the ceramics programme at CSUF was an energy-efficiency project for the state and in response to the oil crisis the class kilns were fired to cone 6. Over the years, new glazes were formulated and in the mid-1980s they voluntarily lowered the firing temperature to cone 3 achieving similar results. It was this education about reducing fuel use and other sustainable studio practices at Fullerton that has led me to my current studio practices as a college professor. The following is a list of changes I have made to reduce, reuse and recycle in the classroom:
>
> 1. I have created paperless classes by building a website for all of my classes. The website includes web PDF documents for students to download including: syllabi, projects, glaze tips and course calendars. In addition to reducing paper waste, I am able to utilise other media including blogs and video creating an enhanced student experience in learning.
>
> 2. I pass out terry cloth towels to every student for drying their hands and I have a no-paper-towel policy in my classes. At the end of each semester I have the

students return the used towels to me so I can clean them and reuse them the following semester.

3. When teaching clean-up practices, I show students how to clean up using very little water. Teaching as an adjunct professor at Chaffey College in California, I have helped start various efforts towards creating less waste. Chaffey College uses sinks that recycle water for cleaning tools and wheel splash pans.

4. In 2010 we converted to a cone 6 studio. We fire cone 6 reduction and oxidation, and in 2011 started firing our soda kiln to the same temperature.

5. Following the model of Humbolt State University in California, I am researching businesses that will accept our unclaimed bisque ware and broken refractories to use as aggregate in concrete and road construction.

6. We have also ramped up our clay recycling to reuse all of our trimmings and unfired clay waste. The recycled clay is sold by the students to generate funds for visiting artists and other student-funded initiatives.

My vision as an educator is to teach students sustainable studio practices, explain why we have these measures in place, and how these practices can lead to a better future. I hope my students take this information into their personal lives and build on the practices that they learned in my classroom. I am committed to sustainability in the field, and will continue to make changes towards the advancement of a more sustainable ceramic future.

Roderick Bamford teaches at the College of Fine Arts (Cofa) in Sydney, Australia. He addresses sustainable issues by creating assignments for his ceramics students. Roderick writes:

In setting course projects, my endeavour is to provide engaging opportunities for students to link conceptual and technical ceramic approaches that address contemporary or historical issues, with the aim of the developing sensitivity to both the process and context of ceramics. As a significant issue, sustainability objectives appear in most project briefs, whether it is developing an exhibition installation or preparing a design entry for a bathware competition. One of these projects, 'spin the table', asked the students to develop a range of tableware engaging the issue of sustainability through the lens of 'propaganda'. The project challenged the students on a number of fronts. Individuals were responsible for creating works for exhibition, and all collaborated on curating the exhibition, which opened at Cofaspace during the First Australian Ceramics Triennial in 2009. A website catalogue of the exhibition prepared by the students can be found at http://spinthetable.wetpaint.com/.

The Leonardo Innovation Transfer Project

Authors: EMA-CNIFOP, Keramike Studio Jarmily, Tyrnerová s.r.o, University of Wolverhampton

The Leonardo Innovation Transfer European Project was set up with four international partners to address a number of issues highlighted by French and European studies. One of its aims was to encourage innovation in the development of ecological practices in relation to ceramic waste materials and alternative firing techniques. The four partners: CNIFOP (National Centre for the Introduction, Training and Improvement in Pottery and Stoneware) in Saint Amand en Puisaye, France, well known for its technical instruction and specialist courses on ceramic techniques and skills; Keramike Studio Jarmily in the Czech Republic, which is a private ceramics school run by Jarmila Tynerove and took the lead in the quest for ecological practices within ceramics; Videoscope at the University of Nancy, France who produced the website and the videos; and Gwen Heeney and Vicky Shaw at the University of Wolverhampton, School of Art and Design, Applied Arts Ceramics.

Gwen Heeney organised the eco element for the university enlisting two MA students, Sid Turner and Allen Richards, who were already heavily involved with eco practices. The 'eco conception' element of the project addressed the existence of eco practices within studio-based ceramics and European teaching institutions and particularly how ecological issues were fundamental to other concerns of the project: the exchange of high-level expertise amongst European potters, and the embedding of design philosophies within skill-based ceramic processes. The main outcome of

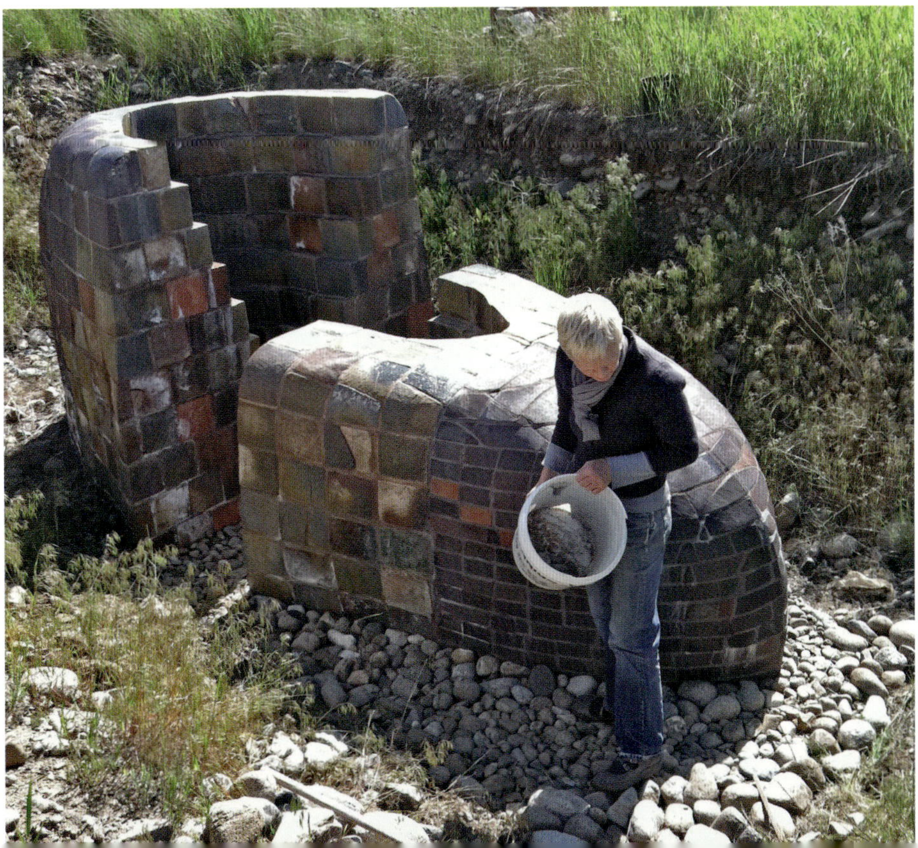

Fossil Pit, Gwen Heeney, 2006–10. Site-specific soda-fired brick sculpture, Archie Bray Foundation for the Cereamic Arts, Helena, Montana. *Photo: courtesy of the artist.*

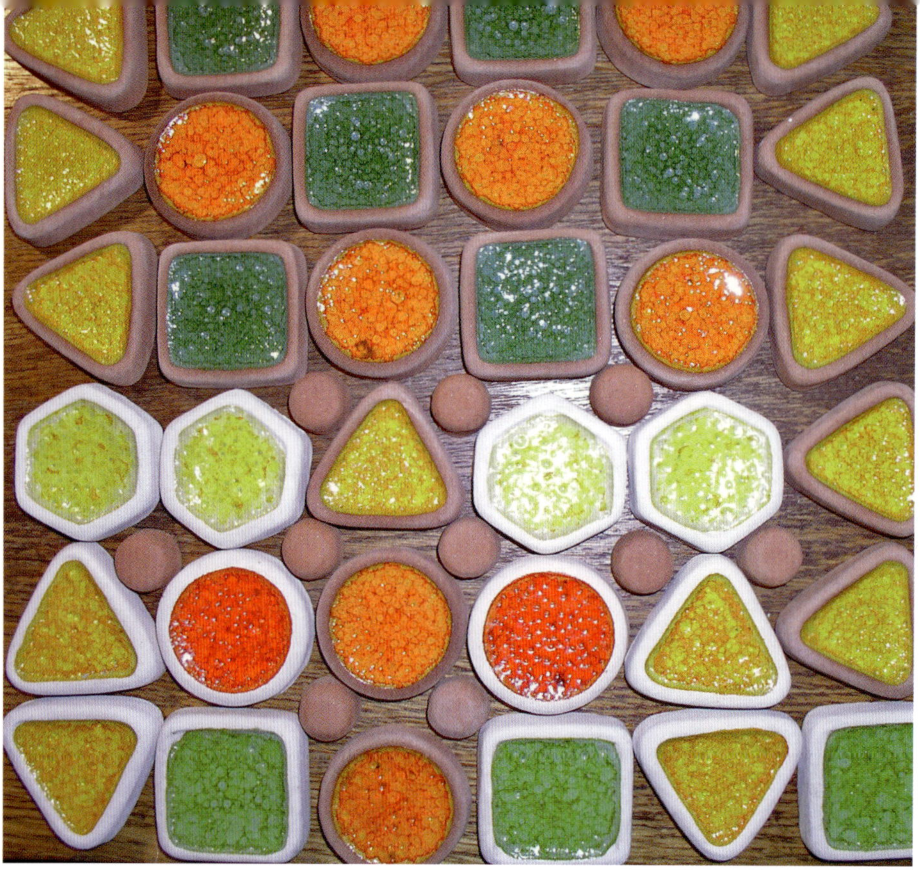

ECOmosaic Tiles, Gwen Heeney, 2011. Recycled waste clay and glazes, Keramike Studio Jarmily, Kohoutov, Czech Republic. *Photo: courtesy of the artist.*

the project was the production of a pedagogic bespoke website: eu-ceramics.eu that links ecological and design issues to training video's explaining a range of ceramic techniques, e.g. brick carving.

Ecological practices ranged from simple recycling of waste glaze, waste additives to clays, developing glazes from residues from incinerators within the city, to the development of eco kilns efficient on the use of power. One of the interesting aspects of the project was the interchange of ideas between the partners. The partner leading the eco practice element of the project, Keramike Studio Jarmily in the Czech Republic, created the ecological research and development plan which at its heart promoted recycling of waste materials and alternative firing methods to cut down fuel consumption. In October 2011 they organised an international eco firing symposium and workshop in Kohoutov in the Czech Republic attended by many international artists, firing enthusiasts and students who built a range of experimental kilns and exchanged eco ideas.

The eco concept developed by the partners of the Leonardo project focused on activities such as recycling materials and energy saving which could easily be put into practice within individual maker's studios or institutions. As small-scale producers it is difficult to compete with industrial ecological production of ceramics. However the eco concept has great potential for the production of individual one-off items or small-scale batch production that excel in creative design and high-quality craftsmanship and also site-specific artworks in the landscape where a substantial reduction in material and energy can actually add to the marketability and public awareness of the quality and intention of the product and maker.

Preheating Air Kiln, Kohoutov 2011

KEY

T	Thermocouple
ST	Stoking Hole
AP	Ash Pit
PPA	Preheating Primary Air
SP	Spy Hole
PPCA	Preheating Postcombustion Air
PSA	Preheating Secondary Air
G	Grate

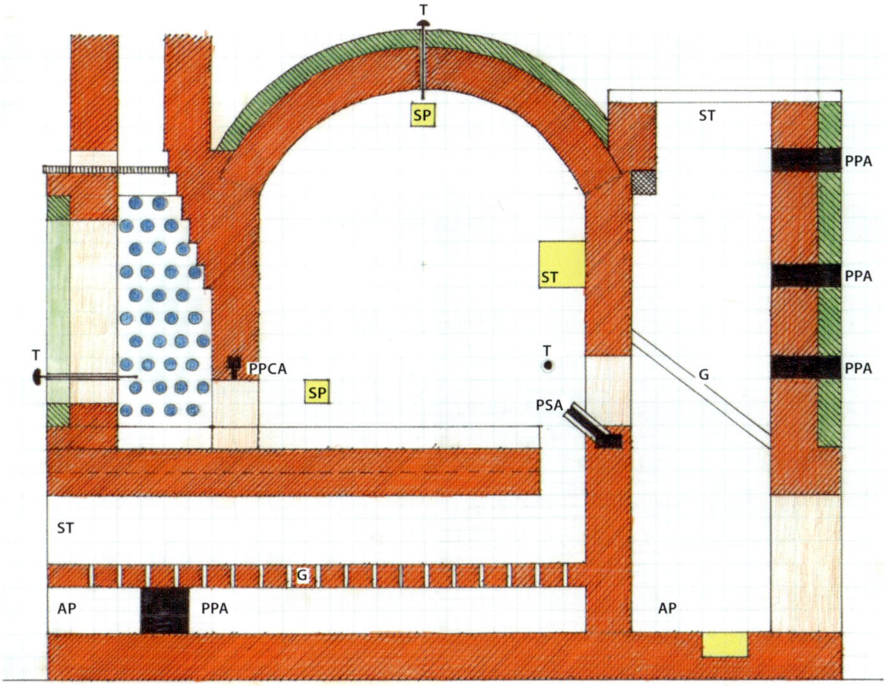

RIGHT: *Eco Wood Kiln Plan*, Gwen Heeney. Drawing for 300-litre wood kiln with pre-heat chamber for air, Petr Toms, Kohoutov, Czech Republic, 2011.

BELOW: Front view of eco wood kiln, Kohoutov, Czech Republic, 2011. *Photos: Gwen Heeney.*

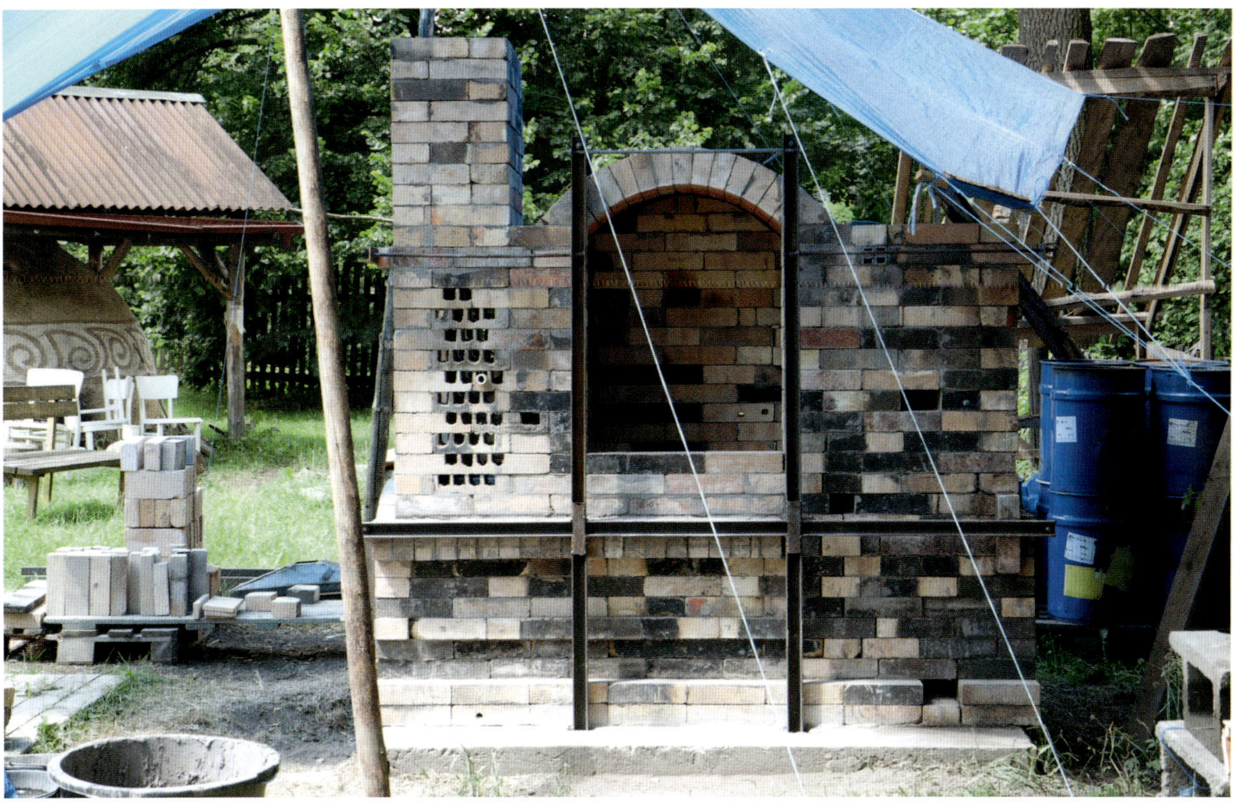

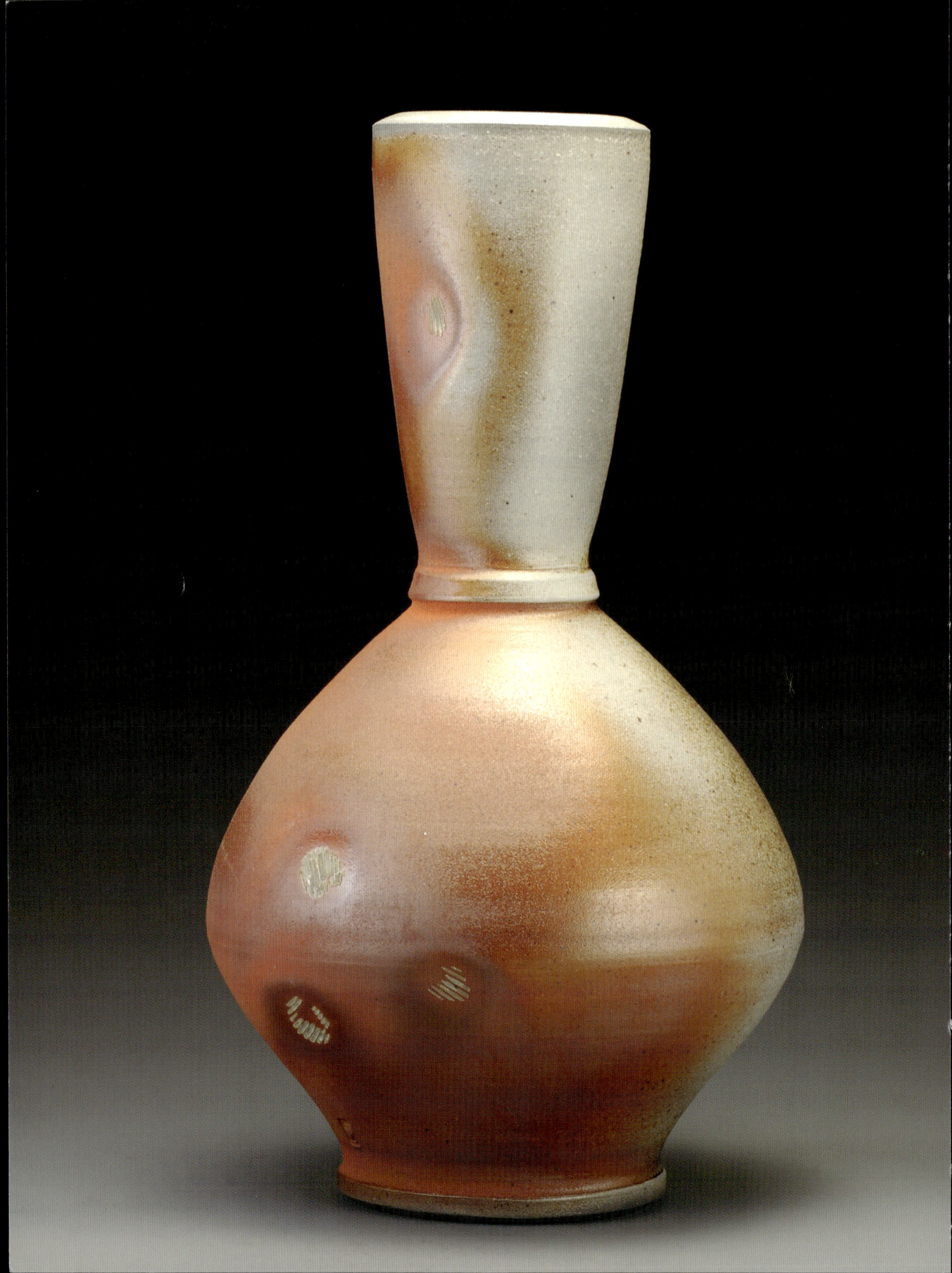

6

Journal leaders: personal approaches

LEFT: *Large Vase,* William Baker, 2011. 46 x 23 cm (18 x 9 in), wheel thrown porcelain, Cone 10 wood/soda fired. *Photo: courtesy of the artist.*

BELOW LEFT: Sherman Hall attaching lugs to a freshly thrown bottle before removing it from the wheel. *Photos: courtesy of the artist.*

RIGHT: Sherman Hall found clay in his Ohio backyard while digging up an old pear-tree stump. Not willing to let the opportunity pass, he dried it out, slaked it down, screened out the sand and uses it to make flower pots to put back out into the backyard.

I have a keen interest in fostering global information and communication in the ceramics field and have personally collected ceramics books and periodicals for the past three decades. The global ceramics field is fortunate to have a collective of dedicated publishers, many of whom have been disseminating information for decades. Representatives from two periodicals that distribute their publications internationally were invited to contribute texts specific to the subject of sustainability for this publication.

Sherman Hall is a maker, the editor of *Ceramics Monthly* magazine and a member of the NCECA Green Task Force. Sherman writes:

> There are two separate perspectives I have when it comes to the issue of sustainability and ceramics. One is based in my own studio and the things I do to make it sustainable, and the other is based on my position as the editor of *Ceramics Monthly* magazine. The two seem quite separate at times, but they do circle back to one another on a regular basis. My studio is one of those small, corner-of-the-basement type studios, while the magazine reaches into all sorts of studios, so the difference in scale between the two can seem insurmountable, but the fact of the matter is that the same things that might make my own studio more sustainable are applicable to a larger studio and, therefore, reasonable fodder for a broad range of readers. Also, because there are so many people from the magazine's readership who are interested in sustainable practices on all sorts of levels, they tend to submit

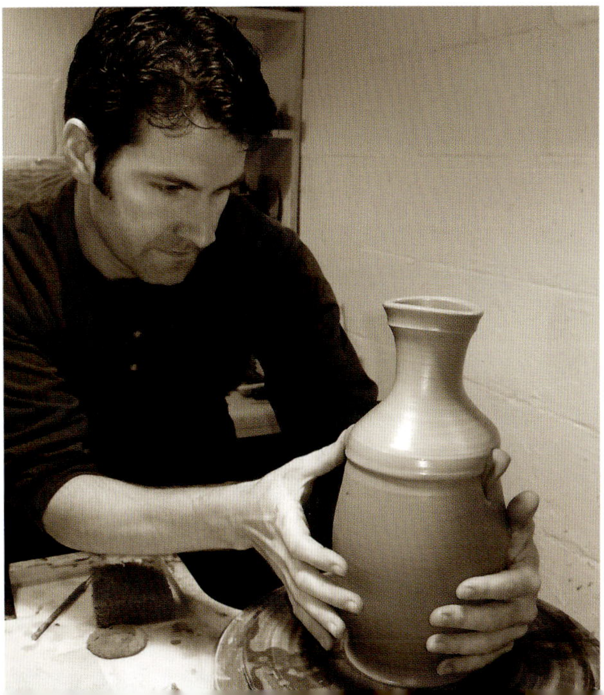

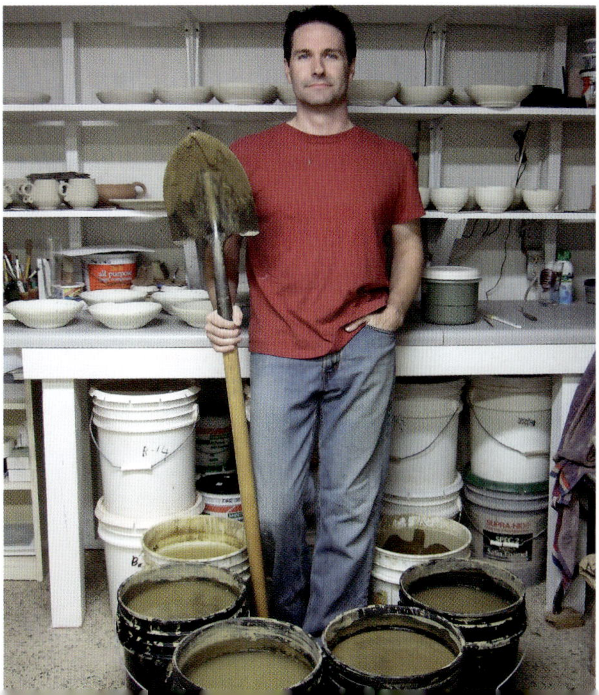

those ideas to the magazine and I get to hear about all kinds of things I can do in my own studio that I may not have considered otherwise.

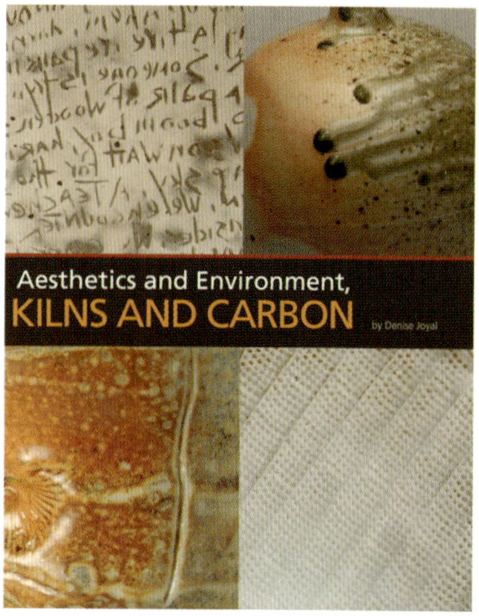

Ceramics Monthly article 'Aesthetics and Environment, Kilns and Carbon' by Denise Joyal, February 2011. *Photo: courtesy of* Ceramics Monthly.

In my studio, I do very simple things, basic things that honestly can seem too simple to mention – but I'll mention a few. I save water in the summer from rain barrels and use it in the studio for mopping up. In the winter, I save water from the humidifier on the furnace using a simple pump (it can be up to 10 gallons [38 litres] per day during a cold winter). I use ash from the fireplace and clay from my backyard to make glazes. These are not the kinds of things that will anchor an entire conversation in the public sphere, partly because those things that have aesthetic effects, like the clay and ash in my glazes, are specific to my own aesthetic, and may not fit everyone's preferences. Also, there are at least 20 ways to get the glazes I make with them, so it's not as if I'm making traditional ash or slip glazes; I'm just making the glazes I like using about half of my materials from extremely local sources. To some, this may be a curiosity, and to others perhaps it is encouragement that you can be true to your own aesthetic while also being somewhat environmentally minded. At best, these practices are the beginning of more in-depth research and conversations that can, and have, happened in print, and so they end up being more significant than is immediately obvious to just one person in just one studio.

Many *Ceramics Monthly* readers inquire about sustainable practices, simply because we do have a store of content on the subject. What almost every person who is relatively new in attempting to 'green' his or her studio wants is a way to use less fuel or energy when firing. A kiln is the biggest, most visible resource hog in the studio, and while reducing its consumption is an admirable goal, I am of the mind that one should use the firing methods necessary to make the work one envisions making; otherwise one is not being honest to the creative process in following it where it leads. There are a myriad of things to be done to offset the carbon footprint of firing, and while it is a good idea to know where your studio stands in that regard, it is often not a good idea to forego all of the other, simpler steps you could take and focus only on the thing that has the potential of fundamentally changing your work.

So, part of my role at the magazine as it pertains to sustainability in ceramics is to provide information and research that has been carried out by others so that practitioners can become more informed about the tools and options available. For instance, we published research done by Denise Joyal on how to calculate the carbon footprint of various kinds of kilns. While there is no single footprint size for a given kiln, because of the variables of cost, source of fuel, effort in obtaining fuel, etc., each person or studio can use Joyal's baseline to calculate consumption and costs according to their own situation. There is no silver bullet or easy answer or simple solution, and that can be less-than-satisfying when you really want to make a difference in your studio. The good news is that all of the individual small things that can be done have immediate results.

I can't personally claim to be doing everything I could be doing, but I started with what was easy and my efforts grew from there. For instance, disseminating the research of others is easier than doing the research myself, and saving water is easier than not using it in the first place. What I found in fairly short order was that, as soon as I did one easy thing, the next steps became easier than I thought they would be. If you do what is easy for you, in your particular situation, more things become obvious and easier in short order.

Ceramics is inherently brown (as in not green). We mine materials from the earth, and often not in what anyone would call a sustainable manner. We ship them all over the world, because we want the options and flexibility that globalisation offers. We consume carbon-based fuel to either directly fire our work or to create electricity to do so. We then (some of us) ship our work long distances to customers or sales venues. We as individuals (me in my own studio), don't make that large of an impact. But we are an industry of sorts, and collectively we have some measurable impact, even if it's well below that of what me might consider traditional industry. We as a field find ourselves somewhere in the middle ground in terms of scale. This is partly due to the sense of community, and responsibility to that community, that has been built into our practice. We are very much aware of our interconnectedness, because we learn through demonstration and first-hand sharing of techniques, information, and studio practices. It is perhaps fitting that, because we work with earth as a material, we are more cognisant of our impact upon it as a body, and therefore worry about our own willingness to adversely affect it.

If I'm honest, I need to admit that I've instituted some of my studio practices partly to make myself feel better about continuing to make pots that, on a specifically utilitarian level, the world really does not need. And, through the magazine, I share the information about what others have done so that everyone in our field who is interested at least has the option of taking steps that make sense for them.

Ceramics will never be what most would consider a green practice, but that is all the more reason to mitigate what we do in areas that may or may not directly impact our studio practice. As with anything, it is difficult to choose a direction and take a first step unless you know where you currently stand. I used to think I stood in my basement and made pots. But because of my exposure to all sorts of research and information through my editorial role at *Ceramics Monthly*, I realise I stand in the middle of a very large group of people who also stand in their basements making pots, and that what each of us does actually matters. No governmental agency will likely attempt to regulate our carbon footprint as an industry, because we simply don't produce enough of a footprint in one place, but that is a pretty bad reason to do nothing. In the end, my hope is that studio ceramics today is more sustainable than it otherwise would be without practitioners attempting to improve our collective knowledge base. We may travel slowly, but I think we are travelling in the right direction.

Elaine Olafson Henry is a maker and the editor and publisher of the international journals, *Ceramics: Art and Perception* and *Ceramics Technical*. As a past-president of the National Council on Education for the Ceramic Arts (NCECA) and an artist member of the International Academy of Ceramics, her work is in international collections and publications. Elaine writes:

> It is our responsibility in the publication of ceramics journals to report on such efforts, whether these efforts are personal or altruistic. In efforts towards sustainability, the personal is altruistic.
>
> It is also our responsibility as publishers to be as green as possible. In this effort, we utilise paper that is partially made from recycled materials and we offer both journals in electronic form to all of our subscribers. It is yet to be seen where these efforts will go as we move forward into a more electronic world. We are heartened by the efforts of others. And we are heartened by the fact that our journals seldom (if ever) add to the landfill. We will continue to work towards greater sustainability and we will continue to encourage articles that bring to our readers information on sustainability efforts internationally.

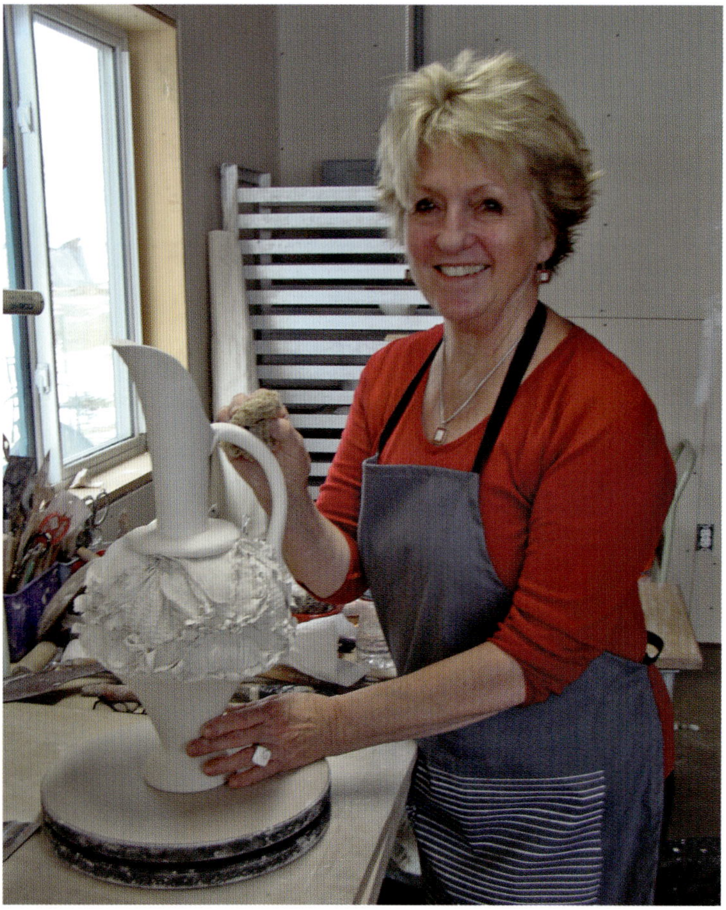

Elaine Olafson Henry working in her studio in Sheridan, Wyoming, 2012. *Photo: courtesy of the artist.*

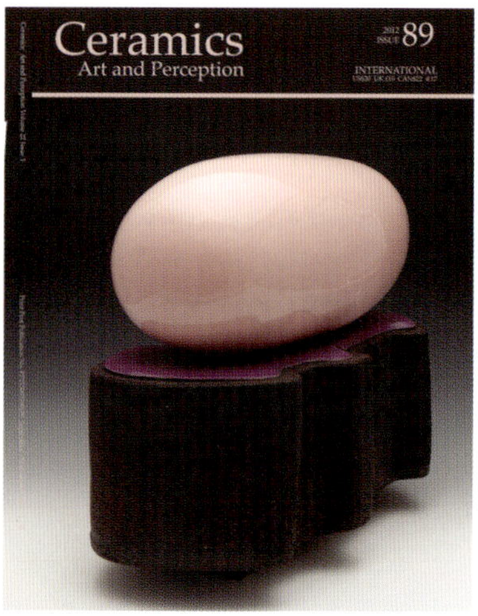

ABOVE: *Ceramics: Art and Perception* cover, Issue 89, 2012. *Photo: courtesy of* Ceramics: Art and Perception.

Sustainable ceramic conferences and symposia

I am heartened by the fact that there have been a number of international conferences, symposia and exhibitions recently focused on the sustainable aspects of ceramic practice. I have been especially impressed with publications from three such events: *The International Ceramics Symposium: Ceramics and Ecology* sponsored by WOCEF, in Gyeonggi, Korea in 2009; *The International Ceramics Symposium: Ceramic Arts and Design for a Sustainable Society*, sponsored by the Frolunda Culture Centre, Gothenburg, Sweden in 2011; and *Thing, Tang, Trash: Upcycling in Contemporary Ceramics*, a ceramics exhibition with a catalogue of essays published by the Bergen National Academy of the Arts in 2011.

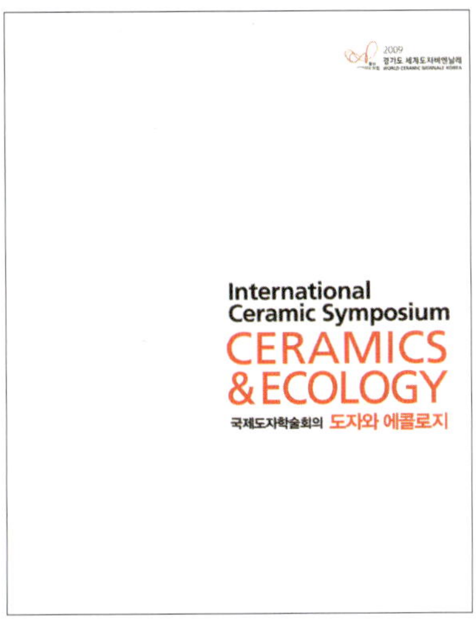

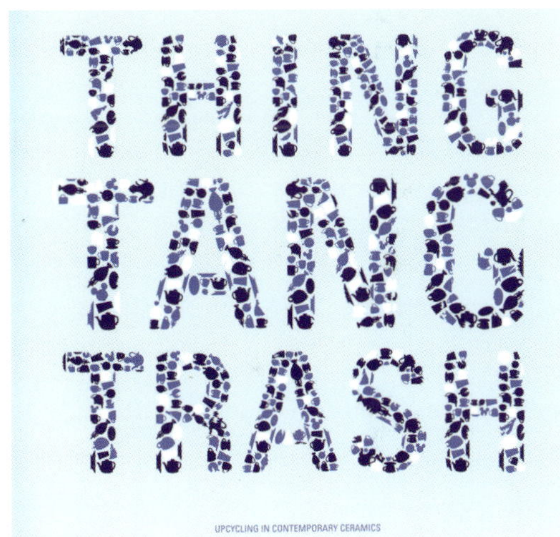

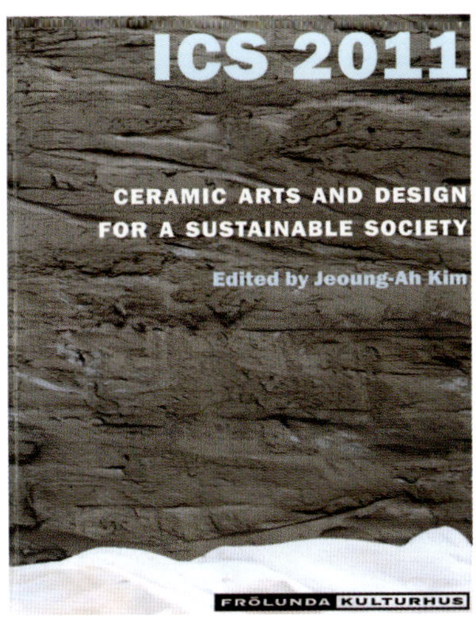

ABOVE LEFT: *International Ceramics Symposium: Ceramics and Ecology*, exhibition catalogue, sponsored by WOCEF, in Gyeonggi, Korea, 2009.

ABOVE: *Thing, Tang, Trash: Upcycling in Contemporary Ceramics*, a ceramics exhibition with a catalogue of essays published by the Bergen National Academy of the Arts, 2011.

LEFT: *The International Ceramics Symposium: Ceramic Arts and Design for a Sustainable Society*, sponsored by the Frolunda Culture Centre, Gothenburg, Sweden, 2011.
Photos: Robert Harrison.

Practical advice – top tips

This is not intended as a complete list of everything in the book – these are just snippets from some of the key issues that feature in the wealth of information in this publication; please go to the main entry for further details on them.

Kilns and firing

- For best firing efficiency, upgrade your kiln from old to new, or replace any degraded elements, etc. to make it fire as efficiently as possible
- You can wrap your entire kiln or draughty sections of it using ceramic fibre to provide better insulation and therefore make it more efficient
- If you have several kilns, it is worth checking their firing schedules and staggering the firings so as not to overload the system (which requires more energy to be drawn down from your power supplier and can be more expensive)
- Reduce your firing temperature if possible
- Reduce the length of drying programmes where possible and speed up your firings
- Use any dampers more efficiently to retain the heat while still oxidising
- As shelves require a lot of energy to heat up, use thinner shelves or get rid of them all together by using different packing methods (such as tumble stacking)
- Try replacing any bag walls with soft brick or stilts/props instead
- Experiment with your packing/stacking – not packing/stacking so tightly may allow a more even temperature rise

* *(These tips are all from the section 'Common-sense firing efficiency' by John Britt, see p.30–32 for full details)*

- Calculate the carbon footprint of your kiln by using Denise Joyal's baseline to work out your individual costs (*See Sherman Hall,* Ceramics Monthly, *p.131*)
- Have your energy supplier run an energy audit on your kilns and electrical use (*See Steve Lee/Archie Bray Foundation, p.29*)
- Single-fire your products where possible to save on fuel and energy (*See Roderick Bamford, p.101*)

Salt/soda kilns

- Try building your kiln from ceramic fibre and HTI bricks (High Thermal Insulators) to increase insulation and then use one of the new surface coatings on the inside of the kiln – this will increase the speed of firing and make it more fuel efficient (*See the section 'Fact and fiction' by Wil Shynkaruk, p.33*)
- Use the most efficient kiln for the purpose – for example try using an electric kiln for your bisque firing and just use a salt kiln for salting (*See the section 'Common-sense firing, by John Britt, see p.30*)

Alternative kilns and fuel

- Try using recycled oil, collected from either mechanics' garages or local cafes (vegetable oil) and adapt your kiln as needed (*See Ben Culbertson p.37 and Joe Finch, p.41*)
- Build a specific oil-drip kiln to fire on waste vegetable oil (*See A Simple Veggie Oil Kiln by Joe Finch, p.41*)
- Try using waste vegetable oil converted into biofuel to fire the kiln (*See Ben Culbertson, p.37*)
- Use any waste products as fuel where possible – such as the pallet kiln, designed specifically around the local waste of wooden pallets as its main source of sustainable fuel and using Methane gas to heat the studio (*See William Baker & Joy Tanner, p.45*)
- Investigate locally available alternative materials for making kilns (*See 'Chianti Wine Bottle Kilns' by Alberto Cavalini and Terry Davies, p. 28*)

Using waste materials/recycling

- Use up your waste as a new material – ash from the wood firing can become glaze or compost fertiliser (*See Steve Harrison, p.36*)
- Only print out information when really necessary, try to use online resources where possible (*See Brian Kohl, p.123*)
- Use terry towels to dry hands rather than paper towels (*See Brian Kohl, p.123*)
- Use ground recycled glass as a component in glazes, as a cheaper alternative to frit (*See Elizabeth Sparks, p.54*)
- Rock dust gathered directly from a mine can be used in glazes, such as limestone to create a celadon glaze (*See Elizabeth Sparks, p.54*)
- Use ground steel dust as a colourant (*See David Peters, p.57*)
- Be vigilant about keeping trimmings and processing reclaim to save on clay (*See Steve Harrison, p.36*)
- Collect waste glaze from specific buckets of rinse water (*See Kristin Schimik, p.68*)
- Keep your rejected bisqueware and grind it up for use as grog (*See David Binns, p.71*)
- Upcycle found ceramic objects into your creative work (*See Paul Scott, p.93, and Bouke de Vries, p.95*)
- If you can't reuse it yourself, try to offload any large quantities of unwanted bisqueware to companies that could use it as aggregate for concrete or road construction (they may even pay you for it!). (*See Brian Kohl, p.123*)

Changing your studio practice

- Track your Carbon Footprint; www.footprintnetwork.org
- Carry out extensive testing on your clays and glazes before actually using it on wares to avoid firing work which then ends with bad results, and ultimately ends up as landfill (*See Steve Harrison, p.59 and Brian Kohl, p.123*)
- Be more critical of work before firing and recycling pieces that are not good enough (*See Steve Harrison, p.59*)
- Try using an adobe mixture instead of purely clay for large-scale sculptural projects

(depending on your end requirements), as it can be made very strong and durable and does not require firing (*See the section 'Sustainable materials: backyard resources' by Robert Harrison, p.46*)

- Make work that incorporates waste products from your studio – such as glaze slop, waste clay or old kiln furniture (*See Rod Bamford, p.101 and Kristin Schimik, p.68*)
- Use bricks as a sustainable creative unit to build with (*See the section 'Working with industry', Robert Harrison, p.113 and Gwen Heeney, p.118*)
- Scale down your work – reduce your material costs and transport costs (*See Richard Notkin, p.108*)
- Encourage students to assess and reflect on work, so the emphasis is placed on critical appraisal and learning, rather than keeping all made objects, regardless of quality. This will reduce waste and firing costs and will prevent the world from filling up with more unwanted objects (*See the section 'Educating with a sustainable perspective' by Ilana Crispi, p.125*)
- Actively engage with ceramic industry to move towards sustainable practices (*See Janet DeBoos, p.88 and Rod Bamford, p.101*)
- Create temporal installations by using unfired clay in your practice (*See Ilana Crispi, p.98*)
- Develop proper working habits to sustain your own body (*See Christel Harrison, p.78 and Liz Sparks, p.81*)

Using local materials

- Sourcing materials from your local area will be cheaper and easier – if you build up a working relationship you can get good deals, and transport costs will be reduced (*See Dave Peters, p.57*)
- Contact local geologists and use your local clay supplier as resources to find locally sourced materials (*See Dave Peters, p.57 and Steve Harrison, p.59*)
- If you have the time and inclination, try digging your own clay and finding your own rocks to crush and use as glaze materials (*See David Peters, p.57 and Steve Harrison, p.59*)
- Try testing materials for multiple uses (clay bodies often make good slips), as this will obviously save time and money (*See David Peters, p.57*)

Building and setting up a studio

- Careful planning of the studio layout and your needs is key to avoid renting or building too large a space, and to make best use of the space. Consider placement of the kiln for possible heating and drying use
- Use solar panels and other energy-efficient technologies wherever possible to reduce outgoing costs. This can initially seem like an expensive outlay but over time will greatly reduce costs, and add to ones sense of sustainable contribution
- Increase the energy efficiency in your studio by replacing your HVAC filter frequently
- Invest or replace old heating/cooling units for more energy-efficient ones
- Use energy-saving lightbulbs; LED's are the current industry standard and provide

excellent *white* light

- Use a thermostat in the studio to regulate the heating so it is not just on or off (particularly useful if the kiln has been on and the heating is not needed that day)
- If building your studio, orientate the building to make best use of any sunlight and passive solar gain
- Consider an under/in-floor water (hydronic) heating system which is ideal for ceramics (less draughts and dust)
- When building, choice of sustainable and affordable materials is important for insulation and reducing costs of heating and cooling

* *See the section 'Building an energy-efficient ceramics studio' by Lee Akins for details on all these tips, p.64.*

- Use purpose-made bricks to build with as part of climate control – to keep cool in summer and insulate in winter (*See the section 'Green walls: growing bricks' by Jacques Kaufmann, p.120*)

Water

- Find your own water footprint (*See Robert Harrison, p.76 and Websites at end of book, p.140*)
- Use water efficiently with a system of buckets to avoid constant use of fresh water (*See Kristin Schimik, p.68*)
- Buckets of water for specific purposes (such as washing-off glaze and rinsing glazing tools) also means that waste glaze can be collected and the same water reused. Use a specific bucket of water just to clean wheel and tools rather than fresh water every time (*See Kristin Schimik, p.68*)
- Rainwater harvesting – collect rainwater in water butts for studio use (*See Kristin Schimik, p.68*)
- CINK – a very useful portable clay and water filtration system; self-contained water recirculation, captures clay, eliminates clogged plumbing and saves water; manufactured by Ci Products (*See Brian Kohl, p.77*)
- Make sure you have a settling tank under your sink, or even two, to collect waste clay and glaze and avoid blocking your drains.

Websites

Makers/contributors

Akins, Lee – www.leeakins.co

Baker, William – www.williambbakerpottery.com

Bamford, Roderick – www.tactile.com.au

Binns, Dave – www.davidbinnsceramics.co.uk

Britt, John – www.johnbrittpottery.com

Crispi, Ilana – www.ilanacrispi.com

Davies, Terry – www.terrydavies.it

DeWeese, Josh – www.deweeseart.com/josh

Finch, Joe – www.joefinchkilns.co.uk

Harrison, Robert – www.robert.harrison.net

Harrison, Steve – www.hotnsticky.com.au

Heeney, Gwen – www.gwenheeneybricksculptor.com

Kohl, Brian – www.briankohlceramics.com

Mansfield, Janet – www.janetmansfield.com

Nelson, Aaron – www.aaronnelson.ca

Schimik, Kristin – www.kristin-schimik.weebly.com

Scott, Paul – www.cumbrianblues.com

Sparks, Elizabeth – www.lizsparks.net

Tanner, Joy – www.joytannerpottery.com

Ecology

David Suzuki Foundation: Environmental Science – www.davidsuzuki.org

Eco Geek: Technology for the Environment – www.ecogeek.org

Global Footprint Network: Footprint Calculator – www.footprintnetwork.org

Guardian Newspaper: Environmental Coverage – www.guardian.co.uk/environment

Nature: International Journal of Science – www.nature.org/nature

Planet Ark: Guide for Reducing your Impact on the Planet – www.planetark.org

Tree Hugger: Sustainable Design, News and Solutions – www.treehugger.com

World Changing Magazine: Tools, Models and Ideas – www.worldchanging.com

Eco products

Creative Industries CINK Product – www.buyciproducts.com

Organisations

Archie Bray Foundation for the Ceramic Arts – www.archiebray.org

EnergyXchange Renewable Energy Center – www.energyxchange.org

International Academy of Ceramics (IAC) – www.aic-iac.org

Medalta International Artist-In-Residence Program – www.medalta/miair.org

National Council on Education for the Ceramic Arts (NCECA) – www.nceca.net

World Association of Brick Artists (WABA) – www.waba-co.com

Periodicals

Ceramics Art & Perception/Ceramics Technical magazines – www.ceramicart.com.au

Ceramics Monthly magazine – www.ceramicartsdaily.org

Ceramic Review magazine – www.ceramicreview.com

Veggie oil

Blanket Creek Pottery: Waste Oil Kiln – www.blanketcreek.com

Delevan Inc.: Manufacturers of Oil Spray Nozzels – www.delavaninc.com

The body

Posture, motion and ergonomics – www.ergonomics.org

Yoga – www.yoga.com

Bibliography

Bach, David, *Go Green, Live Rich*, Broadway Books, 2008

Benyus, Janine M., *Biomimicry*, HarperCollins, 1997

Binns, Charles F., *The Potter's Craft*, D. Van Nostrand, 1947

Cardew, Michael, *Pioneer Pottery*, Longmans, Green and Co. Ltd., 1969

Ceramics & Ecology, International Ceramics Symposium, World Ceramic Exposition Foundation (Korea), 2009

Chiras, Dan and Wann, Dave, *Superbia! 31 Ways to Create Sustainable Neighborhoods*, New Society Publishers, 2003

Coperthwaite, William S., *A Handmade Life: In Search of Simplicity*, Chelsea Green Publishers, 2007

Heinberg, Richard, *The End of Growth: Adapting to Our New Economic Reality*, New Society Publishers, 2011

Hopkins, Rob, *The Transition Handbook: From Oil Dependency to Local Resilience*, Chelsea Green Publishing, 2008

Kemp, William H., *Biodiesel Basics and Beyond: A comprehensive Guide to Production and Use for the Home and Farm*, Aztext Press, 2006

Kemp, William H., *The Renewable Energy Handbook: The Updated Comprehensive Guide to Renewable Energy and Independent Living*, Aztext Press, 2009

Kim, Jeoung-Ah, *Ceramic Arts and Design for a Sustainable Future*, Frolunda Culture Centre (Sweden), 2011

Kostigen, Thomas M., *The Green Blue Book*, Rodale, 2010

Krigger, John and Dorsi, Chris, *The Homeowner's Handbook to Energy Efficiency: A Guide for Big and Small Improvements*, Saturn Resource Management, 2008

Krigger, John and Dorsi, Chris, *Residential Energy: Cost Savings and Comfort for Existing Buildings*, Prentice Hall, 2009

Kunstler, James Howard, *The Long Emergency: Surviving the End of Oil, Climate Change, and Other Converging Catastrophes of the Twenty-First Century*, Atlantic Monthly Press, 2005

Leach, Bernard, *A Potter's Book*, Transatlantic Arts Inc., 1973

Mau, Bruce with Jennifer Leonard and the Institute without Boundaries, *Massive Change*, Phaidon Press, 2004

McDonough, William and Braungart, Michael, *Cradle to Cradle*, North Point Press, 2002

McKay, Kim and Bonnin, Jenny, *true green*, National Geographic Society, 2006

Milbraith, Lester W., *Envisioning A Sustainable Society: Learning Our Way Out*, State University of New York, 1989

Pahl, Greg, *The Citizen-Powered Energy Handbook: Community Solutions to a Global Crisis*, Chelsea Green Publishing, 2007

Rawson, Philip, *Ceramics*, University of Pennsylvania Press, 1984

Riley, Trish, T*he Complete Idiot's Guide to Green Living*, Alpha Books, 2007

Staubach, Suzanne, *Clay: The History and Evolution of Humankind's Relationship with Earth's Most Primal Element*, Berkeley Publishing, 2005

Steffen, Alex, *Worldchanging: A User's Guide for the 21st Century*, Abrams, 2011

Tickell, Joshua, *From the Fryer to the Fuel Tank: The Complete Guide to Using Vegetable Oil as an Alternative Fuel*, Tickell Energy Consulting, 2000

Veiteberg, Jorunn, *Thing, Tang, Trash: Upcycling in Contemporary Ceramics*, Bergen National Academy of the Arts & Art Museums Bergen (Norway), 2011

Ward, Peter D., *The Flooded Earth; Our Future in a World Without Ice Caps*, Basic Books, 2010

Index

Adams, Dean 52
adobe 48–50, 65–6, 137–8
aggregate 72, 75
Akins, Lee 64–8
Archie Bray Foundation *see* schools

Baker, William 130–31
Bamford
  Roderick 101–05, 126
bicycle kiln 19
Binns, Dave 71–5
brick 32, 106–7, 113, 115–21, 139
  firebrick 30, 34, 36, 44
  'growing' 11, 113, 120–21, 139
  HTI (high thermal insulators) 136
  kilns 39, 40, 107
  paver 69, 70
  refractory 36, 37
  repurposed 85, 87, 106, 107, 113, 114
  see also adobe
Britt, John 30–32

carbon
  footprint 16, 76, 137
  offsetting 16
Cardrew, Michael 46
Cavalini, Alberto 28–30
clay 6, 7, 46–58
  Dyce Creek 53
  heavy clay 57–8
  International Wild Clay Project 52, 53
  naturally-occurring 46–7
  threads 54–5
  wild clay in Montana 52–3
  see also adobe
coatings 34 *see also* glaze
conservation *see* restoration
Crispi, Ilana 98–100
Crowan Pottery 20
Culbertson, Ben 37–9

Davies, Terry 28–30
Davis, Harry 20
DeBoos, Janet 88–92
de Vries, Bouke 95–7
DeWeese, Josh 22–3, 52, 53

energy sources
  see kilns; solar; water
EnergyXchange 44–6
ergonomics 78–80

feldspathic stone/porcelain/clay 51, 59, 60
Finch, Joe 41–3
firebrick *see* brick
Forrest, Miranda 62–4
fuels 36–45
  biodiesel 39, 137
  straw waste (camelina straw) 52
  veggie oil 37–43
  wood 36–7
  see also straw; wood

gas *see* kilns
glaze chemistry 70

Hall, Sherman 131
Harrison
  Christel 78–80
  Robert 15, 16, 49–51, 84–7, 113–8
  Steve 59–61
heating 67
  air 129
  ground source heat pumps (GSHPs) 21
  see also kilns; solar power; water
Heeney, Gwen 118–9, 127–9
Henry, Elaine Olafson 134

Joyal, Denise 132–3

Kaufmann, Jacques 106–07, 113, 120–21
kilns 136
  atmospheric 27
  Bailey 27
  Blaauw 27
  bottle 28–30
  brick 39
  build-your-own 27
  down-drought 41
  driftwood 64
  electric, cost to run 24
  Geil car 27
  gas 24, 26, 44
    expanded gas 27
    methane 21, 44–5
    reduction 27
  oil 41, 43, 137
  Pallet 45–6, 137
    use of refractory fibre 27
  salt/soda 27, 32–5, 45–6, 136
    salt and soda firing compared 34
  settings 31
  wood 27, 64, 129, , 129
Kohl, Brian 125
Krusoe, Sana 69–70

Leach, Bernard 46
Lee, Steve 25
Leonardo Innovation Transfer project
    127–9

methane *see* gas
Montana, Helena
  home 9
NCECA/GTF 10, 13, 108, 123–4, 131, 134, 141
Nelson, Aaron 17, 18, 19
Nor, Nybol 118
Notkin, Richard 108–11

oil 37–43
  see also water
Olafson *see* Henry

Peters, Dave 23, 57, 58, 83
potteries *see* schools; studios

repurposing 108
restoration 93–7

salt *see* kilns
Schimik, Kristen 69–70
schools
  Archie Bray Foundation 23–7, 47, 84–5,
    87, 113, 116
  Harrow 20, 21
  Penland 44
Scott, Paul 93–4
Shyankaruk, Wil 33–4, 122–3
soda *see* kilns
solar power 67
Sparks, Elizabeth 54–6, 81
Stepp, Tim 48, 52
straw 48, 52, 65–6
studios, building and designing 64–70,
    138–9
  work station ergonomics 78–80
  see also schools
Swanson, Richard 78–9

Tanner, Joy 46
tiles 73
  drain 84
  mosaic 128
translucency 17

Vehring, Fritz 118–9
Viotti, Ulla 118–9

waste mitigation 68–77
  recycling waste 71–7, 83–7, 137–8
water 139
  conservation 76–7, 139
  filters 11
  mill 20
  radiant heat (hot water) 67
  use with oil 40, 42
wood 27, 36–7
  driftwood 64
  see also kilns

yoga 81